HLM™ 5

Hierarchical Linear and Nonlinear Modeling

Stephen W. Raudenbush
University of Michigan

Anthony S. Bryk
University of Chicago

Yuk Fai Cheong
Emory University

Richard T. Congdon, Jr.
Harvard University

SSI SCIENTIFIC SOFTWARE
INTERNATIONAL

HLM™ 5

Hierarchical Linear and Nonlinear Modeling.

Copyright © 2001 by Scientific Software International, Inc.

All rights reserved. Printed in the United States of America.

Cover by Esse Group based on an original design by M. James Scott.

Elevations of the 880 North Lake Shore Drive building of Mies van der Rohe.

ISBN: 0–89498–050–5

3 4 5 6 7 8 9 0   04 03 02 01 (second edition with addition)

Published by:

Scientific Software International, Inc.
7383 North Lincoln Avenue, Suite 100
Lincolnwood, IL 60712–1704
Tel: +1.847.675.0720
Fax: +1.847.675.2140
Web: *www.ssicentral.com*

Preface

New program features in HLM version 5

HLM version 5 greatly broadens the range of hierarchical models that can be estimated. It also offers further advances over version 4 in convenience of use. It Here is a quick overview of key new features and options:

1. Estimating multivariate linear models from incomplete data. This includes unrestricted models, random-effects models, auto-correlated within-subject errors, heterogeneous within-subject variances; multivariate and multilevel models.
2. Faster, more efficient import of data from statistical packages.
3. Highly accurate Laplace approximation to maximum likelihood for binary outcome models (Bernoulli only for 2-level models).
4. Generalized estimating equations with robust standard errors.
5. Comparison of Ordinary Least Squares (with and without robust standard errors) and HLM estimates (with and without robust standard errors) on every analysis.
6. Multinomial regression for two-level data.
7. Ordinal regression for two-level data.
8. Latent variable analysis — estimating direct and indirect effects of explanatory variables measured with error (not included with three-level multivariate, the HMLM2 module).
9. Log-linear model for heterogeneous level-1 variance (2-level program only).
10. Automated analysis of multiply-imputed data.

Contents

List of examples

Input and data files for the examples are included with the program on the distribution media. For these files we use the following naming conventions. A raw data file in ASCII (plain text) format has the suffix DAT, in SPSS system file format the suffix SAV. The response file that creates the SSM or MDM file has the extension RSP. The command file that has the specifications for a particular analysis has the filename extension HLM for use with the HLM2 or HLM3 analysis module, or the MLM suffix for use with the HMLM or HMLM2 module. The file that contains the list output from an analysis has the extension OUT.

Title of Example	**See page**

1

Conceptual and Statistical Background for Two-Level Models

Behavioral and social data commonly have a nested structure. For example, if repeated observations are collected on a set of individuals and the measurement occasions are not identical for all persons, the multiple observations are properly conceived as nested within persons. Each person might also be nested within some organizational unit such as a school or workplace. These organizational units may in turn be nested within a geographical location such as a community, state, or country. Within the hierarchical linear model, each of the levels in the data structure (*e.g.*, repeated observations within persons, persons within communities, communities within states) is formally represented by its own sub-model. Each sub-model represents the structural relations occurring at that level and the residual variability at that level.

This manual describes the use of the HLM computer program for the statistical modeling of two- and three-level data structures, respectively. It should be used in conjunction with the text *Hierarchical Linear Models: Applications and Data Analysis Methods* (Bryk, A.S. & Raudenbush, S.W., 1992: Newbury Park, CA: Sage Publications).[1] The HLM program has been tailored so that the basic program structure, input specification, and output of results closely coordinate with this textbook. This manual also cross-references the appropriate sections of the textbook for the reader interested in a full discussion of the details of parameter estimation and hypothesis testing. Many of the illustrative examples described in this manual are based on data distributed with the program and analyzed in the Sage text.

---

[1]Also available from SSI.

1

We begin by discussing the two-level model below and the use of the HLM2 program in Chapter 2. Building on this framework, Chapters 3 and 4 introduce the three-level model and the use of the HLM3 program. Chapters 5 and 6 discuss use of hierarchical modeling for non-normal level-1 errors, such as discrete outcomes and count data. Chapters 7 and 8 consider multivariate models that can be estimated from incomplete data. Chapter 9 describes some special features, including analyses for multiply-imputed data, analyses where the level-1 variances are known, and analyses involving latent variables, that is, predictor or outcome variables that are measured with error or are missing.

1.1 The general two-level model

As the name implies, a two-level model consists of two submodels at level 1 and level 2. For example, if the research problem consists of data on students nested within schools, the level-1 model would represent the relationships among the student-level variables and the level-2 model would capture the influence of school-level factors. Formally, there are $i = 1, \ldots, n_j$ level-1 units (e.g., students) nested within $j = 1, \ldots, J$ level-2 units (e.g., schools).

1.1.1 Level-1 model

We represent in the level-1 model the outcome for case i within unit j as:

$$
\begin{aligned}
Y_{ij} &= \beta_{0j} + \beta_{1j} X_{1ij} + \beta_{2j} X_{2ij} + \cdots + \beta_{Qj} X_{Qij} + r_{ij} \\
&= \beta_{0j} + \sum_{q=1}^{Q} \beta_{qj} X_{qij} + r_{ij} \,,
\end{aligned}
\tag{1.1}
$$

where

$\beta_{qj}(q = 0, 1, \ldots, Q)$ are *level-1 coefficients*;

X_{qij} is *level-1 predictor* q for case i in unit j;

r_{ij} is the *level-1 random effect*; and

σ^2 is the variance of r_{ij}, that is the *level-1 variance*.

Here we assume that the random term $r_{ij} \sim N(0, \sigma^2)$.

1.1.2 Level-2 model

Each of the level-1 coefficients, β_{qj}, defined in the level-1 model becomes an outcome variable in the level-2 model:

$$
\begin{aligned}
\beta_{qj} &= \gamma_{q0} + \gamma_{q1}W_{1j} + \gamma_{q2}W_{2j} + \cdots + \gamma_{qS_q}W_{S_qj} + u_{qj} \\
&= \gamma_{q0} + \sum_{s=1}^{S_q} \gamma_{qs}W_{sj} + u_{qj} ,
\end{aligned}
\tag{1.2}
$$

where

γ_{qs} $(q = 0, 1, \ldots, S_q)$ are *level-2 coefficients*;

W_{sj} is a *level-2 predictor*; and

u_{qj} is a *level-2 random effect*.

We assume that, for each unit j, the vector $(u_{0j}, u_{1j}, \ldots, u_{Qj})'$ is distributed as multivariate normal, with each element u_{qj} having a mean of zero and variance of

$$
\mathsf{Var}(u_{qj}) = \tau_{qq} .
\tag{1.3}
$$

For any pair of random effects q and q',

$$
\mathsf{Cov}(u_{qj}, u_{q'j}) = \tau_{qq'} .
\tag{1.4}
$$

These *level-2 variance and covariance components* can be collected into a dispersion matrix, $\mathbf{T}$, whose maximum dimension is $(Q + 1) \times (Q + 1)$.

We note that each level-1 coefficient can be modeled at level 2 as one of three general forms:

1. *a fixed level-1 coefficient; e.g.,*

$$\beta_{qj} = \gamma_{q0} \, , \qquad (1.5)$$

2. *a non-randomly varying level-1 coefficient, e.g.,*

$$\beta_{qj} = \gamma_{q0} + \sum_{s=1}^{S_q} \gamma_{qs} W_{sj} \, , \qquad (1.6)$$

3. *a randomly varying level-1 coefficient, e.g.,*

$$\beta_{qj} = \gamma_{q0} + u_{qj} \qquad (1.7)$$

or a level-1 coefficient with both non-random and random sources of variation,

$$\beta_{qj} = \gamma_{q0} + \sum_{s=1}^{S_q} \gamma_{qs} W_{sj} + u_{qj} \, . \qquad (1.8)$$

The actual dimension of $\mathbf{T}$ in any application depends on the number of level-2 coefficients specified as randomly varying. We also note that a different set of level-2 predictors may be used in each of the $Q + 1$ equations that form the level-2 model.

1.2 Parameter estimation

Three kinds of parameters are estimated in a hierarchical linear model: empirical Bayes estimates of randomly varying level-1 coefficients; generalized least squares estimates of the level-2 coefficients; and maximum-likelihood estimates of the variance and covariance components.

1.2.1 Empirical Bayes ("EB") estimates of randomly varying level-1 coefficients, β_{qj}

These estimates of the level-1 coefficients for each unit j are optimal composites of an estimate based on the data from that unit and an estimate based on data from other similar units. Intuitively, we are borrowing strength from all of the information present in the ensemble of data to improve the level-1 coefficient estimates for each of the J units. These "EB" estimates are also referred to as "shrunken estimates" of the level-1 coefficients. They are produced by HLM as part of the residual file output (see page 13, *Model checking based on the residual file*). (For further discussion see *Hierarchical Linear Models*, pp. 39–44; 76–82.)

1.2.2 Generalized least squares (GLS) estimates of the level-2 coefficients, γ_{qs}

Substitution of the level-2 equations for β_{qj} into their corresponding level-1 terms yields a single-equation linear model with a complex error structure. Proper estimation of the regression coefficients of this model (*i.e.*, the γ's) requires that we take into account the differential precision of the information provided by each of the J units. This is accomplished through generalized least squares. In the program output, the final generalized least squares estimates for the γ's are represented by Gqs. (For further discussion see *Hierarchical Linear Models*, pp. 32–39.)

1.2.3 Maximum likelihood estimates of variance and covariance components, σ^2 at level 1, and T at level 2

Because of the unbalanced nature of the data in most applications of hierarchical linear models (*i.e.*, n_j varies across the J units and the observed patterns on the level-1 predictors also vary), traditional methods for variance-covariance component estimation fail to yield efficient estimates. Through iterative computing techniques, such as the EM algorithm and Fisher scoring, maximum-likelihood estimates for σ^2 and T can be obtained. (For further discussion, see *Hierarchical Linear Models*, pp. 44–48; also Chapter 10). In the program output, these estimates are denoted by SIGMA-SQUARED and TAU respectively.

1.2.4 Some other useful statistics

Based on the various parameter estimates discussed above, HLM2 and HLM3 also compute a number of other useful statistics. These include:

1. *Reliability of $\hat{\beta}_{qj}$.*

   The program computes an overall or average reliability for the least squares estimates of each level-1 coefficient across the set of J level-2 units. These are denoted in the program output as RELIABILITY ESTIMATES and are calculated according to Equation 3.53 in *Hierarchical Linear Models*, p. 43.

2. *Least squares residuals $(\hat{u}_{qj})$.*

   These residuals are based on the deviation of an ordinary least squares estimate of a level-1 coefficient, $\hat{\beta}_{qj}$, from its predicted or "fitted" value based on the level-2 model, *i.e.*,

   $$\hat{u}_{qj} = \hat{\beta}_{qj} - \left(\hat{\gamma}_{q0} + \sum_{s=1}^{S_q} \hat{\gamma}_{qs} W_{sj}\right) . \tag{1.9}$$

   These ordinary least squares residuals are denoted in HLM residual files by the prefix OL before the corresponding variable names.

3. *Empirical Bayes residuals (u_{qj}^*).*

   These residuals are based on the deviation of the empirical Bayes estimates, β_{qj}^*, of a randomly varying level-1 coefficient from its predicted or "fitted" value based on the level-2 model, *i.e.*,

   $$u_{qj}^* = \beta_{qj}^* - \left(\hat{\gamma}_{q0} + \sum_{s=1}^{S_q} \hat{\gamma}_{qs} W_{sj}\right) . \tag{1.10}$$

   These are denoted in the HLM residual files by the prefix EB before the corresponding variable names. (For a further discussion and illustration of OL and EB residuals see *Hierarchical Linear Models*, pp. 41–42; and 76–80).

1.3   Hypothesis testing

Corresponding to the three basic types of parameters estimated in a hierarchical linear model (EB estimates of random level-1 coefficients, GLS estimates of the fixed level-2 coefficients, and the maximum-likelihood estimates of the variance and covariance components), are single-parameter and multi-parameter hypothesis-testing procedures. (See *Hierarchical Linear Models*, pp. 48–56.) The current HLM program executes a variety of hypothesis tests for the level-2 fixed effects and the variance-covariance components. These are summarized in Table 1.1.

1.4   Restricted versus full maximum likelihood

By default, two-level models are estimated by means of restricted maximum likelihood (REML). Using this approach, the variance-covariance components are estimated via maximum likelihood, averaging over all possible values of the fixed effects. The fixed effects are estimated via GLS given these variance-covariance estimates. Under full maximum likelihood (ML), variance-covariance parameters and fixed level-2 coefficients are estimated by maximizing their joint likelihood. One practical consequence is that, under ML, any pair of nested models can be tested using a likelihood-ratio test. In contrast, using REML, the likelihood-ratio test is available only for testing the variance-covariance parameters, as indicated in Table 1.1.

1.5   Generalized estimating equations

Statistical inferences about the fixed level-2 coefficients, γ_{qs}, using HLM are based on the assumption that random effects at each level are normally distributed; and on the assumed structure of variation and covariation of these random effects at each level. Given a reasonably large sample of level-2 units, it is possible to make sound statistical inferences about γ_{qs} that are not based on these assumptions by using the method of generalized estimating equations or "GEE" (Zeger & Liang, 1986). Comparing

Table 1.1

Hypothesis tests for the level-2 fixed effects and the variance-covariance components

Type of Hypothesis	Test Statistic	Program Output
Fixed level-2 effects		
Single-parameter: $H_0 : \gamma_{qs} = 0$ $H_1 : \gamma_{qs} \neq 0$	t-ratio[1]	Standard feature of the Fixed Effects Table for all level-2 coefficients.
Multi-parameter: $H_0 : C'\gamma = 0$ $H_1 : C'\gamma \neq 0$	general linear hypothesis test (Wald test), chi-square test[2]	Optional output specification (see page 59).
Variance-covariance components		
Single-parameter: $H_0 : \tau_{qq} = 0$ $H_1 : \tau_{qq} > 0$	Chi-square test[3]	Standard feature of the Variance Components Table for all level-2 random effects.
Multi-parameter: $H_0 : \mathbf{T} = \mathbf{T}_0$ $H_1 : \mathbf{T} = \mathbf{T}_1$	Difference in deviances, likelihood ratio test.[4]	Optional output specification (see page 61).

[1] See Equation 3.65 in *Hierarchical Linear Models*.
[2] See Equation 3.73 in *Hierarchical Linear Models*.
[3] See Equation 3.82 in *Hierarchical Linear Models*.
[4] Here $\mathbf{T}_0$ is a reduced form of $\mathbf{T}_1$.

these GEE inferences to those based on HLM provides a way of assessing whether the HLM inferences about γ_{qs} are sensitive to the violations of these assumptions.

The simplest GEE model assumes that the outcome, Y_{ij}, for case i in unit j is independent of the outcome $Y_{i'j}$ for some other case, i', in the same unit; and that these outcomes have constant variance. Under these simple assumptions, estimation of the γ coefficients by ordinary least squares (OLS) would be justified. If these OLS assumptions are incorrect, the OLS estimates of γ_{qs} will be consistent (accurate in large samples) but not efficient. However, the standard error estimates produced under OLS will generally be inconsistent (biased, often badly, even in large samples). Version 5 of HLM produces the following tables, often useful for comparative purposes:

- A table of OLS estimates along with the OLS standard errors.
- A table including the OLS estimates, but accompanied by robust standard errors, that is, standard errors that are consistent even when the OLS assumptions are incorrect.
- A table of HLM estimates of γ_{qs}, based on GLS, and standard errors based on the assumptions underlying HLM.
- A table of the same HLM estimates, but now accompanied by robust standard errors, that is, standard errors that are consistent even when the HLM assumptions are mistaken.

By comparing these four tables, it is possible to discern how different the HLM estimates and standard errors are from those based on OLS and to discern whether the HLM inferences are plausibly distorted by incorrect assumptions about the distribution of the random effects at each level. We illustrate the value of these comparisons in Chapter 2. The GEE approach is very useful for strengthening inferences about the fixed level-2 coefficients but does not provide a basis for inferences about the random, level-1 coefficients or the variance-covariance components. Cheong, Fotiu, & Raudenbush (in press) have intensively studied the properties of HLM and GEE estimators in the context of three-level models. GEE results are also available for three-level data.

2 Working with HLM2

Data analysis by means of the HLM2 program will typically involve three stages:

1. Construction of the "SSM file" (the sufficient statistics matrices),
2. Execution of analyses based on the SSM file, and
3. Evaluation of fitted models based on a residual file.

We describe each stage below and then illustrate a number of special options. Data collected from a High School & Beyond (HS&B) survey on 7,185 students nested within 160 US High Schools, as described in Chapter 4 of *Hierarchical Linear Models*, will be used for demonstrations.

2.1 Constructing the SSM file from raw data

We assume that a user has employed a standard computing package to check and clean the data thoroughly, to recode or transform variables as needed, and to conduct relevant exploratory analyses, and that the user now wishes to fit a series of hierarchical linear models. The first task will be to construct the sufficient statistics or SSM file from raw data.

Two raw data files are required as input: a level-1 file and a level-2 file.[1] For the HS&B example, the level-1 units are students and the level-2 units

---

[1]In some cases, all the data may be contained in a single file. The data still have to be sorted by the ID variables representing the different levels of the hierarchy. Simply use the same filename as the data file at the various levels of the hierarchy in the creation of the SSM file. See, for example, the HSBALL.DAT data file that comes with the program, together with the HSBALL.RSP response file. Note the two different data format statements in the RSP file.

are schools. The two files are linked by a common level-2 unit ID, school id in our example, which must appear on every level-1 record that is linked to a particular level-2 unit. In constructing the SSM file, the HLM program will compute summary statistics based on the level-1 unit data and store these statistics together with level-2 data.

The procedure to create an SSM file consists of three major steps. The user needs to:

1. Inform HLM of the input and SSM file type,
2. Supply HLM with the appropriate information for the data, the command and the SSM files, and
3. Check if the data have been properly read into HLM.

2.2   Executing analyses based on the SSM file

Once the SSM file is constructed, all subsequent analyses will be computed using the SSM file as input. It will therefore be unnecessary to read the larger student-level data file in computing these analyses. The efficient summary of data in the SSM file leads to faster computation. The SSM file is like a "system file" in a standard computing package in that it contains not only the summarized data but the names of all of the variables.

Model specification has three steps:

1. Specifying the level-1 model, which defines a set of level-1 coefficients to be computed for each level-2 unit.
2. Specifying a level-2 structural model to predict each of the level-1 coefficients.
3. Specifying the level-1 coefficients to be viewed as random or nonrandom.

The output produced from these analyses includes:

❑ Ordinary least squares and generalized least squares results for the fixed coefficients defined in the level-2 model.

- Estimates of variance and covariance components and approximate chi-square tests for the variance components.
- A variety of auxiliary diagnostic statistics.

Additional output options and hypothesis-testing procedures may be selected.

2.3 Model checking based on the residual file

After fitting a hierarchical model, it is wise to check the tenability of the assumptions underlying the model:

- Are the distributional assumptions realistic?
- Are results likely to be affected by outliers or influential observations?
- Have important variables been omitted or nonlinear relationships been ignored?

These questions and others can be addressed by means of analyses of the HLM residual file.

A residual file includes:

- Fitted values for each level-1 coefficient (that is, values predicted on the basis of the level-2 model)
- Ordinary least squares (OL) and empirical Bayes (EB) estimates of level-2 residuals (discrepancies between level-1 coefficients and fitted values)
- Dispersion estimates useful in exploring sources of variance heterogeneity at level 1
- Expected and observed Mahalanobis distance measures useful in assessing the multivariate normality assumption for the level-2 residuals
- Selected level-2 predictors useful in exploring possible relationships between such predictors and level-2 residuals
- Posterior variances

See Chapter 9 in *Hierarchical Linear Models* for a full discussion of these methods.

2.4 Windows, interactive, and batch execution

Formulation and testing of models using HLM programs can be achieved via Windows, interactive, or batch modes. Most PC users will find the Windows mode preferable. This draws on the visual features of Windows while preserving the speed of use associated with a command-oriented (batch) program. Non-PC users have the choice of interactive and batch modes only. Interactive execution guides the user through the steps of the analysis by posing questions and providing a menu of options. In this chapter, we employ the Windows mode for all the examples. Descriptions and examples on how to use HLM2 in interactive and batch mode are given in Appendix A.

2.5 An example using HLM2 in Windows mode

Chapter 4 in *Hierarchical Linear Models* presents a series of analyses of data from the *High School & Beyond* survey. A level-1 model specifies the relationship between student socioeconomic status (SES) and mathematics achievement in each of 160 schools; at level 2, each school's intercept and slope are predicted by school sector (Catholic versus public) and school mean social class. We reproduce one analysis here (see Table 4.5 in *Hierarchical Linear Models*, p. 72).

2.5.1 Constructing the SSM file from raw data

PC users may construct the SSM file directly from four types of data file formats (SPSS, ASCII, SAS, and SYSTAT) or indirectly from many additional types of data file formats.[2]

Non-PC users may construct the SSM file from one of the following formats: ASCII data file, SYSTAT data file, or SAS 5 transport files.

In order for the program(s) to correctly read the data, the IDs need to conform to the following rules:

---

[2]Through the handling by a third-party software module included in the HLM program.

1. For ASCII data, the ID variables must be read in as character (alphanumeric). These IDs are indicated by the A field(s) in the format statement. For all other types of data, the IDs may be character or numeric.

2. The IDs must be sorted, and properly nested. If there are three levels involved, the level-2 IDs must be sorted within level-3 IDs.

   Note: level-1 cases must be grouped together by their respective level-2 unit id. To assure this, sort the level-1 file by the level-2 unit id field prior to entering the data into HLM2.

3. If the ID variable is numeric, it must be in the range $-(10^{13} + 1)$ to $+(10^{13} - 1)$ (*i.e.*, 12 digits). Although the ID may be a number with a decimal point, only the integer part is used.

4. If the ID variable is character, the length must not exceed 12 characters. Furthermore, the IDs at a given level must all be the same length. *This is often a cause of problems.* For example, imagine your data has IDs ranging from "1" to "100." You will need to recreate the IDs as "001" to "100." In other words, all spaces (blank characters) should be coded as zeros.

For non-ASCII files, the program can only properly deal with numeric variables (with the exception of character ID variables). Other data types, such as a "Date format," will not be processed properly.

For non-ASCII files with missing data, one should only use the "standard" missing value code. Some statistical packages (SAS, for example) allow for a number of missing value codes. The HLM modules are incapable of understanding these correctly, thus these additional missing codes need to be recode to the more common "." (period) code.

2.5.1.1 SPSS file input

We first illustrate the use of SPSS file input and then consider input from ASCII data files. Data input requires a level-1 file and a level-2 file.

	id	minority	female	ses	mathach
1	1224	0	1	-1.528	5.876
2	1224	0	1	-.588	19.708
3	1224	0	0	-.528	20.349
4	1224	0	0	-.668	8.781
5	1224	0	0	-.158	17.898
6	1224	0	0	.022	4.583
7	1224	0	1	-.618	-2.832
8	1224	0	0	-.998	.523
9	1224	0	1	-.888	1.527
10	1224	0	0	-.458	21.521

Figure 2.1   First ten cases in HSB1.SAV

Level-1 file.   For our HS&B example, the level-1 file (HSB1.SAV) has 7,185 cases and four variables (not including the *school id*). The variables are:

- MINORITY, an indicator for student ethnicity (1 = minority, 0 = other)
- FEMALE, an indicator for student gender (1 = female, 0 = male)
- SES, (a standardized scale constructed from variables measuring parental education, occupation, and income)
- MATHACH, a measure of mathematics achievement

Data for the first ten cases in HSB1.SAV are shown in Fig. 2.1.

Note: level-1 cases must be grouped together by their respective level-2 unit id. To assure this, sort the level-1 file by the level-2 unit id field prior to entering the data into HLM2.

Level-2 file.   At level 2, the illustrative data set HSB2.SAV consists of 160 schools with 6 variables per school. The variables are:

- SIZE (school enrollment)
- SECTOR (1 = Catholic, 0 = public)
- PRACAD (proportion of students in the academic track)
- DISCLIM (a scale measuring disciplinary climate)

☐ HIMINTY (1 = more than 40% minority enrollment, 0 = less than 40%)

☐ MEANSES (mean of the SES values for the students in this school who are included in the level-1 file)

The data for the first ten schools are displayed in Fig. 2.2.

	id	size	sector	pracad	disclim	himinty	meanses
1	1224	842	0	.350	1.597	0	-.428
2	1288	1855	0	.270	.174	0	.128
3	1296	1719	0	.320	-.137	1	-.420
4	1308	716	1	.960	-.622	0	.534
5	1317	455	1	.950	-1.694	1	.351
6	1358	1430	0	.250	1.535	0	-.014
7	1374	2400	0	.500	2.016	0	-.007
8	1433	899	1	.960	-.321	0	.718
9	1436	185	1	1.000	-1.141	0	.569
10	1461	1672	0	.780	2.096	0	.683

Figure 2.2   First ten cases in HSB2.SAV

As mentioned earlier, the construction of an SSM file consists of three major steps. This will now be illustrated with the HS&B example.

To inform HLM of the input and SSM file type

1. At the **HLM for Windows** window, open the **File** menu.
2. Choose **SSM... New... Stat package input** (see Fig. 2.3). A **Select SSM/MDM type** dialog box opens (see Fig. 2.4).
3. Select **HLM2** and click **OK**. A **Make SSM – HLM2** dialog box will open (see Fig. 2.5).

To supply HLM with appropriate information for the data, the command, and the SSM files

1. Select **SPSS/Windows** from the **Input File Type** drop-down listbox (see Fig. 2.5).

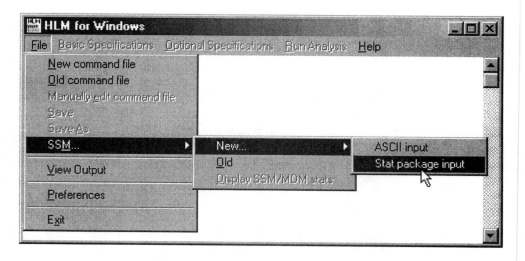

Figure 2.3 HLM for Windows window

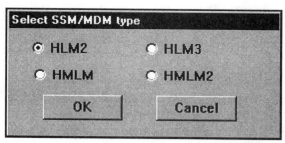

Figure 2.4 Select SSM type dialog box

2. Click **Browse** in the **Level-1 specification** section to open an **Open Data File** dialog box.

3. Open a level-1 SPSS system file in the HLM folder (HSB1.SAV in our example). The **Choose Variables** button below **Browse** will be activated.

4. Click **Choose Variables** to open the **Choose Variables – HLM2** dialog box and choose the ID and variables by clicking the appropriate check boxes (see Fig. 2.6). To de-select, click the box again.

5. Select the options for missing data in the level-1 file (there is no missing data in HSB1.SAV; see Section 2.6 for details).

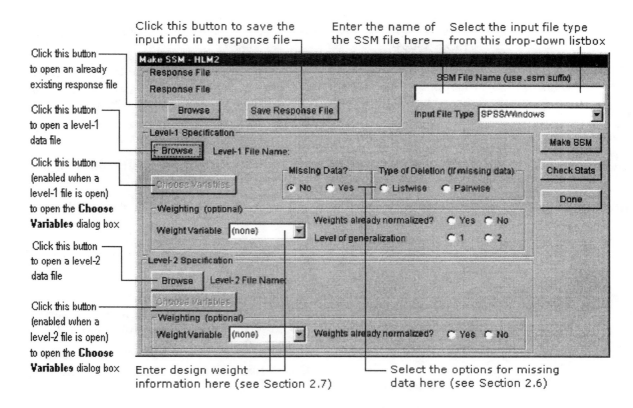

Figure 2.5   Make SSM – HLM2 dialog box

6. (Optional) Enter level-1 design weight information (design weights are not used in the HS&B data set; see Section 2.7 for details).

7. Click **Browse** in the **Level-2 specification** section to open an **Open Data File** dialog box.

8. Open a level-2 SPSS system file in the HLM folder (HSB2.SAV in our example). The **Choose Variables** button below **Browse** will be activated.

9. Click **Choose Variables** to open the **Choose Variables – HLM2** dialog box and choose the ID and variables by clicking the appropriate check boxes (see Fig. 2.7).

10. (Optional) Enter level-2 design weight information (design weights are not used in the HS&B data set; see Section 2.7 for details).

11. Enter a name for the SSM file in the **SSM File Name** box (for example, HSB.SSM).

12. Click **Save Response File** in the **Response File** section to open a **Save Response File** dialog box. Enter a name for the response file (for example, HSBSPSS.RSP). Click **Save** to save the file. The response file saves all the information entered by the user. It can be re-opened by clicking the **Browse** button (see Fig. 2.5) for quick changes.

    Note that HLM will also save the input information into another file called CREATESS.RSP.

13. Click the **MAKE SSM** button. A screen displaying the prompts and responses for SSM creation will appear.

To check if the data have been properly read into HLM

1. Click **Check Stats** to display and check the level-1 and level-2 descriptive statistics (see Fig. 2.8). Close the Notepad window, when done.[3]

2. Click **Done**. The **HLM for Windows** window displays the type and name on its title bar (**hlm2** and **HSB.SSM**) and the level-1 variables in a listbox (see Fig. 2.9).

2.5.1.2   ASCII file input

Below is the procedure for creating a sufficient statistics file with input from ASCII data files.

To inform HLM of the input and SSM file type

1. At the **HLM for Windows** window, open the **File** menu.

2. Choose **SSM. . . New. . . ASCII input**, a **Select SSM type** dialog box will open.

3. Select **HLM2** (see Fig. 2.4) and click **OK**. A **Make SSM – HLM2** dialog box will open (see Fig. 2.10).

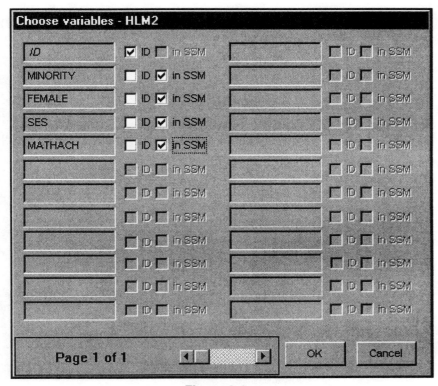

Figure 2.6
Choose Variables – HLM2 dialog box for the level-1 file, HSB1.SAV of the HS&B example

To supply HLM with appropriate information for the data, the command, and the SSM files

1. Click **Browse** in the **Level-1 specification** section to open an **Open Data File** dialog box. Open a level-1 ASCII data file in the HLM examples folder (HSB1.DAT in our example). The file name appears in the **Level-1 File Name** box.

2. Enter the number of variables into the **Number of Variables box** (4 in our example) and the data entry format in the **Data Format** box (A4,4F12.3 in our example).

---

[3]Use "Save As" and give it a new name if you anticipate later use.

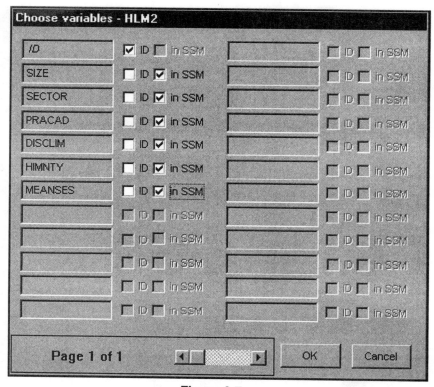

Figure 2.7
Choose Variables – HLM2 dialog box for the level-2 file, HSB2.SAV of the HS&B example

Note that the ID is included in the format statement, but excluded in the **Number of Variables** box. Rules for input format statements are given in Section A.2 in Appendix A.

3. Click **Labels** to open the **Enter Variable Labels** dialog box.

4. Enter the variable names into the boxes (MINORITY, FEMALE, SES, MATHACH for our example, see Fig. 2.11). Click **OK**.

5. Click the **Missing Data** button to enter level-1 missing data info (there is no missing data in HSB1.DAT; see Section 2.6 for details).

6. (Optional) Enter level-1 design weight information (design weights are not used in the HS&B data set; see Section 2.7 for details).

Click here to close Notepad

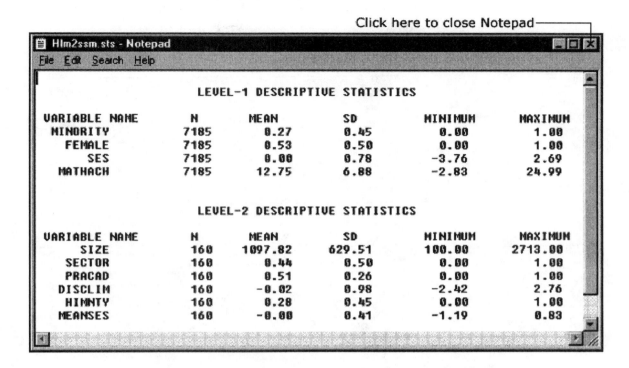

Figure 2.8   Descriptive Statistics for the SSM file, HSB.SSM

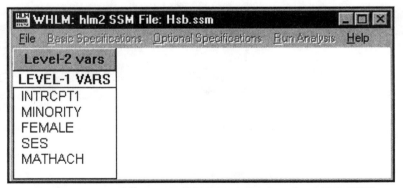

Figure 2.9   WHLM: hlm2 SSM File window for HSB.SSM

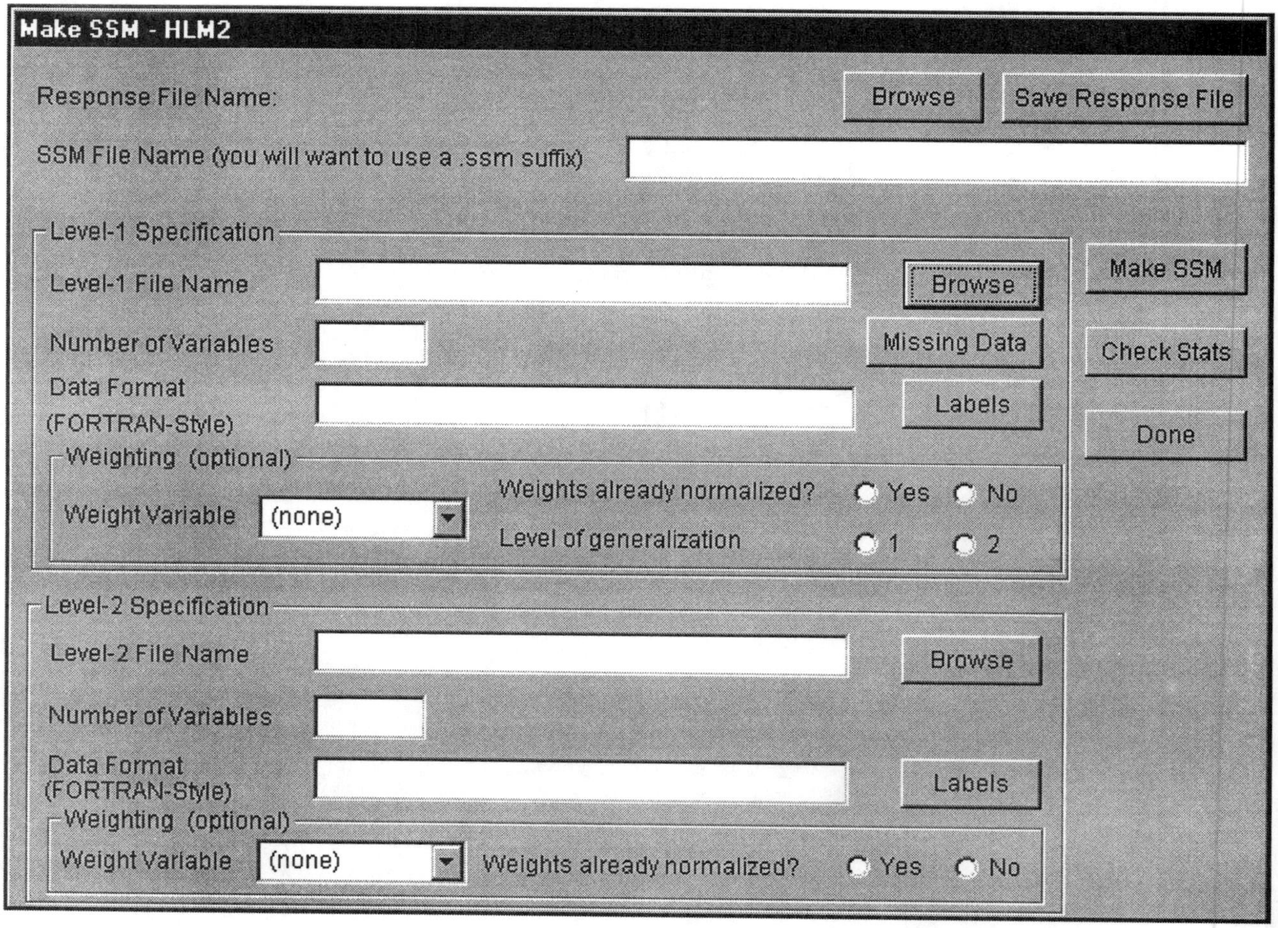

Figure 2.10 Make SSM – HLM2 dialog box

7. Click **Browse** in the **Level-2 specification** section to open an **Open Data File** dialog box. Open a level-2 ASCII data file in the HLM folder (HSB2.DAT in our example). The filename will appear in the **Level-2 File Name** box.

8. Enter the number of variables into the **Number of Variables** box (6 in our example) and the data entry format in the **Data Format** box (A4,6F12.3 in our example).

9. Click **Labels** to open the **Enter Variable Labels** dialog box for the level-2 variables.

10. Enter the variable names into the **Variable** boxes (SIZE, SECTOR, PRACAD, DISCLIM, HIMINTY, MEANSES in our example, see Fig. 2.12). Click **OK**.

11. (Optional) Enter level-2 design weight information (design weights are not used in the HS&B data set; see Section 2.7 for details).

12. Enter an SSM filename in the **SSM File Name** box (for example, HSB.SSM).

13. Click **Save Response File** in the **Response File** section to open a **Save Response File** dialog box. Enter a name for the response file (for example, HSBASCII.RSP). Click **Save** to save the file.

To check if the data have been properly read into HLM

The procedure is the same as above for SPSS file input as described in Section 2.5.1.1.

2.5.1.3 SAS transport and SYSTAT file input and other formats for raw data

For SAS or SYSTAT file input, a user selects either **SAS 5 transport** or **SYSTAT** from the **Input File Type** drop-down menu as appropriate to open the **Make New HLM2/MLM SSM File From non-ASCII Files** dialog box. With the third-party software module included in the current version, HLM will read data from STATA, EXCEL, LOTUS, and many other formats. Select **Anything else** from the **Input File Type** drop-down list box *before* clicking on the **Browse** button in the input file specification sections.

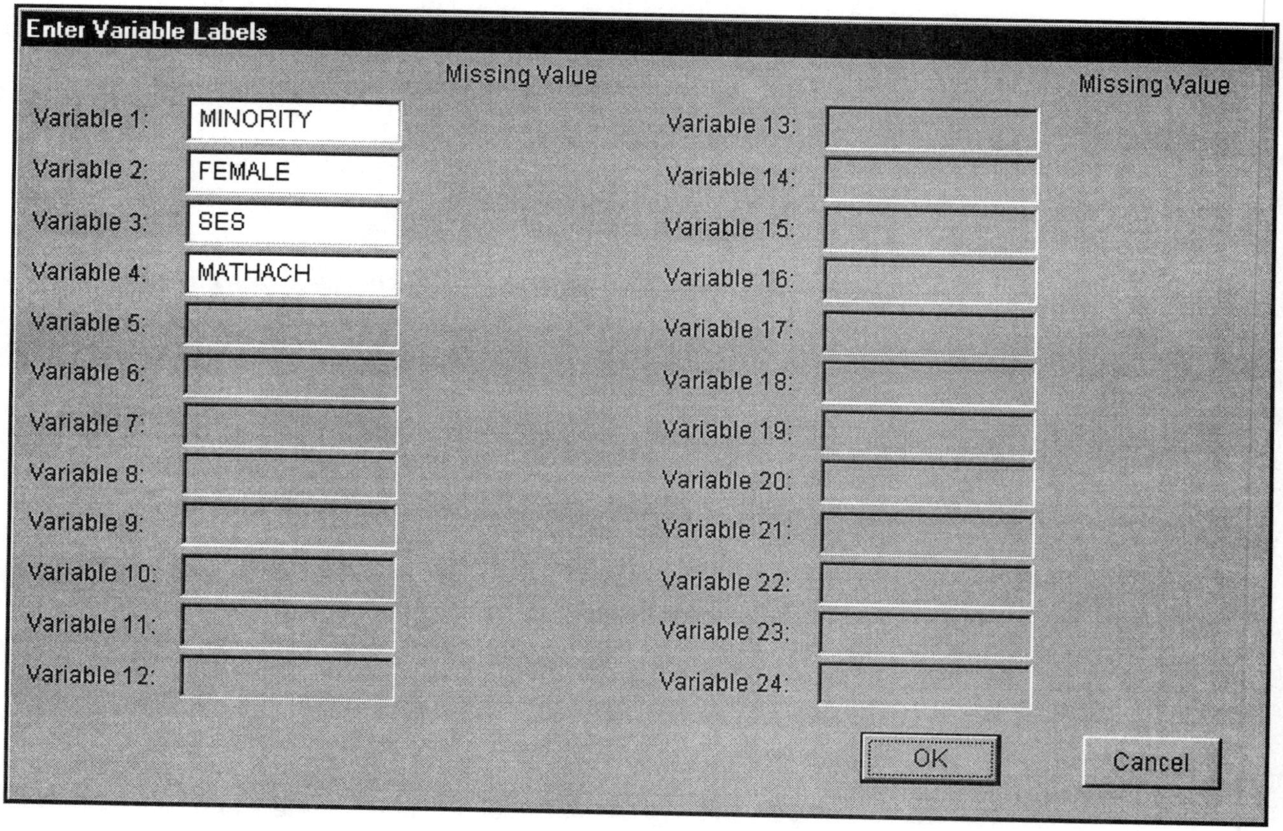

Figure 2.11   Enter Variable Labels dialog box for level-1 file, HSB1.DAT

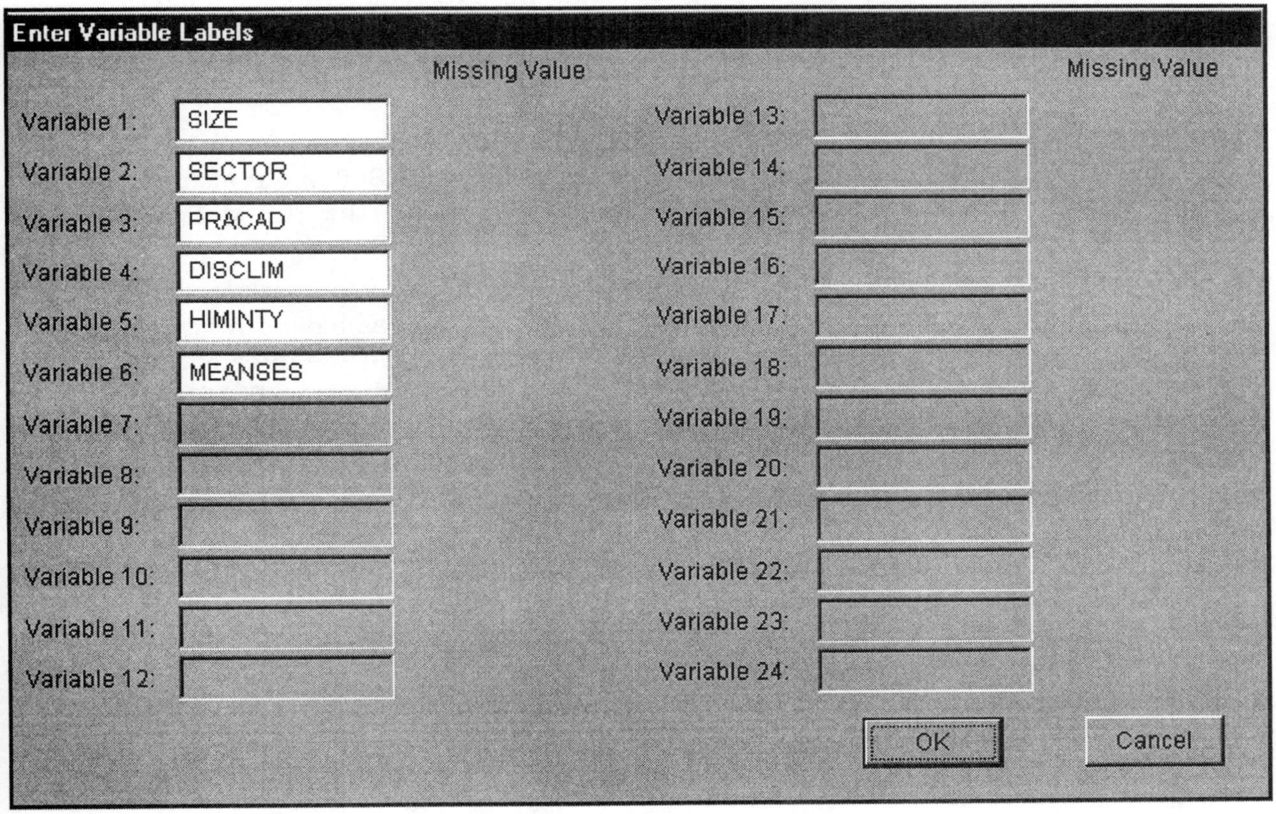

Enter Variable Labels

	Missing Value		Missing Value
Variable 1:	SIZE	Variable 13:	
Variable 2:	SECTOR	Variable 14:	
Variable 3:	PRACAD	Variable 15:	
Variable 4:	DISCLIM	Variable 16:	
Variable 5:	HIMINTY	Variable 17:	
Variable 6:	MEANSES	Variable 18:	
Variable 7:		Variable 19:	
Variable 8:		Variable 20:	
Variable 9:		Variable 21:	
Variable 10:		Variable 22:	
Variable 11:		Variable 23:	
Variable 12:		Variable 24:	

OK   Cancel

Figure 2.12   Enter Variable Labels dialog box for level-2 file, HSB2.DAT

2.5.2 Executing analyses based on the SSM file

Once the SSM file is constructed, it can be used as input for the analysis. As mentioned earlier, model specification has three steps:

1. Specification of the level-1 model. In our example, we shall model mathematics achievement (MATHACH) as the outcome, to be predicted by student SES. Hence, the level-1 model will have two coefficients: the intercept and the SES–MATHACH slope.

2. Specification of the level-2 prediction model. We shall predict each school's intercept by school SECTOR and MEANSES in our example. Similarly, SECTOR and MEANSES will predict the SES–MATHACH slope of each school.

3. Specification of level-1 coefficients as random or non-random. We shall model both the intercept and the slope as having randomly varying residuals. That is, we are assuming that the intercept and slope vary not only as a function of the two predictors, SECTOR and MEANSES, but also as a function of a unique school effect. The two school residuals (*e.g.*, for the intercept and slope) are assumed sampled from a bivariate normal distribution.

The procedure for executing analyses based on the SSM file is described below.

Step 1: To specify the level-1 prediction model

1. From the **HLM for Windows** window, open the **File** menu.

2. Choose **SSM. . . Old** to open an **Open SSM/MDM File** dialog box. Open an existing SSM file (HSB.SSM in our example). The name of the SSM file will be displayed on the title bar of the main window. A listbox for level-1 variables (LEVEL-1 VARS) will appear (see Fig. 2.9).

3. Click on the name of the outcome variable (MATHACH in our example). Click **Outcome Variable** (see Fig. 2.13). The specified model will appear in equation format.[4]

---

[4]The user may switch to batch mode execution after specifying the outcome. The procedure is as follows:

4. Click on the name of a predictor variable and click the type of centering (SES and **add variable group centered**, see Fig. 2.14). The predictor will appear on the equation screen and each regression coefficient associated with it will become an outcome in the level-2 model (see Fig. 2.15).

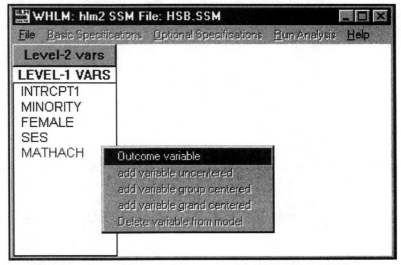

Figure 2.13   Model window for the HS&B example

Step 2: To specify the level-2 prediction model

1. Click the check box in front of the regression coefficient(s) the user intends to model (β_0 (intercept) and β_1 (SES slope) in our HS&B example).

2. Click the **Level-2 vars** button to display the LEVEL-2 VARS listbox. Click to select the variable(s) to be entered as predictor(s) and the

---

(a) Open the **File** menu and choose **Manually edit command file**. A Notepad displaying the model will open.

(b) Edit the command file (see Appendix A for details).

(c) Save the file.

(d) Close the Notepad session using the close button to return to the Model Mode. The screen will display the modified model.

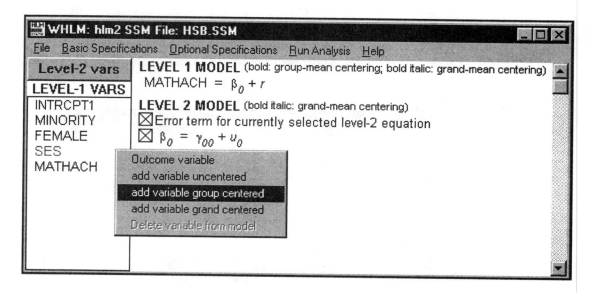

Figure 2.14
Specification of model predictor, SES, for the HS&B example

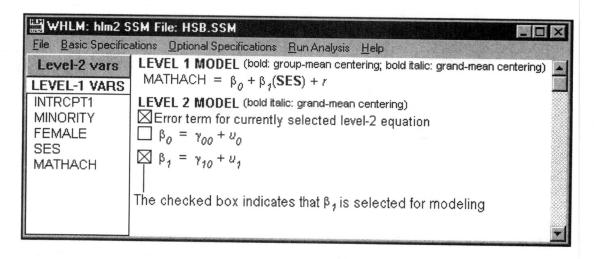

Figure 2.15   Model window for the HS&B example

type of centering (for our example, select SECTOR and **add variable uncentered**, and MEANSES and **add variable grand-mean centered** to model β_0 and β_1, see Fig. 2.16. Fig. 2.17 displays the model specified).

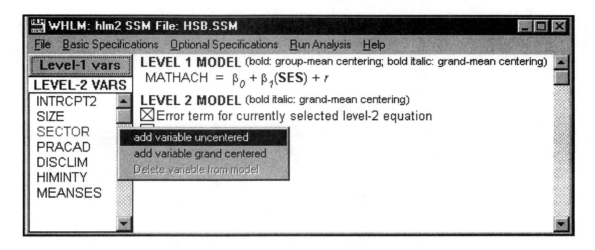

Figure 2.16   Specification of the level-2 model

Step 3: To specify level-1 coefficients as random or non-random

The program begins by assuming that every level-1 coefficient will be treated as random. Click the **Error term for currently selected level-2 equation** box to constrain the u term at the end of an equation to be zero (see Fig. 2.17). The u at the end of the equation will disappear as a result (in the HS&B example, both level-1 coefficients, β_0 and β_1, are to be specified as random). The level-1 coefficient is now specified as "fixed."

Steps 1 to 3 are the three major steps for executing analyses based on the SSM file. Other analytic options are described in Section 2.9. After specifying the model, the user can give a title to the output and name the output filename by the following procedure:

1. Select **Basic Specifications** to open the **Basic Model Specifications – HLM2** dialog box. Enter a title in the **Title** box (for example, *Intercept and slopes-as-Outcomes Model*) and an output filename in **Output file**

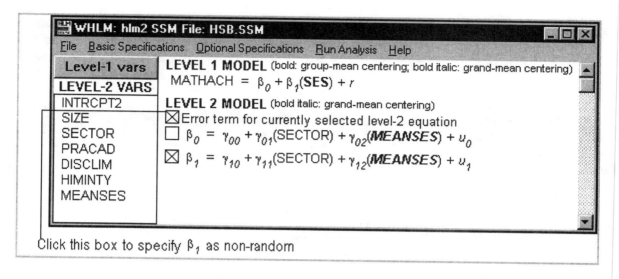

Figure 2.17   Model window for the HS&B example

name box (for example, HSB1.OUT). See Fig. 2.18. Click **OK**. See Section 2.8 for the definitions of entries and options in the **Basic Model Specifications – HLM2** dialog box.

2. Open the **File** menu and choose **Save As** to open a **Save Command File** dialog box.

3. Enter a command file name (for example, HSB1.HLM).

4. Click **Run Analysis**. A box displaying the iterations will appear.

In our example, after the 49th iteration, the user is prompted with the question: *The maximum number of iterations had been reached, but the analysis has not converged. Do you want to continue until convergence?* See Fig. 2.19. Enter Y and press Enter. Convergence is achieved on the 61st iteration.

Note: If you wish to terminate the computations early, press the Ctrl–C key combination once. This will stop the analysis after the current iteration and provide a full presentation of results based on that iteration. If you press Ctrl–C more than once, however, computation is terminated immediately and all output is lost.

5. Open the **File** menu and choose **View Output** to call up Notepad to look at the results.

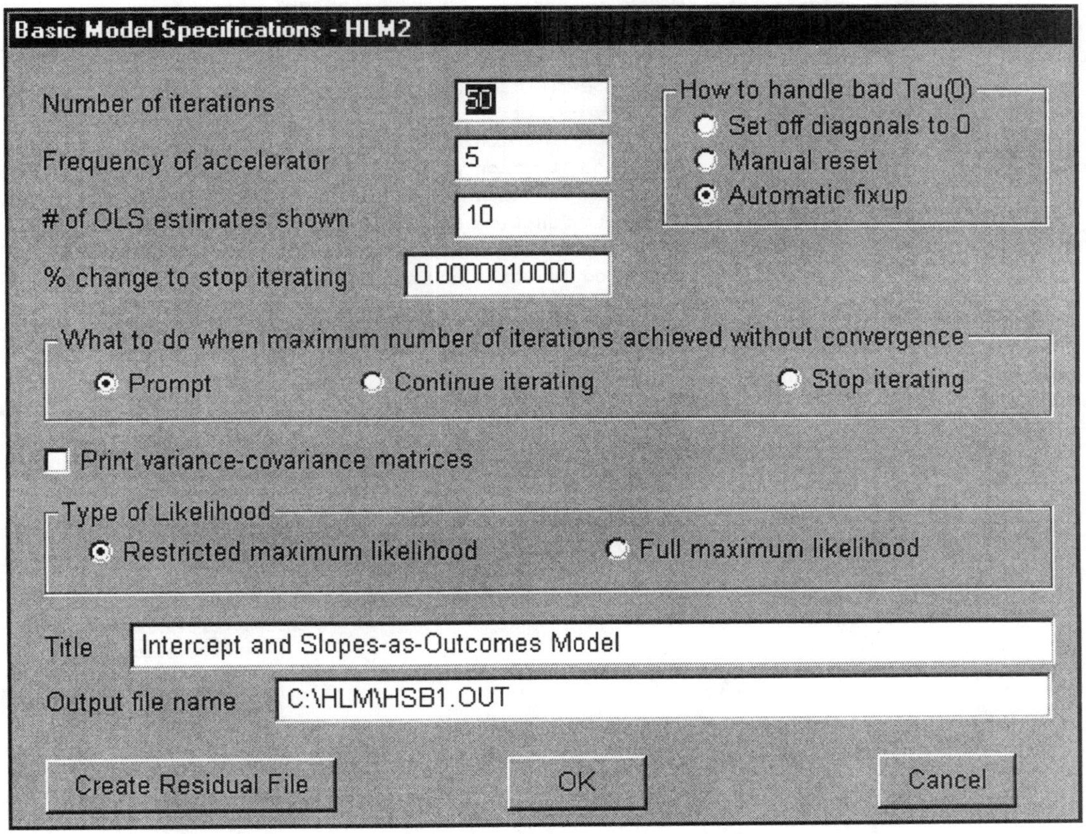

Figure 2.18
Basic Model Specifications – HLM 2 dialog box for the HS&B example (see Section 2.8 for a description of the options)

2.5.3 Annotated HLM2 output

Here is the output produced by the Windows session described above (see example HSB1.HLM).

```
D:\hlm5\HLM2.EXE

The value of the likelihood function at iteration 36 = -2.325094E+004
The value of the likelihood function at iteration 37 = -2.325094E+004
The value of the likelihood function at iteration 38 = -2.325094E+004
The value of the likelihood function at iteration 39 = -2.325094E+004
The value of the likelihood function at iteration 40 = -2.325094E+004
The value of the likelihood function at iteration 41 = -2.325094E+004
The value of the likelihood function at iteration 42 = -2.325094E+004
The value of the likelihood function at iteration 43 = -2.325094E+004
The value of the likelihood function at iteration 44 = -2.325094E+004
The value of the likelihood function at iteration 45 = -2.325094E+004
The value of the likelihood function at iteration 46 = -2.325094E+004
The value of the likelihood function at iteration 47 = -2.325094E+004
The value of the likelihood function at iteration 48 = -2.325094E+004
The value of the likelihood function at iteration 49 = -2.325094E+004


The maximum number of iterations has been reached, but the analysis has
not converged. Do you want to continue until convergence?
```

Figure 2.19   Iteration screen

```
Program:              HLM 5 Hierarchical Linear and Nonlinear Modeling
Authors:              Stephen Raudenbush, Tony Bryk, & Richard Congdon
Publisher:            Scientific Software International, Inc. (c) 2000
                                                   techsupport@ssicentral.com
                                                   www.ssicentral.com
-------------------------------------------------------------------------------
Module:     HLM2.EXE (5.01.2040.2)
Date:       9 February 2000, Wednesday
Time:       12:20:57
-------------------------------------------------------------------------------
```

*The first page of the output lists, after a program header, the specifics for
this analysis. For your convenience, it has the date and time the problem
ran. If you need to contact technical support at SSI, be sure to include the
version number of the module you are using. It is given in parentheses
right after the module name.*

```
SPECIFICATIONS FOR THIS HLM2 RUN

  Problem Title: INTERCEPT AND SLOPES-AS-OUTCOMES MODEL

  The data source for this run  = HSB.SSM
  The command file for this run = HSB1.HLM
  Output file name              = HSB1.OUT
```

```
The maximum number of level-2 units = 160
The maximum number of iterations = 10000
Method of estimation: restricted maximum likelihood
```

Weighting Specification

	Weighting?	Weight Variable Name	Normalized?
Level 1	no		no
Level 2	no		no

```
The outcome variable is  MATHACH
```

```
The model specified for the fixed effects was:
-----------------------------------------------------
```

Level-1 Coefficients	Level-2 Predictors
----------------------	---------------
INTRCPT1, B0	INTRCPT2, G00
	SECTOR, G01
	MEANSES, G02
* SES slope, B1	INTRCPT2, G10
	SECTOR, G11
	MEANSES, G12

```
'*' - This level-1 predictor has been centered around its group mean.
```

```
The model specified for the covariance components was:
-----------------------------------------------------------
```

```
        Sigma squared (constant across level-2 units)

        Tau dimensions
            INTRCPT1
                SES slope
```

```
Summary of the model specified (in equation format)
----------------------------------------------------
```

```
Level-1 Model

Y = B0 + B1*(SES) + R

Level-2 Model
B0 = G00 + G01*(SECTOR) + G02*(MEANSES) + U0
B1 = G10 + G11*(SECTOR) + G12*(MEANSES) + U1
```

The information presented on the first page or two of the HLM2 printout summarizes key details about the SSM file (e.g., number of level-2 units, whether weighting was specified), and about both the fixed and random effects models specified for this run. In this particular case, we are estimating the model specified by Equations 4.11 and 4.15 in Hierarchical Linear Models.

```
Level-1 OLS regressions
-----------------------

Level-2 Unit    INTRCPT1        SES slope
-------------------------------------------------------------------------
        1224     9.71545         2.50858
        1288    13.51080         3.25545
        1296     7.63596         1.07596
        1308    16.25550         0.12602
        1317    13.17769         1.27391
        1358    11.20623         5.06801
        1374     9.72846         3.85432
        1433    19.71914         1.85429
        1436    18.11161         1.60056
        1461    16.84264         6.26650
```

By default, HLM2 prints out the ordinary least squares (OL) regression equations, based on the level-1 model, for the first 10 units. When first analyzing a new data set, examining the OL equations for all of the units may be helpful in identifying possible outlying cases and bad data. The number of OL equations to be printed is selected in the "Basic Model Specifications" dialog box.

```
The average OLS level-1 coefficient for INTRCPT1 =      12.62075
The average OLS level-1 coefficient for      SES =       2.20164
```

This is a simple average of the OL coefficients across all units that had sufficient data to permit a separate OL estimation.

```
Least Squares Estimates
-----------------------

sigma_squared =    39.03409

The outcome variable is  MATHACH

Least-squares estimates of fixed effects
-------------------------------------------------------------------------
                                  Standard
    Fixed Effect      Coefficient Error     T-ratio  d.f.    P-value
-------------------------------------------------------------------------
```

```
For       INTRCPT1, B0
    INTRCPT2, G00          12.084805    0.106898    113.050    7179    0.000
      SECTOR, G01           1.280341    0.157845      8.111    7179    0.000
     MEANSES, G02           5.163791    0.190834     27.059    7179    0.000
For       SES slope, B1
    INTRCPT2, G10           2.935860    0.155284     18.906    7179    0.000
      SECTOR, G11          -1.642102    0.240178     -6.837    7179    0.000
     MEANSES, G12           1.044120    0.299885      3.482    7179    0.001
---------------------------------------------------------------------------

The outcome variable is  MATHACH

Least-squares estimates of fixed effects
(with robust standard errors)
---------------------------------------------------------------------------
                                    Standard
    Fixed Effect      Coefficient   Error      T-ratio   d.f.    P-value
---------------------------------------------------------------------------
For       INTRCPT1, B0
    INTRCPT2, G00          12.084805    0.169517     71.290    7179    0.000
      SECTOR, G01           1.280341    0.299077      4.281    7179    0.000
     MEANSES, G02           5.163791    0.334078     15.457    7179    0.000
For       SES slope, B1
    INTRCPT2, G10           2.935860    0.147580     19.893    7179    0.000
      SECTOR, G11          -1.642102    0.237223     -6.922    7179    0.000
     MEANSES, G12           1.044120    0.332897      3.136    7179    0.002
---------------------------------------------------------------------------
```

The first part of fixed effects tables are based on OL estimation. The second table provides robust standard errors. Note that the conventional OL standard errors associated with G00, G01, and G12 are smaller than their robust counterparts.

```
The least-squares likelihood value = -23362.111326
Deviance =  46724.22265
Number of estimated parameters =    1

STARTING VALUES
---------------
sigma(0)_squared =     36.72025

Tau(0)
INTRCPT1,B0     2.56964       0.28026
     SES,B1     0.28026      -0.01614

New Tau(0)
INTRCPT1,B0     2.56964       0.28026
     SES,B1     0.28026       0.43223
```

The initial starting values failed to produce an appropriate variance-co-variance matrix (Tau(0)). An automatix fix-up was introduced to correct this problem (New Tau(0)).

```
The outcome variable is  MATHACH

Estimation of fixed effects
(Based on starting values of covariance components)
-------------------------------------------------------------------------
                                     Standard           Approx.
       Fixed Effect     Coefficient  Error    T-ratio   d.f.    P-value
-------------------------------------------------------------------------
For        INTRCPT1, B0
   INTRCPT2, G00         12.095864   0.204343  59.194    157    0.000
     SECTOR, G01          1.226266   0.315204   3.890    157    0.000
    MEANSES, G02          5.335184   0.379879  14.044    157    0.000
For        SES slope, B1
   INTRCPT2, G10          2.935410   0.168691  17.401    157    0.000
     SECTOR, G11         -1.634083   0.260672  -6.269    157    0.000
    MEANSES, G12          1.015061   0.323523   3.138    157    0.002
-------------------------------------------------------------------------
```

Above are the initial estimates of the fixed effects. These are not to be used in drawing substantial conclusions.

```
The value of the likelihood function at iteration 1 = -2.325199E+004
The value of the likelihood function at iteration 2 = -2.325182E+004
The value of the likelihood function at iteration 3 = -2.325174E+004
The value of the likelihood function at iteration 4 = -2.325169E+004
The value of the likelihood function at iteration 5 = -2.325154E+004
                                                        .
                                                        .
                                                        .
The value of the likelihood function at iteration 57 = -2.325094E+004
The value of the likelihood function at iteration 58 = -2.325094E+004
The value of the likelihood function at iteration 59 = -2.325094E+004
The value of the likelihood function at iteration 60 = -2.325094E+004

Iterations stopped due to small change in likelihood function
```

Below are the estimates of the variance and covariance components from the final iteration and selected other statistics based on them.

```
****** ITERATION 61 ******

Sigma_squared =    36.70313              Level-1 variance components

Tau
```

```
INTRCPT1,B0      2.37996       0.19058          Level-2 variance-covariance components
     SES,B1      0.19058       0.14892


Tau (as correlations)
 INTRCPT1,B0  1.000  0.320                        Level-2 variance-covariance components
     SES,B1   0.320  1.000                                  expressed as correlations


 --------------------------------------------------
  Random level-1 coefficient   Reliability estimate
 --------------------------------------------------
   INTRCPT1, B0                         0.733        These are average reliability estimates
       SES, B1                          0.073          for the random level-1 coefficients
 --------------------------------------------------

The value of the likelihood function at iteration 61 = -2.325094E+004
```

The next three tables present the final estimates for: the fixed effects with GLS and robust standard errors, variance components at level-1 and level-2, and related test statistics. These results are slightly more precise than those reported in Table 4.5, p. 72 of Hierarchical Linear Models, because they are based on the more efficient computing routines used in versions 3 and higher.

```
The outcome variable is  MATHACH

Final estimation of fixed effects:
 ----------------------------------------------------------------------------
                                   Standard           Approx.
     Fixed Effect     Coefficient  Error     T-ratio  d.f.     P-value
 ----------------------------------------------------------------------------
 For        INTRCPT1, B0
    INTRCPT2, G00      12.096006    0.198734   60.865    157     0.000
      SECTOR, G01       1.226384    0.306272    4.004    157     0.000
     MEANSES, G02       5.333056    0.369161   14.446    157     0.000
 For     SES slope, B1
    INTRCPT2, G10       2.937981    0.157135   18.697    157     0.000
      SECTOR, G11      -1.640954    0.242905   -6.756    157     0.000
     MEANSES, G12       1.034427    0.302566    3.419    157     0.001
 ----------------------------------------------------------------------------


The outcome variable is  MATHACH

Final estimation of fixed effects
(with robust standard errors)
 ----------------------------------------------------------------------------
                                   Standard           Approx.
     Fixed Effect     Coefficient  Error     T-ratio  d.f.     P-value
 ----------------------------------------------------------------------------
 For        INTRCPT1, B0
```

```
    INTRCPT2, G00        12.096006    0.173699    69.638    157    0.000
      SECTOR, G01         1.226384    0.308484     3.976    157    0.000
     MEANSES, G02         5.333056    0.334600    15.939    157    0.000
For       SES slope, B1
    INTRCPT2, G10         2.937981    0.147620    19.902    157    0.000
      SECTOR, G11        -1.640954    0.237401    -6.912    157    0.000
     MEANSES, G12         1.034427    0.332785     3.108    157    0.002
----------------------------------------------------------------------
```

The first table provides model-based estimates of the standard errors while the second table provides robust estimates of the standard errors. Note that the two sets of standard errors are similar. If the robust and model-based standard errors are substantively different, it is recommended that the user further investigate the tenability of key assumptions (see Section 4.3 on examining residuals).

```
Final estimation of variance components:
----------------------------------------------------------------------
Random Effect        Standard     Variance    df   Chi-square  P-value
                     Deviation    Component
----------------------------------------------------------------------
INTRCPT1,      U0     1.54271      2.37996    157   605.29503   0.000
    SES slope, U1     0.38590      0.14892    157   162.30867   0.369
  level-1,     R      6.05831     36.70313
----------------------------------------------------------------------


Statistics for current covariance components model
---------------------------------------------------
Deviance =  46501.87563
Number of estimated parameters =    4
```

Exploratory Analysis: estimated level-2 coefficients and their standard errors
    obtained by regressing EB residuals on level-2 predictors selected for
    possible inclusion in subsequent HLM runs

```
----------------------------------------------------------------------
Level-1 Coefficient         Potential Level-2 Predictors
----------------------------------------------------------------------

                        SIZE    PRACAD   DISCLIM   HIMINTY
          INTRCPT1,B0
Coefficient             0.000    0.690   -0.161    -0.543
Standard Error          0.000    0.404    0.106     0.229
t value                 1.569    1.707   -1.515    -2.372

                        SIZE    PRACAD   DISCLIM   HIMINTY
              SES,B1
Coefficient             0.000    0.039   -0.005    -0.058
Standard Error          0.000    0.044    0.012     0.025
```

```
        t value                1.297    0.899   -0.425   -2.339
```

```
A residual file, called HSB1.SPS, has been created.  Note, some statistics
could not be computed and a value of -99 has been entered. These should be
recoded to 'missing values' before any analyses are performed.

tauvc.dat, containing tau has been created.
gamvc.dat, containing the variance-covariance matrix of gamma has been created.
gamvcr.dat, containing the robust variance-covariance matrix of gamma has
been created.
The above files have been created with a (nE15.7,1X) format.
```

2.5.4 Model checking based on the residual file

The residual file produced by HLM2 provides the data analyst with a means of checking the fit and distributional assumptions of the model. This file will contain the EB residuals (see Eq. 1.10 above), OL residuals (see Eq. 1.9 above), and fitted values, *i.e.*,

$$\hat{\gamma}_{q0} + \Sigma\hat{\gamma}_{qs}W_{sj}$$

for each level-1 coefficient. By adding the OL residuals to the corresponding fitted values, the analyst can also obtain the OL estimate $\hat{\beta}_{qj}$ of the corresponding level-1 coefficient, β_{qj}. Similarly, by adding the EB residuals to the fitted values, we obtain the EB estimate β_{qj}^* of the level-1 coefficient, β_{qj}. Note, OL residuals are only produced for those units which have sufficient data to permit a separate OLS estimation of the level-1 model for that unit. In contrast, EB estimates are provided for all units included in the analysis.

In addition, the file will contain Mahalanobis distances (which are discussed below), estimates of the total and residual standard deviations (log metric) within each unit, the values of the predictors used in the level-2 model, and any other level-2 prediction variables selected by the user.

To create the SPSS residual file type

1. Select **Basic Specifications** to open the **Basic Model Specifications – HLM2** dialog box.

2. Click **Create Residual File** to open a **Create Residual File** dialog box.

3. Double-click the variables to be entered into the residual file (for our example, select DISCLIM, PRACAD, HIMINTY, and SIZE, see Fig. 2.20).

4. Select SPSS as **Residual File Type**. Note that the user can create a SYSTAT or SAS file type as well.

5. Enter a name for the residual file in the **Residual File Name** box (for example RESFIL.SPS, see Fig. 2.20). Click **OK**.

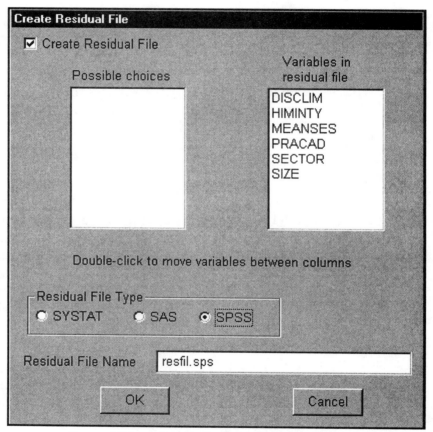

Figure 2.20   Create Residual File dialog box

Below is an example of an SPSS version of a residual file.

```
DATA LIST FIXED RECORDS = 6
```

```
/1 ID NJ CHIPCT MDIST LNTOTVAR OLSRSVAR MDRSVAR (A12,F5,5F11.5)
/2 EBINTRCP EBSES    (2F11.5)
/3 OLINTRCP OLSES    (2F11.5)
/4 FVINTRCP FVSES    (2F11.5)
/5 PV00 PV10 PV11 (3F11.5)
/6   SIZE    SECTOR   PRACAD  DISCLIM  HIMINTY  MEANSES ( 6F11.5).
BEGIN DATA
        1224   47    0.01875    0.00327    2.02739    2.01643    2.00545
   -0.07338  -0.00469
   -0.09801   0.01334
    9.81346   2.49525
    0.614791  0.046355   0.129200
  842.00000   0.00000    0.35000    1.59700    0.00000   -0.42800
        1288   25    0.11875    0.14750    1.94945    1.92016    1.89907
    0.45587   0.04211
    0.73216   0.18506
   12.77864   3.07039
    0.924264  0.071304   0.134372
 1855.00000   0.00000    0.27000    0.17400    0.00000    0.12800
        1296   48    2.73860    2.45979    1.67767    1.67989    1.68407
   -1.71022  -0.22337
   -2.22016  -1.42756
    9.85612   2.50352
    0.605396  0.045421   0.128456
 1719.00000   0.00000    0.32000   -0.13700    1.00000   -0.42000
```

(Only the data from the first three units are reproduced here.)

The residual file above is an SPSS syntax file. It is meant for use with the SPSS package to construct various diagnostic plots.

2.5.4.1 Structure of the residual file

The first part of the SPSS syntax contains data definition information and file and variable definitions. A residual file will generally contain multiple records per unit.

- ❑ The first record contains the variable names ID, NJ, and CHIPCT through MDRSVAR.
- ❑ The second record contains the two EB residuals.
- ❑ The third record contains two OL residuals.
- ❑ The fourth record contains the fitted or predicted values of the level-1 coefficients based on the estimated level-2 models.

- The fifth record contains the posterior variances and covariances of the estimates of intercept and the SES slopes.
- The last record contains the level-2 predictors used in the analysis plus those additional level-2 predictors requested by the user for inclusion in the file.

While most of this is straightforward, the information contained in the first record for each unit merits elaboration. NJ is the number of cases for level-2 unit j. It is followed by two variables, CHIPCT and MDIST. If we model q level-1 coefficients, MDIST would be the Mahalanobis distance (*i.e.*, the standardized squared distance of a unit from the center of a v-dimensional distribution, where v is the number of random effects per unit). Essentially, MDIST provides a single, summary measure of the distance of a unit's EB estimates, β_{qj}^*, from its "fitted value," $\hat{\gamma}_{q0} + \Sigma\hat{\gamma}_{qs}W_{sj}$.

Note that the units in the residual file are sorted in ascending order by MDIST. If the normality assumption is true, then the Mahalanobis distances should be distributed approximately $\chi^2(v)$. Analogous to univariate normal probability plotting, we can construct a Q–Q plot of MDIST vs. CHIPCT. CHIPCT are the expected values of the order statistics for a sample of size J selected from a population that is distributed $\chi^2(v)$. If the Q–Q plot resembles a 45 degree line, we have evidence that the random effects are distributed v-variate normal. In addition, the plot will help us detect outlying units (*i.e.*, units with large MDIST values well above the 45 degree line). It should be noted that such plots are good diagnostic tools only when the level-1 sample sizes, NJ, are at least moderately large. (For further discussion see *Hierarchical Linear Models*, p. 218.)

After MDIST, record 1 contains three estimates of the level-1 variability:

- The natural logarithm of the total standard deviation within each unit, LNTOTVAR.
- The natural logarithm of the residual standard deviation within each unit based on its least squares regression, OLSRSVAR.

  Note, this estimate exists only for those units which have sufficient data to compute level-1 OL estimates.
- The MDRSVAR, the natural logarithm of the residual standard deviation from the final fitted fixed effects model.

The natural log of these three standard deviations with the addition of a bias-correction factor for varying degrees of freedom is reported (see *Hierarchical Linear Models*, p. 169). We note that these statistics can be used as input for the V-known program in research on group-level correlates of diversity (Raudenbush & Bryk, 1987).

2.5.4.2 Some possible residual analyses

We illustrate below some of the possible uses of a residual file in examining the adequacy of fitted models and in considering other possible level-2 predictor variables. (For a full discussion of this topic see Chapter 9 of *Hierarchical Linear Models*.)

Here are the basic statistics for each of the variables created as part of the HLM2 residual file.

```
Descriptive Statistics
```

	N	Minimum	Maximum	Mean	Std. Deviation
NJ	160	14	67	44.91	11.85
CHIPCT	160	.00625	11.53664	1.9911459	1.9670473
MDIST	160	.00286	13.21842	2.0072714	2.1447755
LNTOTVAR	160	1.26524	2.13817	1.8205691	.1504338
OLSRSVAR	160	1.27157	2.08749	1.7898266	.1374496
MDRSVAR	160	1.31413	2.07195	1.7903878	.1349678
EBINTRCP	160	-3.71820	4.16209	1.875000E-07	1.3125839
EBSES	160	-.37793	.43750	3.750000E-07	.1415770
OLINTRCP	160	-7.71388	5.54525	-1.0794563E-02	1.8473861
OLSES	160	-3.56028	3.80348	-1.8229500E-02	1.4605545
FVINTRCP	160	5.76034	17.75416	12.6315498	2.4908064
FVSES	160	.51500	3.64967	2.2198701	.7756902
PV00	160	.48564	1.25479	.6678536	.1406214
PV10	160	.03612	.09787	5.033184E-02	1.137835E-02
PV11	160	.12086	.13835	.1289982	3.583093E-03
SIZE	160	100.00000	2713.00000	1097.8250000	629.5064309
SECTOR	160	.00000	1.00000	.4375000	.4976359
PRACAD	160	.00000	1.00000	.5139375	.2558967
DISCLIM	160	-2.41600	2.75600	-1.5125000E-02	.9769777
HIMNTY	160	.00000	1.00000	.2750000	.4479162
MEANSES	160	-1.18800	.83100	-1.8750000E-04	.4139731
Valid N (listwise)	160				

Examining heterogeneity of level-1 variance. Fig. 2.21 displays a histogram of the residual dispersions for the 160 schools based on the final fitted model.

This can be helpful in suggesting possible causes of heterogeneity of level-1 variances. (See the section *Testing homogeneity of level-1 variances* on page 60 for how to test this hypothesis within HLM2.) We see from the information below that there are three schools where the within-school standard deviation, σ_j, is considerably smaller than we would expect under a homogeneity hypothesis. (For a further discussion see *Hierarchical Linear Models*, pp. 207–210.)

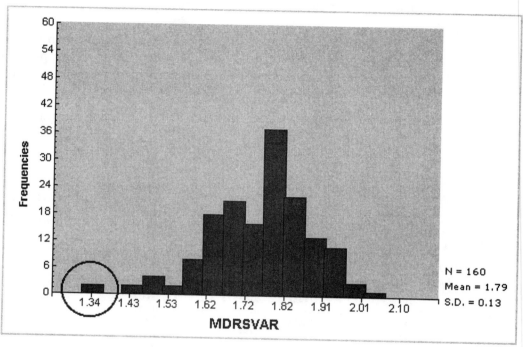

Figure 2.21   A histogram of within-school standard deviations

Examining OL and EB residuals.   Figure 2.22 shows a plot of the OL vs. EB residuals for the SES slopes. As expected, the EB residuals for the SES slope are much more compact than the OL residuals. While the latter range between $(-4.0, 4.0)$, the range for the EB residuals is only $(-0.5, 0.5)$. (For a further discussion see *Hierarchical Linear Models*, pp. 76–82.)

Next, in Fig. 2.23, we see a plot of the OL vs. EB residuals for the intercepts. Notice that while the EB intercepts are "shrunk" as compared to

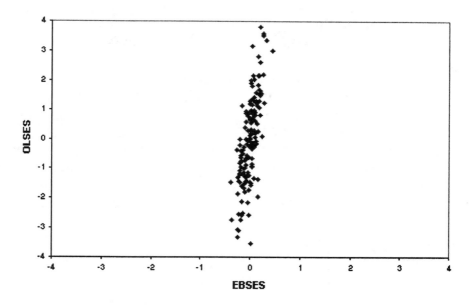

Figure 2.22   OL versus EB residuals for the SES slopes

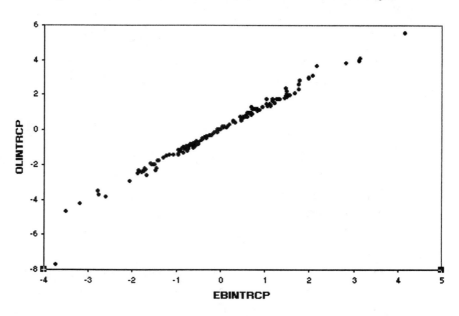

Figure 2.23   OL versus EB residuals for the intercepts

the OL estimates, the amount of shrinkage for the intercepts is far less than for the SES slopes in Fig. 2.22.

Exploring the potential of other possible level-2 predictors. Fig. 2.24 shows a plot of EB residuals against a possible additional level-2 predictor, PRACAD, for the intercept model. Although the relationship appears slight (a correlation of 0.15), PRACAD will enter this model as a significant predictor. (For a further discussion of the use of residual plots in identifying possible level-2 predictors see *Hierarchical Linear Models*, pp. 212–214.)

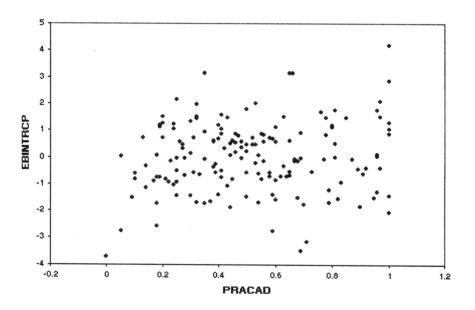

Figure 2.24
EB residuals against a possible additional level-2 predictor, PRACAD, for the intercept model

Examining possible nonlinearity of a level-2 predictor's relationship to an outcome. Next, in Fig. 2.25, is an example of a plot of EB residuals, in this case for the SES slope, against a variable included in the model. This plot suggests that the assumption of a linear relationship between the SES slope

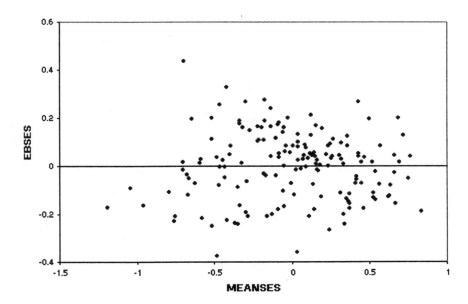

Figure 2.25   EB residuals for SES slope against MEANSES

and MEANSES is appropriate. (That is, the residuals appear randomly distributed around the zero line without regard to values of MEANSES.)

2.6   Handling of missing data

HLM2 provides two options[5] for handling missing data at level 1: pairwise deletion and listwise deletion of cases (see Fig. 2.5). The pairwise and listwise deletion follow the conventional routines used in standard statistical packages for regression analysis and the general linear model. Although the pairwise option is included, we caution against its use, especially when the amount of missing data is substantial.

At level 2, HLM2 assumes complete data. If you have missing data at level 2, you should either impute a value for the missing information, delete the units in question, or preferably use methods described in Section 9.2. **Prior to entering data into HLM2 it is important to check**

---

[5]See also Section 9.2.

that the level-2 file does not contain blanks or missing data codes as the program will read these as legitimate values.

For ASCII file input, click **Missing Data** in the **Make SSM – HLM2** dialog box. The dialog box displayed in Fig. 2.26 will open.

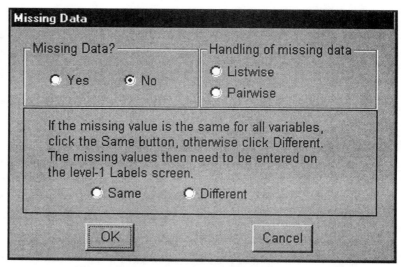

Figure 2.26   Missing Data dialog box

Assuming you have missing data, you should click the **Yes** box in the **Missing Data?** section, and almost certainly click **Listwise** in the **Handling of missing data** section. Then, if you have coded all of your missing values for all of the variables to the same number, check the **Same** button. When you specify the variable names, enter this number in the box to the right of the first variable in the **Enter Variable Labels** dialog box. If you have more than one missing value code, check the **Different** button, and enter these codes for each respective variable on the **Enter Variable Labels** dialog box.

For non-ASCII data at level 1, you should click **Yes** in the **Missing Data?** section, and almost certainly click **Listwise** in the **Type of Deletion** section. Then, when HLM2 encounters values coded as missing, it will recognize these properly. It is important to note that some statistics packages (*e.g.*, SAS) allow for more than one kind of missing data code. HLM2 (and HLM3 etc.) will only recognize the standard, "system-missing" code.

How HLM2 handles missing data differs a bit in the ASCII and non-ASCII cases. For ASCII data, it is very important that you do not have any missing data codes or blanks in the level-2 file. HLM2 will read these as valid data; missing data codes as they are coded and blanks will be read as zeros. For non-ASCII data, the program will skip over cases that have missing data in them.

Note: For non-ASCII file input, the user has to prepare either system-missing values or use missing values for the missing data.

2.7   Using design weights

In many studies, data arise from sample surveys in which units have been selected with known but unequal probabilities. In these cases it will often be desirable to weight observations in order to produce unbiased estimates of population parameters. According to standard practice in such cases, observations are weighted inversely proportional to their probability of selection.

For example, suppose that in a pre-election poll, ethnic minority voters are oversampled to guarantee that various ethnic groups are represented in the sample. Without weighting, the over-sampled groups would exert undue influence on population estimates of the proportion of voters favoring a specific candidate. Using design weights produces unbiased population estimates.

Note: design weights may not be used when specifying nonlinear models as discussed in Chapters 5 and 6.

2.7.1   Design weighting in the hierarchical context

When the data have a two-level hierarchical structure, several possibilities arise. Consider the problem of studying educational achievement in U.S. high schools. A two-stage cluster sampling procedure will commonly be utilized in which schools are first sampled and then, within schools, students are selected. Over-sampling may occur at the school level, at the student level, or both. For example, schools might be stratified on the basis of region of the country, sector (public versus private) and location (urban versus suburban versus rural). Within schools, students may be stratified on the basis of grade or ethnicity. Selection of schools or students — or both — with unequal probability may be required to achieve the purposes of a study. How can the data be appropriately weighted to produce unbiased population estimates?

The appropriate weighting scheme will depend not only on the sampling plan but also on the conceptual orientation of the study. In some cases, researchers will aim to supply generalizations that apply to a population of level-1 units, *e.g.*, students. In other cases, the goal may be to make statements about the population of level-2 units, *e.g.*, schools. We shall consider implementation of weighting with HLM2 for these two purposes.

2.7.2 Generalizing to a population of level-1 units

Suppose the purpose of a study is to make inferences about a population of students (level-1 units). Suppose that these units have been sampled with unequal but known probability from the population of interest. The user may then wish to compute a design weight, that is, a level-1 variable taking on values inversely related to the probability of selection for each level-1 unit. Often the user will wish to normalize these weights in order to preserve the effective sample size. This is accomplished by multiplying them by a constant such that the sum of the weights is N, the total number of students. If P_{ij} is the probability of selection of student i in school j, one might compute

$$w_{ij} = \frac{N/P_{ij}}{\sum_{j=1}^{J} \sum_{i=1}^{n_j} 1/P_{ij}} \ , \tag{2.1}$$

in which case

$$\sum_{j=1}^{J} \sum_{i=1}^{n_j} w_{ij} = N \ . \tag{2.2}$$

Alternatively, HLM2 will normalize weights supplied by the user. Either way, the user may ask HLM2 to weight level-1 variables by w_{ij} so that the resulting parameter estimates will be unbiased with respect to parameters defined on the population of level-1 units.

To weight for level-1 population estimates

1. Select the level-1 user-defined weight variable from the **Weight Variable** drop-down listbox (see Fig. 2.5).
2. Select an answer (yes or no) to the **Weight already normalized** question.
3. Select an answer (1 or 2) to the **Level of generalization** question.

Note the weighting options selected are directly incorporated into the computation of the sufficient statistics saved in the SSM file, and will be applied in every analysis using the SSM file. (The front page of each HLM2 output reminds the user of the weighting specification chosen during the SSM file creation.) If an alternative weighting scheme is desired (including the possibility of no weighting), the SSM file must be recreated accordingly.

2.7.3 Generalizing to a population of level-2 units

The procedures to apply design weights to aid making unbiased estimation over the population of level-2 units differ when the level-1 units have been sampled according to a simple random sample or with unequal probability within each level-2 units.

2.7.3.1 Simple random sample within level-2 units

Suppose now that the purpose of a study is to make inferences about a population of schools (level-2 units). Suppose that schools have been sampled with unequal but known probability from the population of interest while students have been sampled within schools according to a simple random sample. The user may then wish to compute a level-2 design weight, that is, a school-level variable having values inversely related to the probability of selection of the schools from the population of schools. The user may again wish to normalize these, that is, to multiply them by a constant such that the sum of the weights is J, the total number of schools. If P_j is the probability of selection of school j, one might compute

$$w_j = \frac{J/P_j}{\sum_{j=1}^{J} 1/P_j} \; ,$$
(2.3)

in which case

$$\sum_{j=1}^{J} w_j = J \; .$$
(2.4)

Again, HLM2 will, as an option, normalize conventional design weights supplied by the user. Either way, the user may ask HLM2 to weight level-2 variables by w_j so that the resulting parameter estimates will be unbiased with respect to parameters defined on the population of level-2 units.

2.7.3.2 Unequal probability of selection among level-2 units

In some cases, level-2 units may first be selected with unequal probability from the population of all level-2 units. Then, within level-2 units, level-1 units are selected with unequal probability within each level-2 unit. Assuming that the purpose of a study is to make inferences about a population of level-2 units, the weighting problem becomes a bit more complex. In most cases (*e.g.*, in the case of the national survey data collected by the US National Center for Education Statistics) two types of weights will be available: school weights and student weights. HLM2 enables the user simultaneously to use both types of weights to compute unbiased estimates of parameters defined on the population of schools.

The procedure works as follows. Again, consider the case of students nested within schools. First, the student data are weighted using level-1 weights that are normalized within each school. This weighting guarantees unbiased estimates of school-specific parameters. Also, school-level data are weighted by level-2 weights that are normalized across schools. This guarantees unbiased estimation over the population of schools.

Normalization of level-1 weights within schools works as follows. Within schools we compute

$$\omega_{ij} = \frac{n_j/w_{ij}}{\sum_{i=1}^{n_j} w_{ij}} \ , \tag{2.5}$$

where w_{ij} is, as before, the level-1 weight, guaranteeing that

$$\sum_{i=1}^{n_j} \omega_{ij} = n_j \ . \tag{2.6}$$

Then, the school weights are normalized as in Eq. 2.3. The simultaneous use of both weights is required to guarantee unbiased estimation.

Below is the procedure to apply weights for both levels.

To apply weights for both levels

1. Select the level-1 user-defined weight variable from the **Weight Variable** drop-down listbox (see Fig. 2.5).
2. Select an answer (yes or no) to the **Weight already normalized** question.
3. Select 2 for the **Level of generalization**.
4. Select the level-2 user-defined weight variable from the **Weight Variable** drop-down listbox (see Fig. 2.5).
5. Select an answer (yes or no) to the **Weight already normalized** question.

Note that the front page of each HLM2 analysis printout reminds the user of the weighting specification chosen during the SSM file creation.

2.8 Definitions of entries and options in Basic Model Specifications – HLM2 dialog box

Table 2.1 lists the definitions and options in the **Basic Model Specifications – HLM2** dialog box. See Fig. 2.27; note the linking numbers (1 through 7) in figure and table.

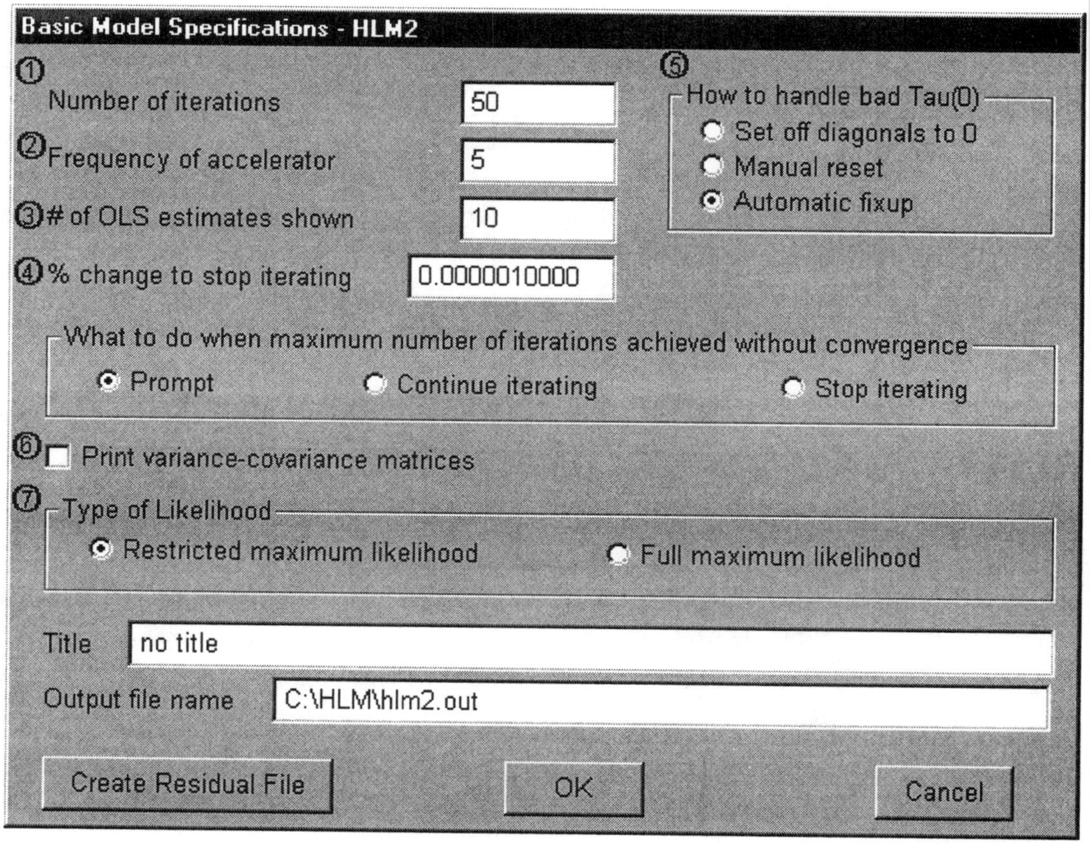

Figure 2.27   Basic Model Specifications – HLM2 dialog box

Table 2.1
Definitions and options in the Basic Model Specifications – HLM2 dialog box

	Key Terms	Function	Option	Definition
1	Number of iterations	Maximum number of iterations	*positive integer*	
2	Frequency of accelerator	Controls frequency of use of acceleration	*integer* ≥ 3	Selects how often the accelerator is used. Default is 5.
3	# of OLS estimates shown	Number of units for which OLS equations should be printed	*positive integer*	Default is 10.
4	% change to stop iterating	Convergence criterion for maximum likelihood estimation	*positive real number*	Default: 0.000001. Can be specified to be more (or less) restrictive
5	How to handle bad Tau(0)	Method of correcting unacceptable starting values	*3 choices*	1. Set off-diagonal to 0 2. Manual reset (starting values) 3. Automatic fix-up (default)
6	Print variance-covariance matrices	Requests files containing the variance-covariance matrices of Tau and Gammas as well as the inverse of the information matrix for Tau	*Selected*	See Section A.6 in Appendix A for format information for the files.
7	Type of Likelihood	Method of Estimation	*2 choices*	1. Restricted maximum likelihood 2. Full maximum likelihood (see Section 1.4 and p. 57 of *Hierarchical Linear Models*)

2.9 Other analytic options

2.9.1 Exploratory analysis of potential level-2 predictors

The user may be interested in computing "t-to-enter" statistics for potential level-2 predictors to guide specification of subsequent HLM2 models. The implementation procedure is as follows.

To implement exploratory analysis of potential level-2 predictors

1. Open the **Optional Specifications** menu and choose **Exploratory Analysis (level 2)**. The program switches to **Select Variables For Exploratory Analysis** mode.
2. Click the box in front of the regression coefficient to model the corresponding coefficient. Click to select variables for exploratory analysis. (Fig. 2.28 displays the level-2 predictors chosen for our HS&B example).
3. Click **Return to Model Mode** to return to the model window.

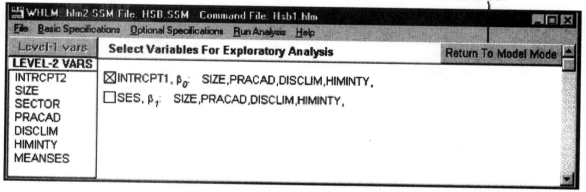

Figure 2.28
Select Variables For Exploratory Analysis dialog box for the HS&B example

The following contains selected HLM2 output to illustrate exploratory analysis of potential level-2 predictors.

Exploratory Analysis: estimated level-2 coefficients and their standard errors
obtained by regressing EB residuals on level-2 predictors selected for
possible inclusion in subsequent HLM runs

```
-------------------------------------------------------------------------
Level-1 Coefficient          Potential Level-2 Predictors
-------------------------------------------------------------------------

                         SIZE    PRACAD  DISCLIM  HIMINTY
       INTRCPT1,B0
Coefficient              0.000   0.690   -0.161   -0.543
Standard Error           0.000   0.404    0.106    0.229
t value                  1.569   1.707   -1.515   -2.372

                         SIZE    PRACAD  DISCLIM  HIMINTY
         SES,B1
Coefficient              0.000   0.039   -0.005   -0.058
Standard Error           0.000   0.044    0.012    0.025
t value                  1.297   0.899   -0.425   -2.339
-------------------------------------------------------------------------
```

*The results of this exploratory analysis suggest that HIMINTY might be a
good candidate to include in the INTRCPT1 model. The t-values represent
the approximate result that will be obtained when one additional predictor is added to any of the level-2 equations. This means that if HIMINTY is
added to the model for the INTRCPT1, for example, the apparent relationship suggested above for HIMINTY in the SES slope model might disappear.
(For a further discussion of the use of these statistics see discussion in Hierarchical Linear Models, p. 214 on "Approximate t-to-Enter Statistics.")*

2.9.2 Multivariate hypothesis tests for fixed effects

HLM allows multivariate hypothesis tests for the fixed effects. For example, for the model displayed in Fig. 2.29, a user can test the following
composite null hypothesis:

$$H_0 : \gamma_{01} = \gamma_{11} = 0 ,$$

where γ_{01} is the effect of SECTOR on the intercept and γ_{11} is the effect of
SECTOR on the SES slope.

Below is a procedure that illustrates a Windows execution of the hypothesis test.

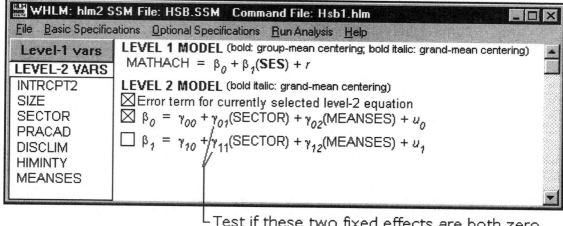

LEVEL 1 MODEL (bold: group-mean centering; bold italic: grand-mean centering)

$$MATHACH = \beta_0 + \beta_1(SES) + r$$

LEVEL 2 MODEL (bold italic: grand-mean centering)

☒ Error term for currently selected level-2 equation

☒ $\beta_0 = \gamma_{00} + \gamma_{01}(SECTOR) + \gamma_{02}(MEANSES) + u_0$

☐ $\beta_1 = \gamma_{10} + \gamma_{11}(SECTOR) + \gamma_{12}(MEANSES) + u_1$

Test if these two fixed effects are both zero

Figure 2.29   Model windows

To pose a multivariate hypothesis test among the fixed effects

1. Open the **Optional Specifications** menu.
2. Choose **Optional Hypothesis Testing/Estimation** to open the **Optional Hypothesis Testing/Estimation** dialog box (see Fig. 2.30).
3. Click **1** to open the **General Linear Hypothesis: Hypothesis 1** dialog box to specify the first hypothesis (see Fig. 2.31 for the contrast comparing the effect of SECTOR on the intercept and on the SES slope).

The HLM2 output associated with this test appears on page 61 below. (For a further discussion of this multivariate hypothesis test for fixed effects see *Hierarchical Linear Models*, pp. 50–52, 74–75).

2.9.3 Testing homogeneity of level-1 variances

HLM2 assumes homogeneity of residual variance at level 1. That is, it specifies a common σ^2 within each of the J level-2 units. As an option, HLM2 tests the adequacy of this assumption.

To test the homogeneity of level-1 variances

Check the **Test homogeneity of level-1 variance** box (Fig. 2.30).

The HLM2 output associated with this test also appears on page 61 below. (For a further discussion of this test see *Hierarchical Linear Models*, pp. 207–211. We advise that users review these pages carefully before using this procedure.)

2.9.4 Multivariate tests of variance-covariance components specification

HLM2 also provides, as an option, a multi-parameter test for the variance-covariance components. This likelihood-ratio test compares the deviance statistics of a restricted model with a more general alternative. The user must input the value of the deviance statistic and related degrees of freedom for the alternative specification. Below we compare the variance-covariance components of two *Intercept and Slope as Outcome* models. One treats β_1 as random and the other does not.

To specify a multivariate test of variance-covariance components

Enter the deviance and the number of parameters in the **Deviance Statistic** text box and in the **Number of Parameters** text box, respectively (the two numbers for our example are 46501.87563 and 4, as obtained in Section 2.5.3).

The HLM2 output associated with this test appears on page 61 below. (For a further discussion of this multi-parameter test see *Hierarchical Linear Models*, pp. 55–56, 75–76).

Below is an example of selected HLM2 output that illustrates optional hypothesis testing procedures (see example HSB2.HLM).

```
Module:      HLM2.EXE (5.01.2040.2)
Date:        9 February 2000, Wednesday
Time:        12:21: 1
-----------------------------------------------------------------------

SPECIFICATIONS FOR THIS HLM2 RUN

  Problem Title: NO TITLE

  The data source for this run  = HSB.SSM
  The command file for this run = HSB2.HLM
```

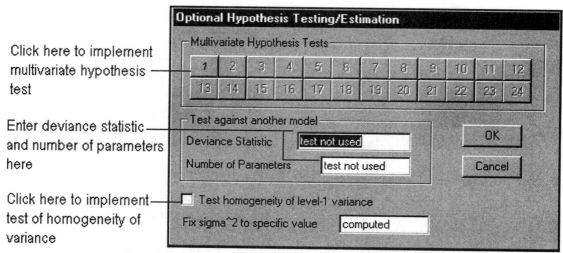

Click here to implement multivariate hypothesis test

Enter deviance statistic and number of parameters here

Click here to implement test of homogeneity of variance

Figure 2.30   Optional Hypothesis Testing/Estimation dialog box

```
Output file name              = HSB2.OUT
The maximum number of level-2 units = 160
The maximum number of iterations = 50
Method of estimation: restricted maximum likelihood

Weighting Specification
-----------------------

                        Weight
                        Variable
            Weighting?  Name        Normalized?
Level 1     no                      no
Level 2     no                      no

 The outcome variable is  MATHACH

 The model specified for the fixed effects was:
 -------------------------------------------------------

     Level-1                Level-2
     Coefficients           Predictors
     ---------------------  ---------------
            INTRCPT1, B0     INTRCPT2, G00
                               SECTOR, G01
                              MEANSES, G02
 #*     SES slope, B1       INTRCPT2, G10
                               SECTOR, G11
                              MEANSES, G12

'#' - The residual parameter variance for this level-1 coefficient has been set
      to zero.
```

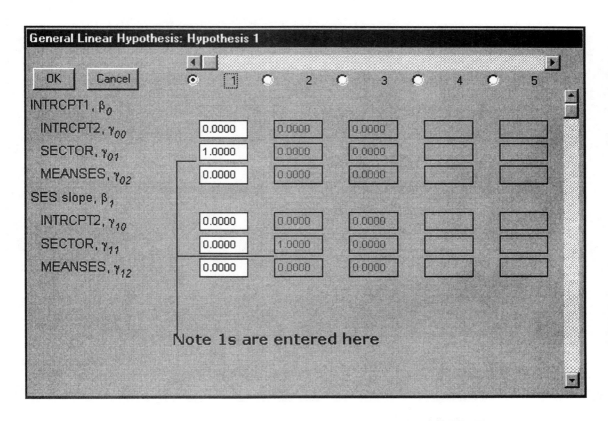

Figure 2.31   General Linear Hypothesis: Hypothesis 1 dialog box

```
'*' - This level-1 predictor has been centered around its group mean.

   The model specified for the covariance components was:
   ------------------------------------------------------------

         Sigma_squared (constant across level-2 units)

         Tau dimensions
            INTRCPT1


   Summary of the model specified (in equation format)
   ----------------------------------------------------

Level-1 Model

Y = B0 + B1*(SES) + R

Level-2 Model
B0 = G00 + G01*(SECTOR) + G02*(MEANSES) + U0
B1 = G10 + G11*(SECTOR) + G12*(MEANSES)
```

Note, the middle section of output has been deleted. We proceed directly to the final results page.

```
   Final estimation of fixed effects:
   -----------------------------------------------------------------------
                                      Standard          Approx.
      Fixed Effect       Coefficient  Error    T-ratio  d.f.    P-value
   -----------------------------------------------------------------------
   For       INTRCPT1, B0
      INTRCPT2, G00        12.096251  0.198643  60.894     157   0.000
        SECTOR, G01         1.224401  0.306117   4.000     157   0.000
       MEANSES, G02         5.336698  0.368978  14.463     157   0.000
   For       SES slope, B1
      INTRCPT2, G10         2.935860  0.150705  19.481    7179   0.000
        SECTOR, G11        -1.642102  0.233097  -7.045    7179   0.000
       MEANSES, G12         1.044120  0.291042   3.588    7179   0.001
   -----------------------------------------------------------------------

   The outcome variable is  MATHACH

   Final estimation of fixed effects
   (with robust standard errors)
   -----------------------------------------------------------------------
                                      Standard          Approx.
      Fixed Effect       Coefficient  Error    T-ratio  d.f.    P-value
   -----------------------------------------------------------------------
   For       INTRCPT1, B0
      INTRCPT2, G00        12.096251  0.173691  69.642     157   0.000
        SECTOR, G01         1.224401  0.308507   3.969     157   0.000
       MEANSES, G02         5.336698  0.334617  15.949     157   0.000
```

```
For      SES slope, B1
    INTRCPT2, G10        2.935860    0.147580    19.893     7179    0.000
     SECTOR, G11        -1.642102    0.237223    -6.922     7179    0.000
    MEANSES, G12         1.044120    0.332897     3.136     7179    0.002
    ---------------------------------------------------------------------

Final estimation of variance components:
    ---------------------------------------------------------------------
Random Effect              Standard     Variance    df    Chi-square  P-value
                           Deviation    Component
    ---------------------------------------------------------------------
INTRCPT1,      U0          1.54118      2.37524     157   604.29893   0.000
  level-1,     R           6.06351     36.76611
    ---------------------------------------------------------------------


Statistics for current covariance components model
    --------------------------------------------------
Deviance =  46502.95273
Number of estimated parameters =     2
```

For the likelihood-ratio test, the deviance statistic reported above is compared with the value from the alternative model input by the user. The result of this test appears below.

```
Variance-Covariance components test
    -----------------------------------
Chi-square statistic       =    10.02527
Number of degrees of freedom =    2
P-value                    = 0.007
```

A model that constrains the residual variance for the SES slopes, B1, to zero appears appropriate. (For a further discussion of this application see Hierarchical Linear Models, pp. 75–76. Note: the statistics reported here differ slightly from those in the text because of the improved computing routines in versions 3 and higher of HLM2.)

```
Test of homogeneity of level-1 variance
    ---------------------------------------
Chi-square statistic       =   244.08641
Number of degrees of freedom =   159
P-value                    = 0.000
```

These results indicate that there is variability among the $(J = 160)$ level-2 units in terms of the residual within-school (i.e., level-1) variance. (For a full discussion of these results see Hierarchical Linear Models, pp. 207–211.)

```
                Results of General Linear Hypothesis Testing
--------------------------------------------------------------------------
                                    Coefficients      Contrast
--------------------------------------------------------------------------
For          INTRCPT1, B0
       INTRCPT2, G00                 12.096251      0.000   0.000
         SECTOR, G01                  1.224401      1.000   0.000
        MEANSES, G02                  5.336698      0.000   0.000
For          SES slope, B1
       INTRCPT2, G10                  2.935860      0.000   0.000
         SECTOR, G11                 -1.642102      0.000   1.000
        MEANSES, G12                  1.044120      0.000   0.000

Chi-square statistic = 65.626400
Degrees of freedom   = 2
P-value              = 0.000000
```

The table above reminds the user of the multivariate contrast specified. The chi-square statistic and associated p-value indicate that it is highly unlikely that the observed estimates for G01 and G11 could have occurred under the specified null hypothesis.

2.9.5 Modeling heterogeneity of level-1 variances

Users may wish to estimate models that allow for heterogeneous level-1 variances. A simple example (see HSB3.HLM) using the HS&B data would be a model that postulates that the two genders have different means and variances for the math achievement scores. To specify a model that hypothesizes different central tendency and variability in math achievement for the two genders, a user first sets up the model displayed in Fig. 2.32.

To model heterogeneity of level-1 variances

1. Open the **Optional Specifications** menu.
2. Choose **Optional Hypothesis Testing/Estimation** to open the **Heterogeneous sigma^2 variable for C** dialog box. Double-click FEMALE to enter as a variable in C (See Fig. 2.33). Click **OK**.

The model estimated is a loglinear model for the level-1 variances, which can be generally stated as:

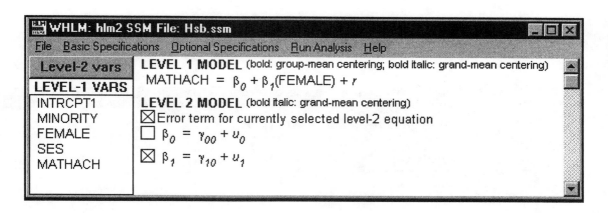

Figure 2.32
Model window for the modeling heterogeneity of level-1 variances example

$$\sigma_{ij}^2 = \exp\{\alpha_0 + \alpha_1 \mathsf{FEMALE}_{ij}\} \ .$$

The following is selected annotated output of the model run (see example HSB3.HLM).

```
The outcome variable is  MATHACH

Final estimation of fixed effects:
----------------------------------------------------------------------------
                                       Standard         Approx.
          Fixed Effect      Coefficient   Error    T-ratio    d.f.    P-value
----------------------------------------------------------------------------
For        INTRCPT1, B0
     INTRCPT2, G00        13.345654   0.261011   51.131     159     0.000
For     FEMALE slope, B1
     INTRCPT2, G10        -1.381356   0.185852   -7.433     159     0.000
----------------------------------------------------------------------------

The outcome variable is  MATHACH

Final estimation of fixed effects
(with robust standard errors)
----------------------------------------------------------------------------
                                       Standard         Approx.
          Fixed Effect      Coefficient   Error    T-ratio    d.f.    P-value
----------------------------------------------------------------------------
For        INTRCPT1, B0
     INTRCPT2, G00        13.345654   0.261027   51.127     159     0.000
```

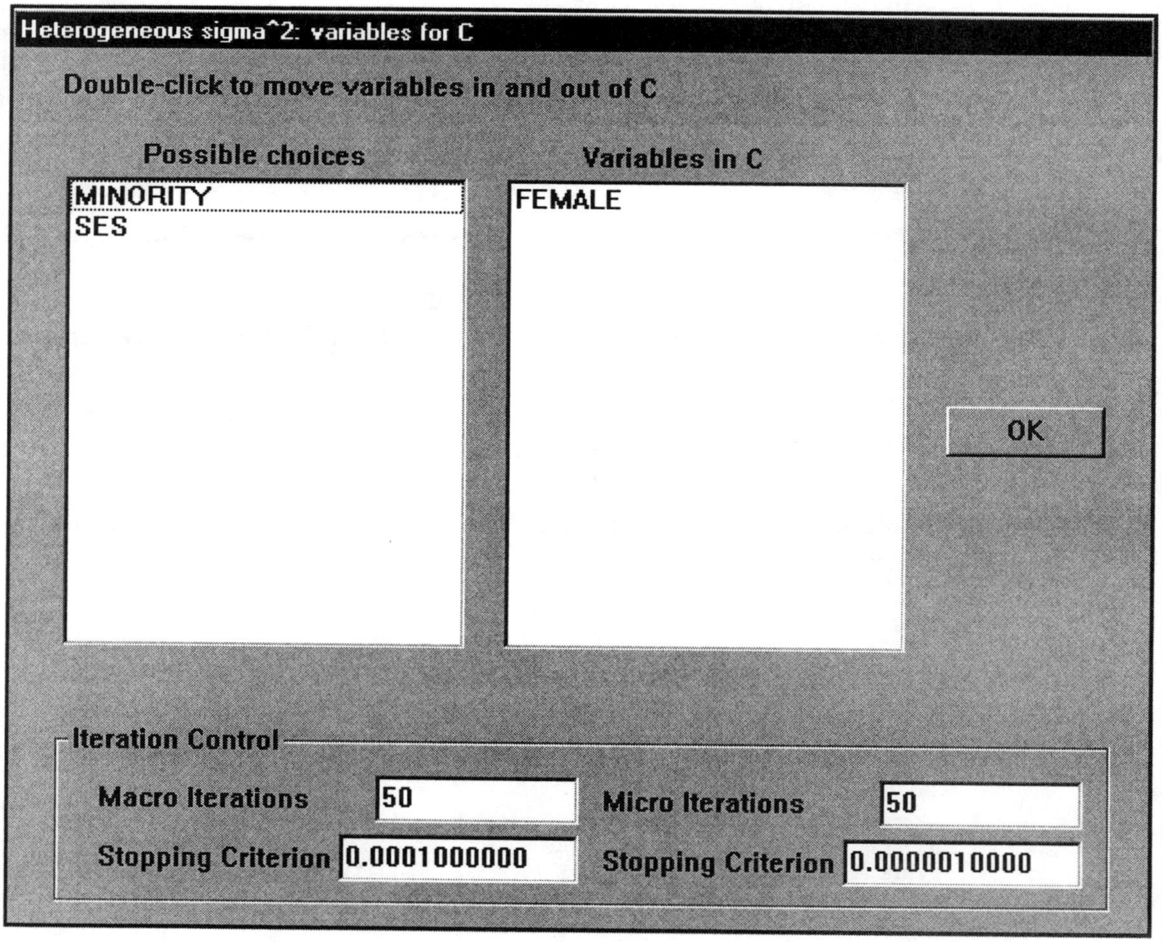

Figure 2.33   Heterogeneous sigma^2 variable for C dialog box

```
For   FEMALE slope, B1
      INTRCPT2, G10          -1.381356   0.185897    -7.431      159    0.000
---------------------------------------------------------------------------


 . . .
 . . .
 . . .

RESULTS FOR HETEROGENEOUS SIGMA-SQUARED
(macro iteration 4)

Var(R) = Sigma_squared and
log(Sigma_squared) = alpha0 + alpha1(FEMALE)

Model for level-1 variance
-----------------------------------------------------------------------
                                     Standard
        Parameter     Coefficient     Error      Z-ratio    P-value
-----------------------------------------------------------------------
INTRCPT1  ,alpha0       3.70388       0.024798    149.364    0.000
   FEMALE ,alpha1      -0.09127       0.034089     -2.677    0.008
-----------------------------------------------------------------------
```

Summary of Model Fit

```
-----------------------------------------------------------------------
Model                           Number of            Deviance
                                Parameters
-----------------------------------------------------------------------
1. Homogeneous sigma_squared         6              47049.46273
2. Heterogeneous sigma_squared       7              47042.27726
-----------------------------------------------------------------------
Model Comparison               Chi-square       df     P-value
-----------------------------------------------------------------------
Model 1 vs Model 2               7.18547          1     0.007
```

The T-ratio for γ_{10} (T = −7.433) and Z-ratio for α_1 (Z = −2.677) for FEMALE indicate that the math achievement scores of males are on average higher as well as more variable than those for females. Furthermore, a comparison of the fits of the models suggests that the model with heterogeneous within-school variances appears appropriate ($\chi^2 = 7.18547$, df = 1). See Chapter 7 for details on model comparison.

2.9.6   Models without a level-1 intercept

In some circumstances, researchers may wish to estimate models without a level-1 intercept. Consider, for example, a hypothetical study in which three alternative treatments are implemented within each of J hospitals. One might estimate the following level-1 (within-hospital) model:

$$Y_{ij} = \beta_{1j}X_{1ij} + \beta_{2j}X_{2ij} + \beta_{3j}X_{3ij} + r_{ij} \, ,$$

where X_{qij} ($q = 1, 2, 3$) are indicator variables taking on a value of 1 if patient i in hospital j has received treatment q, 0 otherwise; and β_{qj} is the mean outcome in hospital j of those receiving treatment q. At level 2, the treatment means β_{qj} are predicted by characteristics of the hospitals. Of course, the same data could alternatively be modeled by a level-1 intercept and two treatment contrasts per hospital, but users will sometimes find the no-intercept approach convenient.

Let us suppose that the variable names TREAT1, TREAT2, and TREAT3 represent the dummy variables indicating whether a subject received treatment one, treatment two, or treatment three, respectively. The level-1 intercept is deleted from the model. The level-2 predictor, PUBLIC, indicates whether a hospital is public (as opposed to private). We shall model each treatment mean as depending on the public versus private status of the hospital. Also, we wish to estimate the residual variance in these means over hospitals.

An example of a no-intercept model appears on page 144 of *Hierarchical Linear Models*. The vocabulary growth of young children is of interest. Both common sense and the data indicated that children could be expected to have no vocabulary at 12 months of age. Hence, the level-1 model contained no intercept:

$$Y_{ti} = \pi_{1i}(\mathsf{AGE}_{ti} - 12) + \pi_{2i}(\mathsf{AGE}_{ti} - 12)^2 + e_{ti} \, ,$$

where AGE_{ti} is the age of child i at time t in months and Y_{ti} is the size of that child's vocabulary at that time.

To delete an intercept from a level-1 model

Click INTRCPT1 on the LEVEL-1 VARS listbox. Click **delete variable from model**.

2.9.7 Level-1 coefficients having a random effect with no corresponding fixed effect

A user may find it useful at times to model a level-1 predictor as having a random effect but no fixed effect. For example, it might be that gender differences in educational achievement are, on average, null across a set of schools; yet, in some schools females outperform males while in other schools males outperform females. In this case, the fixed effect of gender could be set to zero while the variance of the gender effect across schools would be estimated.

The vocabulary analysis in *Hierarchical Linear Models* supplies an example of a level-1 predictor having a random effect without a corresponding fixed effect. For the age interval under study, it was found that, on average, the linear effect of age was null. Yet this effect varied significantly across children. The level-1 model estimated was:

$$Y_{ti} = \pi_{1i}(\text{AGE}_{ti} - 12) + \pi_{2i}(\text{AGE}_{ti} - 12)^2 + e_{ti} .$$

However, the level-2 model was:

$$\begin{aligned} \pi_{1i} &= r_{1i} \\ \pi_{2i} &= \beta_{20} + r_{2i} \end{aligned}$$

Note that AGE – 12 has a random effect but no fixed effect.

To delete the fixed effect from a level-2 model

1. Select the equation from which the fixed effect is to be removed.

2. Click INTRCPT2 on the LEVEL-2 VARS listbox. Click **delete variable from model**.

2.9.8 Constraints on the fixed effects

A user may wish to constrain two or more fixed effects to be equal. For example, Barnett, Marshall, Raudenbush, & Brennan (1993) applied this approach in studying correlates of psychological distress in married couples. Available for each person were two parallel measures of psychological distress. Hence, for each couple, there were four such measures (two per person). At level-1 these measures were modeled as the sum of a "true score" plus error:

$$Y_{ij} = \beta_{1j} X_{1ij} + \beta_{2j} X_{2ij} + r_{ij} \; ,$$

where X_{1ij} is an indicator for females, X_{2ij} is an indicator for males, and r_{ij} is a measurement error. Hence β_{1j} is the "true score" for females and β_{2j} is the "true score" for males. At level 2, these true scores are modeled as a function of predictor variables, one of which was marital role quality, W_j, a measure of one's satisfaction with one's marriage. (Note that this is also a model without a level-1 intercept.) A simple level-2 model is then:

$$\begin{aligned}
\beta_{1j} &= \gamma_{10} + \gamma_{11} W_j + u_{1j} \\
\beta_{2j} &= \gamma_{20} + \gamma_{21} W_j + u_{2j} \; .
\end{aligned}$$

The four coefficients to be considered are

$$\gamma_{10}, \gamma_{11}, \gamma_{20}, \gamma_{21} \; .$$

We may, for example, wish to specify some constraints of fixed effects.

To put constraints on fixed effects

1. Open the **Optional Specifications** menu.
2. Choose **Constraint of Gammas** to open the **Constrain Gammas** dialog box. Enter **1**s in the edit boxes for the first constraint (see Fig. 2.34 for an example). Click **OK**. The constraint imposed is:

$$\gamma_{11} = \gamma_{21} \; .$$

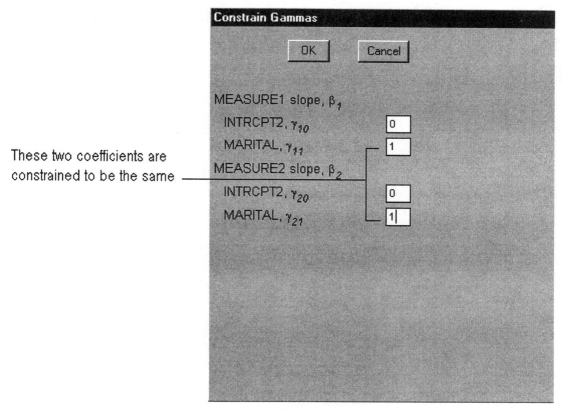

These two coefficients are constrained to be the same

Figure 2.34
Constrain Gammas dialog box for the Barnett, et al. (1993) example

You can impose multiple constraints. Coefficients with zeros are not constrained, and those with positive integers are. Because each set of constraints consists of at least a pair of gammas, the maximum number of constraints equals the number of gammas divided by two. The maximum number of gammas within a constraint is equal to all the gammas.

Each set of constrained coefficients will share the same value. Note that the program expects you to use consecutive integers for the sets, starting with one: $1, 2, 3, \ldots$

3

Conceptual and Statistical Background for Three-Level Models

The models estimated by HLM3 are applicable to hierarchical data structure with three levels of random variation in which the errors of prediction at each level can be assumed approximately normally distributed. Consider, for example, a study in which achievement test scores are collected from a sample of children nested within classrooms that are in turn nested within schools. This data structure is hierarchical (each child belongs to one and only one classroom and each classroom belongs to one and only one school); and there are three levels of random variation: variation among children within classrooms, variation among classrooms within schools, and variation among schools. The outcome (achievement test scores) makes the normality assumption at level 1 reasonable, and the normality assumption at the classroom and school levels will often also be a sensible one.

Chapter 8 of *Hierarchical Linear Models* discusses several applications of a three-level model. The first is a three-level cross-sectional study as described above. A second case involves time-series data collected on each subject where the subjects are nested within organizations. This latter example is from the US Public Schools Study, where achievement data were collected at five time points for each child. Here the time-series data are nested within children and the children are nested within schools. A third example in Chapter 8 involves measures taken on each of the multiple classes taught by secondary school teachers. The classes are nested within teachers and the teachers within schools. A final example involves multiple items from a questionnaire administered to teachers. The items vary "within teachers" at level 1, the teachers vary within schools at level 2, and the schools vary at level 3. In effect, the level-1 model is a model for the measurement error associated with the questionnaire. Clearly, there are many interesting applications of a three-level model.

3.1 The general three-level model

The three-level model consists of three submodels, one for each level. For example, if the research problem consists of data on students nested within classrooms and classrooms within schools, the level-1 model will represent the relationships among the student-level variables, the level-2 model will capture the influence of class-level factors, and the level-3 model will incorporate school-level effects. Formally there are $i = 1, \ldots, n_{jk}$ level-1 units (*e.g.*, students), which are nested within each of $j = 1, \ldots, J_k$ level-2 units (*e.g.*, classrooms), which in turn are nested within each of $k = 1, \ldots, K$ level-3 units (*e.g.*, schools).

3.1.1 Level-1 model

In the level-1 model we represent the outcome for case i within level-2 unit j and level-3 unit k as:

$$
\begin{aligned}
Y_{ijk} &= \pi_{0jk} + \pi_{1jk} a_{1ijk} + \pi_{2jk} a_{2ijk} + \cdots + \pi_{pjk} a_{pijk} + e_{ijk} \\
&= \pi_{0jk} + \sum_{p=1}^{P} \pi_{pjk} a_{pijk} + e_{ijk} ,
\end{aligned}
\tag{3.1}
$$

where

π_{pjk} $(p = 0, 1, \ldots, P)$ are *level-1 coefficients*,

a_{pijk} is a *level-1 predictor* p for case i in level-2 unit j and level-3 unit k,

e_{ijk} is the *level-1 random effect*, and

σ^2 is the variance of e_{ijk}, that is the *level-1 variance*.

Here we assume that the random term $e_{ijk} \sim N(0, \sigma^2)$.

3.1.2 Level-2 model

Each of the π_{pjk} coefficients in the level-1 model becomes an outcome variable in the level-2 model:

$$\begin{aligned}
\pi_{pjk} &= \beta_{p0k} + \beta_{p1k}X_{1jk} + \beta_{p2k}X_{2jk} + \cdots + \beta_{pQ_pk}X_{Q_pjk} + r_{pjk} \\
&= \beta_{p0k} + \sum_{q=1}^{Q_p} \beta_{pqk}X_{qjk} + r_{pjk} ,
\end{aligned} \tag{3.2}$$

where

β_{pqk} $(q = 0, 1, \ldots, Q_p)$ are *level-2 coefficients*,

X_{qjk} is a *level-2 predictor*, and

r_{pjk} is a *level-2 random effect*.

We assume that, for each unit j, the vector $(r_{0jk}, r_{1jk}, \ldots, r_{Pjk})'$ is distributed as multivariate normal where each element has a mean of zero and the variance of r_{pjk} is:

$$\mathsf{Var}(r_{pjk}) = \tau_{\pi pp} . \tag{3.3}$$

For any pair of random effects p and p',

$$\mathsf{Cov}(r_{pjk}, r_{p'jk}) = \tau_{\pi pp'} . \tag{3.4}$$

These *level-2 variance and covariance components* can be collected into a dispersion matrix, $\mathbf{T}_\pi$ with a maximum dimension of $(P+1) \times (P+1)$.

We note that each level-1 coefficient can be modeled at level 2 as one of three general forms:

1. *a level-1 coefficient that is fixed at the same value for all level-2 units*; e.g.,

$$\pi_{pjk} = \beta_{p0k} , \tag{3.5}$$

2. *a level-1 coefficient that varies non-randomly among level-2 units*, e.g.,

$$\pi_{pjk} = \beta_{p0k} + \sum_{q=1}^{Q_p} \beta_{pqk}X_{qjk} , \tag{3.6}$$

3. *a level-1 coefficient that varies randomly among level-2 units, e.g.,*

$$\pi_{pjk} = \beta_{p0k} + r_{pjk} \tag{3.7}$$

or

$$\pi_{pjk} = \beta_{p0k} + \sum_{q=1}^{Q_p} \beta_{pqk} X_{qjk} + r_{pjk} \ . \tag{3.8}$$

The actual dimension of $\mathbf{T}_\pi$ in any application depends on the number of level-1 coefficients specified as randomly varying. We also note that a different set of level-2 predictors may be used in each of the $P+1$ equations that form the level-2 model.

3.1.3 Level-3 model

Each of the level-2 coefficients, β_{pqk}, defined in the level-2 model, becomes an outcome variable in the level-3 model:

$$
\begin{aligned}
\beta_{pqk} &= \gamma_{pq0} + \gamma_{pq1}W_{1k} + \gamma_{pq2}W_{2k} + \cdots + \gamma_{pqS_{pq}}W_{S_{pq}k} + u_{pqk} \\
&= \gamma_{pq0} + \sum_{s=1}^{S_{pq}} \gamma_{pqs}W_{sk} + u_{pqk} \ ,
\end{aligned}
\tag{3.9}
$$

where

$\gamma_{pqs} \ (s = 0, 1, \ldots, S_{pq})$ are *level-3 coefficients*,

W_{sk} is a *level-3 predictor*, and

u_{pqk} is a *level-3 random effect*.

We assume that, for each level-3 unit, the vector of level-3 random effects (the u_{pqk} terms) is distributed as multivariate normal, with each having a mean of zero and with covariance matrix $\mathbf{T}_\beta$, which has as maximum dimension:

$$\sum_{p=0}^{p}(Q_p + 1) \times \sum_{p=0}^{p}(Q_p + 1) \ . \tag{3.10}$$

We note that each level-2 coefficient can be modeled at level-3 as one of three general forms:

1. *as a fixed effect, e.g.,*

$$\beta_{pqk} = \gamma_{pq0} \ , \tag{3.11}$$

2. *as non-randomly varying, e.g.,*

$$\beta_{pqk} = \gamma_{pq0} + \sum_{s=1}^{S_{pq}} \gamma_{pqs} W_{sk} \ , \tag{3.12}$$

3. *as random varying, e.g.,*

$$\beta_{pqk} = \gamma_{pq0} + u_{pqk} \tag{3.13}$$

or

$$\beta_{pqk} = \gamma_{pq0} + \sum_{s=1}^{S_{pq}} \gamma_{pqs} W_{sk} + u_{pqk} \ . \tag{3.14}$$

The actual dimension of $\mathbf{T}_\beta$ in any application depends on the number of level-3 coefficients specified as randomly varying. We also note that a different set of level-3 predictors may be used in each equation of the level-3 model.

3.2 Parameter estimation

Three kinds of parameter estimates are available in a three-level model: empirical Bayes estimates of randomly varying level-1 and level-2 coefficients; maximum-likelihood estimates of the level-3 coefficients (note: these are also generalized least squares estimates); and maximum-likelihood estimates of the variance-covariance components. The maximum-likelihood estimate of the level-3 coefficients and the variance-covariance components are printed on the output for every run. The empirical Bayes estimates for the level-1 and level-2 coefficients may optionally be saved in the "residual files" at levels 2 and 3, respectively. Reliability estimates for each random level-1 and level-2 coefficient are always produced.

The actual estimation procedure for the three-level model differs a bit from the default two-level model. By default, HLM2 uses a "restricted maximum likelihood" approach in which the variance-covariance components are estimated by means of maximum likelihood and then the fixed effects (level-2 coefficients) are estimated via generalized least squares given those variance-covariance estimates. In HLM3, not only the variance-covariance components, but also the fixed effects (level-3 coefficients) are estimated by means of maximum likelihood. This procedure is referred to as "full" as opposed to "restricted" maximum likelihood. (For a further discussion of this see *Hierarchical Linear Models*, pp. 44–48. The actual computational formulas appear on pp. 245–248.) Note that full maximum-likelihood is also available as an option for HLM2.

3.3 Hypothesis testing

As in the case of the two-level program, the three-level program routinely prints standard errors and t-tests for each of the level-3 coefficients (the "fixed effects") as well as a chi-square test of homogeneity for each random effect. In addition, optional "multivariate hypothesis tests" are available in the three-level program. Multivariate tests for the level-3 coefficients enable both omnibus tests and specific comparisons of the parameter estimates just as described in the section *Multivariate hypothesis tests for fixed effects* on page 59. Multivariate tests regarding alternative variance-covariance structures at level 2 or level 3 proceed just as in the section *Multivariate tests of variance-covariance components specification* on page 61.

The use of full maximum likelihood for parameter estimation in HLM3 has a consequence for hypothesis testing. For both restricted and full maximum likelihood, one can test alternative variance-covariance structures by means of the likelihood-ratio test as described in the section *Multivariate tests of variance-covariance components specification* on page 61. However, in the case of full maximum likelihood, it is also possible to test alternative specifications of the fixed coefficients by means of a likelihood-ratio test. In fact, any pair of nested models can be compared using the likelihood-ratio test under full maximum likelihood. By nested models, we refer to a pair of models in which the more complex model includes all of the parameters of the simpler model plus one or more additional parameters. Any pair of nested two-level models can be compared using a likelihood ratio test.

4

Working with HLM3

As in the case of the two-level program, data analysis by means of the HLM3 program will typically involve three stages:

1. Construction of an SSM file (the sufficient statistics matrix)
2. Execution of analyses based on the SSM file
3. Evaluation of fitted models based on residual files

As in HLM2, HLM3 analyses can be executed in Windows, interactive, and batch modes. We describe a Windows execution below. We consider interactive and batch execution in Appendix B. A number of special options are presented at the end of the chapter.

4.1 An example using HLM3 in Windows mode

Chapter 8 in *Hierarchical Linear Models* presents a series of analyses of data from the US *Sustaining Effects Study*, a longitudinal study of children's growth in academic achievement during the primary years. A level-1 model specifies the relationship between age and academic achievement for each child. At level 2, the coefficients describing each child's growth vary across children within schools as a function of demographic variables. At level 3, the parameters that describe the distribution of growth curves within each school vary across schools as a function of school-level predictors.

To illustrate the operation of the HLM3 program, we analyze another data set having a similar structure. The level-1 data are time-series observations on 1721 students nested within 60 urban public primary schools and mathematics achievement is the outcome. These data are provided along with the HLM software so that users may replicate our results in order to assure that the program is operating correctly.

4.1.1 Constructing the SSM file from raw data

In constructing the SSM file, the user has the same range of options for data input for HLM3 as for HLM2 (see page 11). We first describe the use of SPSS file input and then consider ASCII, SYSTAT, SAS, and other data file formats.

4.1.1.1 SPSS input

Data input requires a level-1 file (in our illustration a time-series data file), a level-2 (child-level) file, and a level-3 (school level) file.[1]

Level-1 file. The level-1 file, EG1.SAV, has 7242 observations collected on 1721 children beginning at the end of grade one and followed up annually thereafter until grade six. There are four level-1 variables (not including the schoolid and the childid). Time-series data for the first two children are shown in Fig. 4.1.

There are eight records listed, three for the first child and five for the second. (Typically there are four or five observations per child with a maximum of six.) The first ID is the level-3 (*i.e.*, school) ID and the second ID is the level-2 (*i.e.*, child) ID. We see that the first record comes from school 2020 and child 273026452 within that school. Notice that this child has three records, one for each of three measurement occasions. Following the two ID fields are that child's values on four variables:

---

[1]In some cases, all the data may be contained in a single file. The data still have to be sorted by the ID variables representing the different levels of the hierarchy. Simply use the same filename as the data file at the various levels of the hierarchy in the creation of the SSM file.

❑ YEAR (year of the study minus 3.5)

This variable can take on values of -2.5, -1.5, -0.5, 0.5, 1.5, and 2.5 for the six years of data collection.

❑ GRADE

The grade level minus 1.0 of the child at each testing occasion. Therefore, it is 0 at grade 1, 1.0 at grade 2, etc.

❑ MATH

A math test in an IRT scale score metric.

❑ RETAINED

An indicator that a child is retained in grade for a particular year (1 = retained, 0 = not retained).

	schoolid	childid	year	grade	math	retained
1	2020	273026452	.50	2.00	1.15	.00
2	2020	273026452	1.50	3.00	1.13	.00
3	2020	273026452	2.50	4.00	2.30	.00
4	2020	273030991	.50	2.00	2.43	.00
5	2020	273030991	1.50	3.00	2.25	.00
6	2020	273030991	2.50	4.00	3.87	.00
7	2020	273030991	-.50	1.00	.44	.00
8	2020	273030991	-1.50	.00	-1.30	.00

Figure 4.1   First eight cases in EG1.SAV

We see that the first child, child 27306452 in school 2020 had values of 0.5, 1.5, and 2.5 on YEAR. Clearly, that child had no data at the first three data collection waves (because we see no values of -2.5, -1.5, or -0.5 on YEAR), but did have data at the last three waves. We see also that this child was not retained in grade during this period since the values for GRADE increase by 1 each year and since RETAINED takes on a value of 0 for each year. The three MATH scores of that child (1.146, 1.134, 2.300) show no growth in time period 1.5. Oddly enough, the time-series record for the second child (child 273030991 in school 2020) displays a similar pattern in the same testing.

Note: The level-1 and level-2 files must also be sorted in the same order of level-2 ID nested within level-3 ID, *e.g.*, children within schools. If this nested sorting is not performed, an incorrect sufficient statistics file will result.

Level-2 file. The level-2 units in the illustration are 1721 children. The data are stored in the file EG2.SAV. The level-2 data for the first eight children are listed in Fig. 4.2. The first field is the schoolid and the second is the childid. Note that each of the first eight children is in school 2020. There are three variables:

- ❑ FEMALE (1 = female, 0 = male)
- ❑ BLACK (1 = African-American, 0 = other)
- ❑ HISPANIC (1= Hispanic, 0 = other)

We see, for example, that child 273026452 is a Hispanic male (FEMALE = 0, BLACK = 0, HISPANIC = 1).

	schoolid	childid	female	black	hispanic
1	2020	273026452	.00	.00	1.00
2	2020	273030991	.00	.00	.00
3	2020	273059461	.00	.00	1.00
4	2020	278058841	.00	.00	.00
5	2020	292017571	.00	.00	1.00
6	2020	292020281	.00	.00	.00
7	2020	292020361	.00	.00	.00
8	2020	292025081	.00	.00	.00

Figure 4.2   First eight children in EG2.SAV

Level-3 file. The level-3 units in the illustration are 60 schools. Level-3 data for the first seven schools are displayed in Fig. 4.3. The full data are in the file EG3.SAV. The first field on the left is the SCHOOLID. There are three level-3 variables:

- ❑ SIZE, number of students enrolled in the school
- ❑ LOWINC, the percent of students from low income families
- ❑ MOBILITY, the percent of students moving during the course of a single academic year

We see that the first school, school 2020 has 380 students, 40.3% of whom are low income. The school mobility rate is 12.5%.

	schoolid	size	lowinc	mobility
1	2020	380.00	40.30	12.50
2	2040	502.00	83.10	18.60
3	2180	777.00	96.60	44.40
4	2330	800.00	78.90	31.70
5	2340	1133.00	93.70	67.00
6	2380	439.00	36.90	39.30
7	2390	566.00	100.00	39.90

Figure 4.3   First seven schools in EG3.SAV

In sum, there are four variables at level 1, three at level 2, and three at level 3. Note that the ID variables do not count as variables. Once the user has identified the two sets of IDs, the number of variables in each file, the variable names, and the filenames, creation of the SSM file is exactly analogous to the procedure described in the section *SPSS file input* on page 15 for the two-level program. The user first informs HLM that the input files are SPSS system files and the SSM is a three-level file. Then the user supplies HLM with the appropriate information for the data. Note that the three files are linked by level-2 and level-3 ids here.

Note: The program can handle missing data at level 1 only, with the same options available as discussed in HLM2. Like HLM2, HLM3 will delete cases listwise with missing data at the highest level, *i.e.*, level 3. If HLM3 encounters missing data at level 2, it will exit with an error message. The three-level program handles design weights only at level 1.

When using stat package input, we recommend that the package's system missing value be used to indicate missingness. This will minimize errors in creating the SSM file.

The response file, EGSPSS.RSP, contains a log of the input responses used to create the SSM file, EG.SSM, using EG1.SAV, EG2.SAV, and EG3.SAV. Fig. 4.4 displays the dialog box used to create the SSM file. Fig. 4.5 shows the dialog box for the level-1 file, EG1.SAV.

Note that in this example, SCHOOLID and CHILDID are string or character variables and therefore cannot be in the SSM file. In general, IDs can either be numeric or character variables.

Note: As in the case of HLM2, after constructing the SSM file, the user should check whether the data have been properly read into HLM by examining the descriptive statistics of the SSM file.

4.1.1.2 ASCII input

The procedure for constructing an SSM file from ASCII data files is similar to that for SPSS file input. The major difference is that the user has to enter the format statements for the three data files, variable names, and missing value codes, if applicable. Rules about the format are given in Section A.2 in Appendix A. An example is included in the response file, EGASCII.RSP, which constructs the SSM file, EGASCII.SSM, using EG1.DAT, EG2.DAT, and EG3.DAT. Fig. 4.6 shows the dialog box for creating the SSM file, displaying the input responses of EGASCII.RSP.

4.1.1.3 SYSTAT or SAS file input

For SAS and SYSTAT file input, a user selects either SAS 5 transport or SYS-TAT from the **Input File Type** drop-down listbox as appropriate *before* click-

—Click here to select the response file, EGSPSS.RSP

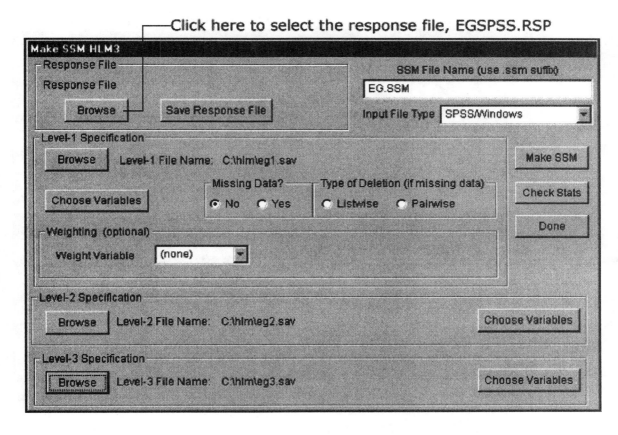

Figure 4.4   Make SSM – HLM3 dialog box for EG.SSM

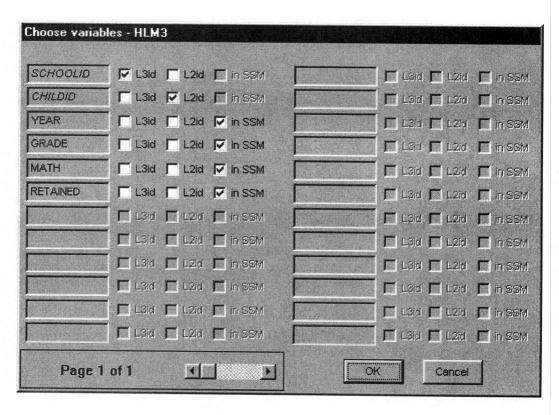

Figure 4.5   Choose Variables HLM3 dialog box for level-1 file, EG1.SAV

Click here to open the response file, EGASCII.RSP——

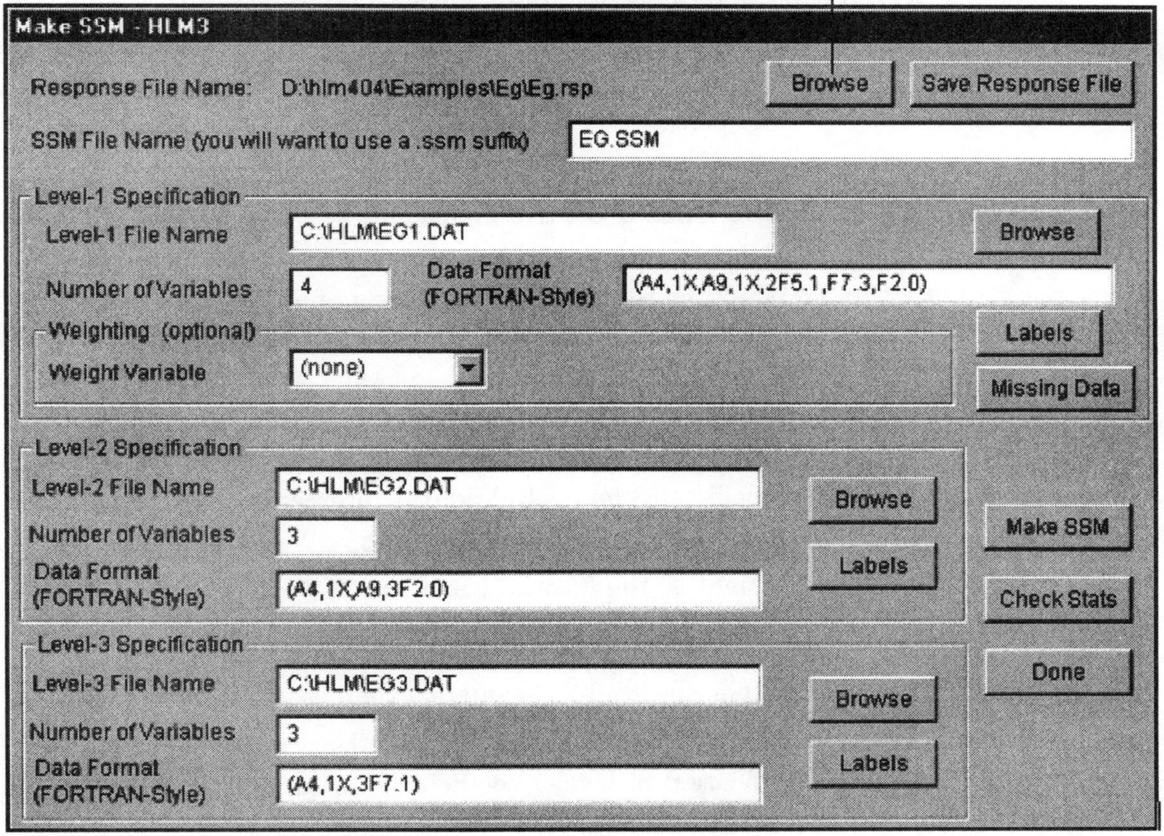

Make SSM - HLM3		
Response File Name: D:\hlm404\Examples\Eg\Eg.rsp	Browse	Save Response File

SSM File Name (you will want to use a .ssm suffix) EG.SSM

Level-1 Specification

Level-1 File Name C:\HLM\EG1.DAT Browse

Number of Variables 4 Data Format (FORTRAN-Style) (A4,1X,A9,1X,2F5.1,F7.3,F2.0)

Weighting (optional)

Weight Variable (none) Labels

Missing Data

Level-2 Specification

Level-2 File Name C:\HLM\EG2.DAT Browse

Number of Variables 3 Make SSM

Data Format (FORTRAN-Style) (A4,1X,A9,3F2.0) Labels Check Stats

Level-3 Specification

Level-3 File Name C:\HLM\EG3.DAT Browse Done

Number of Variables 3

Data Format (FORTRAN-Style) (A4,1X,3F7.1) Labels

Figure 4.6   Make SSM – HLM3 dialog box for EGASCII.SSM

ing the **Browse** buttons in the file specification sections and follows the same steps for SPSS input type to create SSM files.

4.1.1.4 Other file type input

HLM3 has the same range of options for data input as HLM2. In addition to SYSTAT and SAS, the Windows version (through a third-party module) allows numerous other data formats from, for example, STATA, EXCEL, and LOTUS input. See Section 2.5.1 for details.

4.2 Executing analyses based on the SSM file

Once the SSM file is constructed, model fitting analyses use this SSM file as input. Model specification via the Windows mode has five steps:

Step 1: Specification of the level-1 model. In our case we shall model mathematics achievement (MATH) as the outcome, to be predicted by YEAR in the study. Hence, the level-1 model will have two coefficients for each child: the intercept and the YEAR slope.

Step 2: Specification of the level-2 prediction model. Here each level-1 coefficient — the intercept and the YEAR slope in our example — becomes an outcome variable. We may select certain child characteristics to predict each of these level-1 coefficients. In principle, the level-2 parameters then describe the distribution of growth curves within each school.

Step 3: Specification of level-1 coefficients as random or non-random across level-two units. We shall model the intercept and the YEAR slope as varying randomly across the children within schools.

Step 4: Specification of the level-3 prediction model. Here each level-2 coefficient becomes an outcome, and we can select level-3 variables to predict school-to-school variation in these level-2 coefficients. In principle, this model specifies how schools differ with respect to the distribution of growth curves within them.

Step 5: Specification of the level-2 coefficients as random or non-random across level-3 units.

Following the five steps above, we first specified a model with no child- or school-level predictors. The Windows execution is very similar to the one for HLM2 as described in Section 2.5.2. The command file, EG1.HLM, contains the model specification input responses. To open the command file, open **File** menu and choose **Old Command File**. Fig. 4.7 displays the model specified.

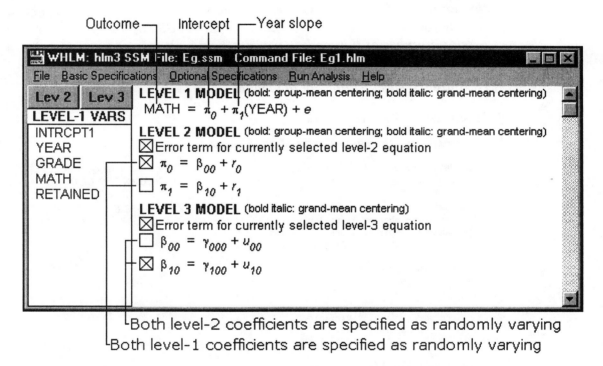

Figure 4.7   Unconditional model for the public school example

4.2.1 An annotated example of HLM3 output

Here is the output produced by the model described above (see example EG1.HLM).

```
Program:              HLM 5 Hierarchical Linear and Nonlinear Modeling
Authors:              Stephen Raudenbush, Tony Bryk, & Richard Congdon
Publisher:            Scientific Software International, Inc. (c) 2000
                                              techsupport@ssicentral.com
                                                        www.ssicentral.com
-------------------------------------------------------------------------
Module:     HLM3.EXE (5.01.2040.2)
Date:       9 February 2000, Wednesday
Time:       12:31:33
-------------------------------------------------------------------------
```

The first page of the output lists, after a program header, the specifics for this analysis. For your convenience, it has the date and time the problem ran. If you need to contact technical support at SSI, be sure to include the version number of the module you are using. It is given in parentheses right after the module name.

Next are the specifications of the model.

```
SPECIFICATIONS FOR THIS HLM3 RUN

  Problem Title: UNCONDITIONAL LINEAR GROWTH MODEL

  The data source for this run    = EG.SSM
  The command file for this run    = EG1.HLM
  Output file name                = EG1.OUT
  The maximum number of level-2 units = 1721
  The maximum number of level-3 units = 60
  The maximum number of iterations = 100
  Method of estimation: full maximum likelihood
```

Name of the SSM file
Name of the command file
Name of this output file
There are 1721 children
There are 60 schools

```
Weighting Specification
-----------------------

                          Weight
                          Variable
            Weighting?    Name        Normalized?
  Level 1      no                        no

  The outcome variable is      MATH

  The model specified for the fixed effects was:
  ------------------------------------------------------


    Level-1            Level-2          Level-3
    Coefficients       Predictors       Predictors
  ---------------    --------------   ----------------
      INTRCPT1, P0     INTRCPT2, B00    INTRCPT3, G000
      YEAR slope, P1   INTRCPT2, B10    INTRCPT3, G100
```

```
Summary of the model specified (in equation format)
----------------------------------------------------
Level-1 Model

    Y = P0 + P1*(YEAR) + E

Level-2 Model

        P0 = B00 + R0
        P1 = B10 + R1

Level-3 Model

        B00 = G000 + U0
        B10 = G100 + U1
```

Next come the initial parameter estimates or "starting values." Users should not base inferences on these values, their sole purpose is to get the iterations started.

```
For starting values, data from 7230 level-1 and 1721 level-2 records were used

   STARTING VALUES
   ---------------
   Sigma_squared(0) =        0.29710

Tau(pi)(0)
  INTRCPT1,P0       0.71125        0.05143
      YEAR,P1       0.05143        0.01582

Tau(beta)(0)
  INTRCPT1        YEAR
  INTRCPT2,B00 INTRCPT2,B10
     0.14930        0.01473
     0.01473        0.01196

The value of the likelihood function at iteration 1 = -8.169527E+003
The value of the likelihood function at iteration 2 = -8.165377E+003
The value of the likelihood function at iteration 3 = -8.165024E+003
The value of the likelihood function at iteration 4 = -8.164872E+003
The value of the likelihood function at iteration 5 = -8.164748E+003
The value of the likelihood function at iteration 6 = -8.163118E+003
The value of the likelihood function at iteration 7 = -8.163116E+003
The value of the likelihood function at iteration 8 = -8.163116E+003

Iterations stopped due to small change in likelihood function

******* ITERATION 9 *******

  Sigma_squared =        0.30148
  Standard Error of Sigma_squared =        0.00660
```

Final estimate of the level-1 variance.

```
Tau(pi)
  INTRCPT1,P0    0.64049    0.04676
      YEAR,P1    0.04676    0.01122
```

Final estimates of the level-2 variances and covariances.

```
Tau(pi) (as correlations)
  INTRCPT1,P0  1.000  0.551
      YEAR,P1  0.551  1.000
```

Note that the estimated correlation between true status at YEAR = 3.5 (halfway through third grade) and true rate of change is estimated to be 0.551 for children in the same school.

```
Standard Errors of Tau(pi)
  INTRCPT1,P0    0.02515    0.00499
      YEAR,P1    0.00499    0.00196

  ---------------------------------------------------
  Random level-1 coefficient   Reliability estimate
  ---------------------------------------------------
    INTRCPT1, P0                      0.839
        YEAR, P1                      0.190
  ---------------------------------------------------
```

Reliabilities of child parameter estimates.

```
Tau(beta)
  INTRCPT1            YEAR
  INTRCPT2,B00  INTRCPT2,B10
    0.16531         0.01705
    0.01705         0.01102
```

Final estimates of the level-3 variances and covariances.

```
Tau(beta) (as correlations)
  INTRCPT1/INTRCPT2,B00  1.000  0.399
      YEAR/INTRCPT2,B10  0.399  1.000
```

Notice that the estimated correlation between true school mean status at YEAR = 3.5 and true school-mean rate of change is 0.398.

```
Standard Errors of Tau(beta)
INTRCPT1        YEAR
INTRCPT2,B00 INTRCPT2,B10
   0.03641      0.00720
   0.00720      0.00252
```

```
-------------------------------------------------------
Random level-2 coefficient   Reliability estimate
-------------------------------------------------------
INTRCPT1/INTRCPT2, B00               0.821
     YEAR/INTRCPT2, B10              0.786
-------------------------------------------------------
```

Reliabilities of school-level parameter estimates. These indicate the reliability with which we can discriminate among level-2 units using their least-squares estimates of β_0, β_1. Low reliabilities do not invalidate the HLM analysis. Very low reliabilities (e.g., $< .10$), often indicate that a random coefficient might be considered fixed in subsequent analyses.

```
The value of the likelihood function at iteration 9 = -8.163116E+003
The outcome variable is    MATH
```

Final estimation of fixed effects:

	Fixed Effect	Coefficient	Standard Error	T-ratio	Approx. d.f.	P-value
For	INTRCPT1, P0					
	For INTRCPT2, B00					
	INTRCPT3, G000	-0.779309	0.057829	-13.476	59	0.000
For	YEAR slope, P1					
	For INTRCPT2, B10					
	INTRCPT3, G100	0.763029	0.015263	49.993	59	0.000

The above table indicates that the average growth rate is significantly positive at 0.763 logits per year, $t = 49.993$.

```
The outcome variable is    MATH
```

Final estimation of fixed effects (with robust standard errors)

	Fixed Effect	Coefficient	Standard Error	T-ratio	Approx. d.f.	P-value
For	INTRCPT1, P0					
	For INTRCPT2, B00					
	INTRCPT3, G000	-0.779309	0.057830	-13.476	59	0.000

```
For      YEAR slope, P1
   For INTRCPT2, B10
      INTRCPT3, G100     0.763029     0.015260     50.000     59     0.000
----------------------------------------------------------------------------
```

Note that the results with and without robust standard errors are nearly identical. If the robust and model-based standard errors are substantively different, it is recommended that the user further investigate the tenability of key assumptions (see Section 4.3 on examining residuals).

Final estimation of level-1 and level-2 variance components:

Random Effect		Standard Deviation	Variance Component	df	Chi-square	P-value
INTRCPT1,	R0	0.80030	0.64049	1661	6046.38220	0.000
YEAR slope,	R1	0.10595	0.01122	1661	2083.62406	0.000
level-1,	E	0.54907	0.30148			

Final estimation of level-3 variance components:

Random Effect	Standard Deviation	Variance Component	df	Chi-square	P-value
INTRCPT1/INTRCPT2, U00	0.40658	0.16531	59	488.34499	0.000
YEAR/INTRCPT2, U10	0.10498	0.01102	59	377.40852	0.000

The results above indicate significant variability among schools in terms of mean status at YEAR = 3.5 (chi-square = 488.34499, df = 59) and in terms of school-mean rates of change (chi-square of 377.40852, df = 59).

```
Statistics for current covariance components model
--------------------------------------------------
Deviance                = 16326.231327

Number of estimated parameters = 9

Exploratory Analysis: estimated level-2 coefficients and their standard errors
      obtained by regressing EB residuals on level-2 predictors selected for
      possible inclusion in subsequent runs
```

```
----------------------------------------------------------------------
Level-1 Coefficient          Potential Level-2 Predictors
----------------------------------------------------------------------

                        FEMALE    BLACK HISPANIC
INTRCPT1, P0
    Coefficient         -0.011   -0.362   -0.033
    Standard Error       0.036    0.067    0.070
    t value             -0.312   -5.432   -0.465

                        FEMALE    BLACK HISPANIC
    YEAR, P1
    Coefficient          0.001   -0.029    0.005
    Standard Error       0.003    0.006    0.006
    t value              0.369   -4.835    0.761
```

Exploratory Analysis: estimated level-3 coefficients and their standard errors
        obtained by regressing EB residuals on level-3 predictors selected for
        possible inclusion in subsequent runs

```
----------------------------------------------------------------------
Level-2 Predictor            Potential Level-3 Predictors
----------------------------------------------------------------------

                         SIZE   LOWINC MOBILITY
INTRCPT1/INTRCPT2, B00
    Coefficient         -0.000   -0.009   -0.016
    Standard Error       0.000    0.002    0.004
    t value             -1.651   -5.100   -4.324

                         SIZE   LOWINC MOBILITY
    YEAR/INTRCPT2, B10
    Coefficient         -0.000   -0.001   -0.002
    Standard Error       0.000    0.000    0.001
    t value             -1.525   -2.871   -1.962
```

Just as in the case of the two-level program, the potential predictors not included in the model may be employed as significant predictors in subsequent models. This potential is indicated approximately by the "t-values" given above. Note: because of the metric of school size (100s and 1000s), significant digits of the actual coefficients and standard errors are too small to be printed. The t-values are not, however.

4.3 Model checking based on the residual files

HLM3 produces two residual files, one at level-2 (containing estimates of the π's) and one at level-3 (containing estimates of the β's). These files will contain the EB residuals defined at levels 2 and 3, fitted values, and OL residuals. By adding the EB residuals to the corresponding fitted values, the analyst can also obtain the EB estimate for the corresponding coefficients. In addition, level-2 predictors can be included in the level-2 residual file and level-3 predictors in the level-3 residual file. However, other statistics provided in the residual file of HLM2, for example, the Mahalanobis distance measures, are not available in the residual files produced by HLM3. The procedures for requesting level-2 and level-3 residual files are similar to that for HLM2 as described in Section 2.5.4.

An example of a level-2 residual file produced in the above analysis is illustrated below. Only the data from the first and last pairs of children are given. See example EG2.HLM.

The files in this example are structured as SPSS command files and can be directly read into that program to create SPSS system files. As with HLM2, the user can also specify SYSTAT or SAS command file format for the residual file. The result will be executable SYSTAT or SAS programs. (For more details see Section 2.3.) Alternatively, the data defining information at the top of the file can be used to read these residual files into any other computing package.

We see that the level-3 ID (group ID or L3ID) is the first variable and the level-2 ID (person ID or L2ID) is the second. Each is to be read as a character variable with a width of 12. The rest of the variables are numeric and include NJK, the number of observations associated with child j in school k. The empirical Bayes estimates of the residuals, r_{pjk}, are given next, including, respectively, the intercept (EBINTRCP) and the YEAR effect (EBYEAR). The ordinary least squares estimates of the same quantities (OLINTRCP and OLYEAR); the fitted values, that is, the predicted values of the π_{pjk}'s for a given child based on the fixed effects (FVINTRCP and FVYEAR) and random school effect follow. Finally, the posterior variances and covariances (PV200, PV210, and PV211) of the empirical Bayes estimates are given.

```
DATA LIST FIXED RECORDS = 6
 /1 L3ID L2ID NJK (A12,A12,F5)
 /2 EBINTRCP EBYEAR   ( 2F11.5)
 /3 OLINTRCP OLYEAR   ( 2F11.5)
 /4 FVINTRCP FVYEAR   ( 2F11.5)
 /5 PV200 PV210 PV211 ( 3F11.5)
 /6   BLACK HISPANIC  ( 2F11.5).
BEGIN DATA
         2020   273026452     3
   0.29336    0.00823
   0.97102   -0.40282
  -0.30986    0.97982
   0.100587  -0.000867   0.006459
   0.00000    1.00000
         2020   273030991     5
   0.93886    0.11570
   0.92072    0.27996
   0.00953    0.93674
   0.072017   0.002066   0.006104
   0.00000    0.00000
 . . .
 . . .
 . . .
         4450   310621871     3
  -0.67126   -0.03988
  -0.73077    0.07880
  -0.95073    0.65420
   0.102936   0.010464   0.008173
   1.00000    0.00000
         4450   314542551     3
   0.17393   -0.02376
  -0.10311   -0.70720
  -0.95073    0.65420
   0.102936   0.010464   0.008173
   1.00000    0.00000
END DATA.
MISSING VALUES NJK TO OLYEAR     (-99).
SAVE OUTPUT = 'resfil2.sys'.
```

We see that the first child in the data set has SCHOOLID 2020 and CHIL-
DID 273026452. That child has 3 time-series observations. The predicted
growth rate for that child (the YEAR effect) is the fitted value 0.97982.
That child's empirical Bayes residual YEAR effect is 0.00823. Thus, the investigator can construct the empirical Bayes estimate of that child's YEAR
effect as:

$$\pi^*_{1jk} = \beta^*_{10k} + r^*_{1jk}$$
$$= \text{FVYEAR} + \text{EBYEAR}$$
$$= 0.97982 + 0.00823 = 0.98805 \; .$$

In a similar fashion, the investigator can also compute the empirical Bayes estimate for the child's intercept, π_{0jk}^*, using FVINTRCP + EBINTRCP.

The level-3 residual file, printed below, has a similar structure. Only the data from the first and last schools are given. We see that the level-3 id (group id or L3ID) is the first alphanumeric variable with a width of 12. The rest of the variables are numeric and include NK, the number of children in school k. This is followed by the empirical Bayes estimates of the β's, including, respectively, the intercept (EB00) and the YEAR effect (EB10). The ordinary least squares estimates of the same quantities (OL00 and OL10); the fitted values are given next, that is, the predicted values of the β's for a given school based on that school's effect and the fixed effects (FV00 and FV10). Finally, the posterior variances and covariances (PV30000, PV31000, and PV31010) of the estimates are given.

```
DATA LIST FIXED RECORDS = 6
 /1 L3ID NK (A12,F5)
 /2 EB00 EB10 ( 2F11.5)
 /3 OL00 OL10 ( 2F11.5)
 /4 FV00 FV01 FV02 FV10 FV11 FV12 ( 6F11.5)
 /5 PV30000 PV31000 PV31010 ( 3F11.5)
 /6   LOWINC ( 1F11.5).
BEGIN DATA
        2020   21
    0.17428    0.11739
    0.21922    0.11685
   -0.16475   -0.50212   -0.31938    0.81934   -0.03092    0.04309
    0.023192   0.000978   0.001715
   40.30000
  . . .
  . . .
  . . .
        4450   45
   -0.08760   -0.09877
   -0.15287   -0.17859
   -0.36101   -0.50212   -0.31938    0.78389   -0.03092    0.04309
    0.012965   0.000691   0.001290
   66.20000
END DATA.
MISSING VALUES NK TO OL10 (-99).
SAVE OUTPUT = 'resfil3.sys'.
```

We see that the first unit, school 2020, has NK = 21 children. The predicted YEAR effect for school 2020 is the fitted value 0.81934, that is, the maximum-likelihood estimate of the school mean growth rate in the case of this unconditional model. That school's empirical Bayes residual YEAR effect is 0.11739. Thus, the investigator can construct the empirical Bayes estimate of that school's YEAR effect (mean rate of growth) as

$$
\begin{aligned}
\beta_{10k}^* &= \gamma_{100}^* + u_{1k}^* \\
&= \text{FV01} + \text{EB10} \\
&= 0.81934 + 0.11739 = 0.93673 \; .
\end{aligned}
$$

Similarly, the investigator can construct the empirical Bayes estimate for the school's intercept, β_{00k}^*, using FV00 + EB00.

Note that the empirical Bayes estimate of the school YEAR effect, 0.93673, is the fitted value for each child in that school (in the level-2 residual file). This will be true in any model that is unconditional at level 2, that is, any model with no child-level predictors such as race black, ethnicity hispanic, or gender female. When level-2 predictors are in the model, the level-2 fitted values will also depend on those predictors.

4.4 Specification of a conditional model

The above example involves a model that is "unconditional" at levels 2 and 3; that is, no predictors are specified at each of those levels. Such a model is useful for partitioning variation in intercepts and growth rates into components that lie within and between schools (see *Hierarchical Linear Models*, Chapter 8), but provides no information on how child or school characteristics relate to the growth curves. Fig. 4.8 shows a model that incorporates information about a child's race and ethnicity and a school's percent low income. Moreover, we explore the possibility that several other predictors (gender, school enrollment, and percent mobility) might help account for variation in subsequent models.

The results of the analysis are given below (see example EG2.HLM).

```
Module:     HLM3.EXE (5.01.2040.2)
Date:       9 February 2000, Wednesday
Time:       12:31:40
-------------------------------------------------------------------------------

SPECIFICATIONS FOR THIS HLM3 RUN
```

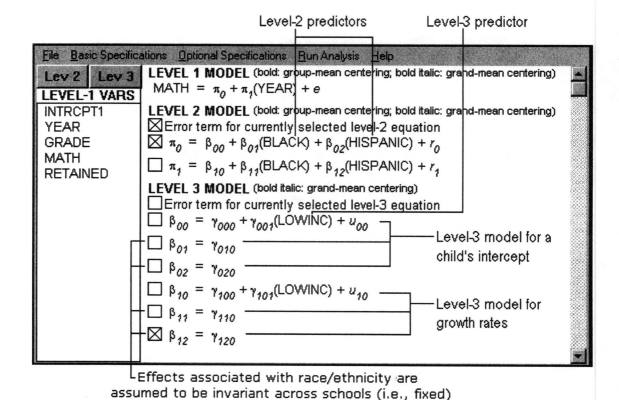

Level-2 predictors   Level-3 predictor

LEVEL 1 MODEL (bold: group-mean centering; bold italic: grand-mean centering)

$$\text{MATH} = \pi_0 + \pi_1(\text{YEAR}) + e$$

LEVEL 2 MODEL (bold: group-mean centering; bold italic: grand-mean centering)

☒ Error term for currently selected level-2 equation

☒ $\pi_0 = \beta_{00} + \beta_{01}(\text{BLACK}) + \beta_{02}(\text{HISPANIC}) + r_0$

☐ $\pi_1 = \beta_{10} + \beta_{11}(\text{BLACK}) + \beta_{12}(\text{HISPANIC}) + r_1$

LEVEL 3 MODEL (bold italic: grand-mean centering)

☐ Error term for currently selected level-3 equation

☐ $\beta_{00} = \gamma_{000} + \gamma_{001}(\text{LOWINC}) + u_{00}$

☐ $\beta_{01} = \gamma_{010}$

☐ $\beta_{02} = \gamma_{020}$

☐ $\beta_{10} = \gamma_{100} + \gamma_{101}(\text{LOWINC}) + u_{10}$

☐ $\beta_{11} = \gamma_{110}$

☒ $\beta_{12} = \gamma_{120}$

— Level-3 model for a child's intercept

— Level-3 model for growth rates

LEVEL-1 VARS
INTRCPT1
YEAR
GRADE
MATH
RETAINED

Lev 2 Lev 3

└ Effects associated with race/ethnicity are assumed to be invariant across schools (i.e., fixed)

Figure 4.8   Conditional model for the public school example

```
Problem Title: LINEAR GROWTH OVER GRADE, MINORITY, LOW INCOME

The data source for this run  = EG.SSM
The command file for this run = EG2.HLM
Output file name              = EG2.OUT
The maximum number of level-2 units = 1721
The maximum number of level-3 units = 60
The maximum number of iterations = 50
Method of estimation: full maximum likelihood

Weighting Specification
-----------------------
                            Weight
                            Variable
               Weighting?   Name       Normalized?
     Level 1      no                       no
```

```
The outcome variable is      MATH

The model specified for the fixed effects was:
--------------------------------------------------------
    Level-1                   Level-2            Level-3
    Coefficients              Predictors         Predictors
--------------------         ---------------    ----------------
        INTRCPT1, P0          INTRCPT2, B00      INTRCPT3, G000
                                                 LOWINC, G001
                          #       BLACK, B01     INTRCPT3, G010
                          #    HISPANIC, B02     INTRCPT3, G020
        YEAR slope, P1        INTRCPT2, B10      INTRCPT3, G100
                                                 LOWINC, G101
                          #       BLACK, B11     INTRCPT3, G110
                          #    HISPANIC, B12     INTRCPT3, G120
```

'#' - The residual parameter variance for the parameter has been set to zero

Summary of the model specified (in equation format)

Level-1 Model

$$Y = P0 + P1*(YEAR) + E$$

Level-2 Model

$$P0 = B00 + B01*(BLACK) + B02*(HISPANIC) + R0$$
$$P1 = B10 + B11*(BLACK) + B12*(HISPANIC) + R1$$

Level-3 Model

$$B00 = G000 + G001(LOWINC) + U00$$
$$B01 = G010$$
$$B02 = G020$$
$$B10 = G100 + G101(LOWINC) + U10$$
$$B11 = G110$$
$$B12 = G120$$

For starting values, data from 7230 level-1 and 1721 level-2 records were used

STARTING VALUES

Sigma_squared(0) =   0.29710

```
Tau(pi)(0)
  INTRCPT1,P0       0.69259        0.04914
      YEAR,P1       0.04914        0.01481

Tau(beta)(0)
  INTRCPT1           YEAR
  INTRCPT2,B00  INTRCPT2,B10
     0.05922        0.00290
     0.00290        0.01057
```

```
The value of the likelihood function at iteration 1 = -8.127397E+003
The value of the likelihood function at iteration 2 = -8.121908E+003
The value of the likelihood function at iteration 3 = -8.121269E+003
The value of the likelihood function at iteration 4 = -8.121059E+003
                                                    .
                                                    .
                                                    .
The value of the likelihood function at iteration 33 = -8.119608E+003
The value of the likelihood function at iteration 34 = -8.119608E+003
The value of the likelihood function at iteration 35 = -8.119603E+003

Iterations stopped due to small change in likelihood function


******* ITERATION 36 *******

 Sigma_squared =      0.30162

Tau(pi)
  INTRCPT1,P0      0.62223       0.04665
     YEAR,P1       0.04665       0.01108

Tau(pi) (as correlations)
  INTRCPT1,P0  1.000  0.562
     YEAR,P1   0.562  1.000


 ----------------------------------------------------
  Random level-1 coefficient   Reliability estimate
 ----------------------------------------------------
   INTRCPT1, P0                      0.835
      YEAR, P1                       0.188
 ----------------------------------------------------

Tau(beta)
  INTRCPT1         YEAR
  INTRCPT2,B00 INTRCPT2,B10
     0.07809      0.00082
     0.00082      0.00798

Tau(beta) (as correlations)
  INTRCPT1/INTRCPT2,B00  1.000  0.033
     YEAR/INTRCPT2,B10   0.033  1.000


 ----------------------------------------------------
  Random level-2 coefficient   Reliability estimate
 ----------------------------------------------------
   INTRCPT1/INTRCPT2, B00            0.702
      YEAR/INTRCPT2, B10            0.735
 ----------------------------------------------------


The value of the likelihood function at iteration 36 = -8.119603E+003
```

The outcome variable is   MATH

Final estimation of fixed effects:

Fixed Effect	Coefficient	Standard Error	T-ratio	Approx. d.f.	P-value
For INTRCPT1, P0					
For INTRCPT2, B00					
INTRCPT3, G000	0.140635	0.127490	1.103	58	0.275
LOWINC, G001	-0.007578	0.001691	-4.482	58	0.000
For BLACK, B01					
INTRCPT3, G010	-0.502115	0.077874	-6.448	1718	0.000
For HISPANIC, B02					
INTRCPT3, G020	-0.319385	0.086092	-3.710	1718	0.000
For YEAR slope, P1					
For INTRCPT2, B10					
INTRCPT3, G100	0.874511	0.039140	22.343	58	0.000
LOWINC, G101	-0.001369	0.000523	-2.619	58	0.012
For BLACK, B11					
INTRCPT3, G110	-0.030920	0.022456	-1.377	1718	0.169
For HISPANIC, B12					
INTRCPT3, G120	0.043087	0.024656	1.748	1718	0.080

The outcome variable is   MATH

Final estimation of fixed effects (with robust standard errors)

Fixed Effect	Coefficient	Standard Error	T-ratio	Approx. d.f.	P-value
For INTRCPT1, P0					
For INTRCPT2, B00					
INTRCPT3, G000	0.140635	0.113804	1.236	58	0.222
LOWINC, G001	-0.007578	0.001396	-5.429	58	0.000
For BLACK, B01					
INTRCPT3, G010	-0.502115	0.076837	-6.535	1718	0.000
For HISPANIC, B02					
INTRCPT3, G020	-0.319385	0.081919	-3.899	1718	0.000
For YEAR slope, P1					
For INTRCPT2, B10					
INTRCPT3, G100	0.874511	0.037287	23.454	58	0.000
LOWINC, G101	-0.001369	0.000499	-2.744	58	0.008
For BLACK, B11					
INTRCPT3, G110	-0.030920	0.022273	-1.388	1718	0.165
For HISPANIC, B12					
INTRCPT3, G120	0.043087	0.024368	1.768	1718	0.077

Final estimation of level-1 and level-2 variance components:

Random Effect		Standard Deviation	Variance Component	df	Chi-square	P-value
INTRCPT1,	R0	0.78881	0.62223	1659	7983.59660	0.000
YEAR slope,	R1	0.10526	0.01108	1659	2090.58661	0.000
level-1,	E	0.54920	0.30162			

Final estimation of level-3 variance components:

Random Effect		Standard Deviation	Variance Component	df	Chi-square	P-value
INTRCPT1/INTRCPT2,	U00	0.27945	0.07809	58	255.02131	0.000
YEAR/INTRCPT2,	U10	0.08933	0.00798	58	277.16437	0.000

Statistics for current covariance components model

Deviance   = 16239.206966
Number of estimated parameters = 15

Exploratory Analysis: estimated level-2 coefficients and their standard errors
        obtained by regressing EB residuals on level-2 predictors selected for
        possible inclusion in subsequent runs

Level-1 Coefficient	Potential Level-2 Predictors

	FEMALE
INTRCPT1, P0	
Coefficient	-0.010
Standard Error	0.036
t value	-0.273

	FEMALE
YEAR, P1	
Coefficient	0.001
Standard Error	0.003
t value	0.453

Exploratory Analysis: estimated level-3 coefficients and their standard errors
        obtained by regressing EB residuals on level-3 predictors selected for
        possible inclusion in subsequent runs

```
-------------------------------------------------------------------------------
Level-2 Predictor              Potential Level-3 Predictors
-------------------------------------------------------------------------------
                               SIZE  MOBILITY
INTRCPT1/INTRCPT2, B00
    Coefficient               -0.000   -0.007
    Standard Error             0.000    0.002
    t value                   -0.716   -2.824

YEAR/INTRCPT2, B10
    Coefficient               -0.000   -0.000
    Standard Error             0.000    0.001
    t value                   -1.155   -0.540
```

4.5 Other program features

Like HLM2, HLM3 provides options for multivariate hypothesis tests for the fixed effects and the variance-covariance components. A "no-intercept" model is available at level 1 or level 2 (but not at level 3). Like HLM2, missing data options are available at level 1 (but not at levels 2 or 3). Fig. 4.9 displays the **Basic Model Specifications – HLM3** dialog box. The options are similar to the corresponding dialog box for HLM2 (see Section 2.8). Unlike HLM2, the user has the option to create a level-2 as well as a level-3 residual file (see Section 4.3). The TAUVC.DAT file written out by the program contains estimates of level-2 and level-3 variances and covariances (see Section B.2 in Appendix B for format information). Finally, there is a separate but similar set of options for the way to handle initial estimates of level-2 and level-3 variances.

Note: Initial estimates simply start the iteration process that leads to final computation of maximum likelihood estimates. Occasionally these initial estimates are unacceptable and must be replaced to begin the iteration process.

The **Mode of iteration acceleration** section of this dialog box is primarily intended for people that have data large enough to cause the accelerator (and final) iterations to take a prohibitive amount of time. While for most data, the 2nd derivative option is recommended, users with large amounts of data (particularly with large ratios of level-1 to level-2 data) may find the 1st derivative Fisher useful, although this will make the standard errors of σ^2 and the tau matrices less precise. If the third option, **No accelerator**, is selected, there will be no Fisher iterations preformed. This will make large SSMs run faster, but will have the side effect of not producing standard errors of σ^2 and the tau matrices. If you want to suppress any Fisher iterations, but do want to have the above mentioned standard errors, choose 1st or 2nd derivative Fisher, and set the value in the **Frequency of accelerator** edit box one higher than the number of iterations in the edit box above it.

Note: Options available with HLM2 but not with HLM3 include the test of homogeneity of variance at level 1, and the specification of a random effect having no corresponding fixed effect.

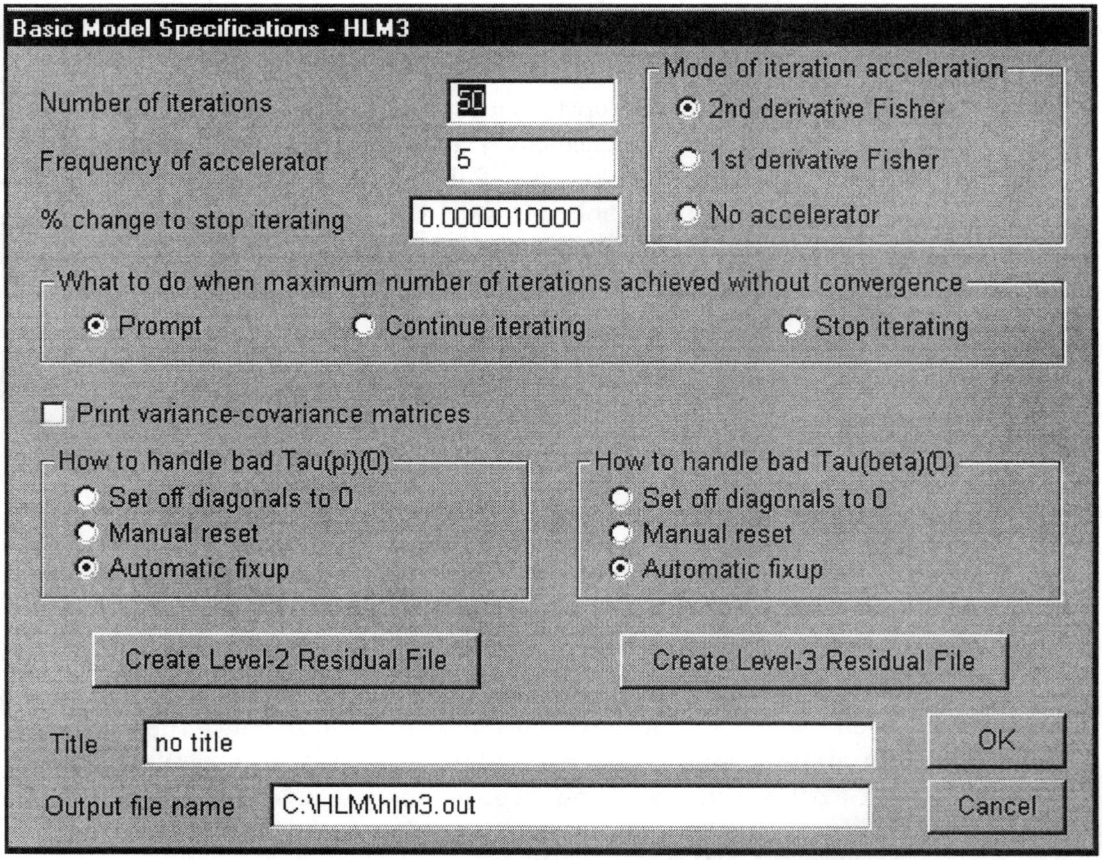

Basic Model Specifications – HLM3

Number of iterations	50
Frequency of accelerator	5
% change to stop iterating	0.0000010000

Mode of iteration acceleration
- ◉ 2nd derivative Fisher
- ○ 1st derivative Fisher
- ○ No accelerator

What to do when maximum number of iterations achieved without convergence
- ◉ Prompt   ○ Continue iterating   ○ Stop iterating

☐ Print variance-covariance matrices

How to handle bad Tau(pi)(0)
- ○ Set off diagonals to 0
- ○ Manual reset
- ◉ Automatic fixup

How to handle bad Tau(beta)(0)
- ○ Set off diagonals to 0
- ○ Manual reset
- ◉ Automatic fixup

Create Level-2 Residual File   Create Level-3 Residual File

Title: no title

Output file name: C:\HLM\hlm3.out

OK   Cancel

Figure 4.9   Basic Model Specifications – HLM3 dialog box

5

Conceptual and Statistical Background for Hierarchical Generalized Linear Models (HGLM)

The hierarchical linear model (HLM) as described in the previous four chapters is appropriate for two- and three-level data where the random effects at each level are normally distributed. The assumption of normality at level 1 is quite widely applicable when the outcome variable is continuous. Even when a continuous outcome is highly skewed, a transformation can often be found that will make the distribution of level-1 random effects (residuals) at least roughly normal. Methods for assessing the normality of random effects at higher levels are discussed on page 41 above and on page 218 of *Hierarchical Linear Models*.

There are important cases, however, where the assumption of normality at level 1 is clearly not realistic and no transformation can make it so. An example is a binary outcome, Y, indicating the presence of a disease ($Y = 1$ if the disease is present, $Y = 0$ if the disease is absent), graduation from high school ($Y = 1$ if a student graduates on time, $Y = 0$ if not), or the commission of a crime ($Y = 1$ if a person commits a crime during given time interval, $Y = 0$ if not). The use of the standard level-1 model in this case would be inappropriate for three reasons:

- Given the predicted value of the outcome, the level-1 random effect can only take on one of two values, and therefore cannot be normally distributed;
- The level-1 random effect cannot have homogeneous variance. Instead, the variance of this random effect depends on the predicted value as specified below.

□ Finally, there are no restrictions on the predicted values of the level-1 outcome in the standard model: they can legitimately take on any real value. In contrast, the predicted value of a binary outcome Y, if viewed as the predicted probability that $Y = 1$, cannot meaningfully be less than zero or greater than unity. Thus, an appropriate model for predicting Y ought to constrain the predicted values to lie in the interval $(0, 1)$. Without this constraint, the effect sizes estimated by the model are, in general, uninterpretable.

Another example involves count data, where Y is the number of crimes a person commits during a year or Y is the number of questions a child asks during the course of a one-hour class period. In these cases, the possible values of Y are non-negative integers $0, 1, 2, \ldots$ Such data will typically be positively skewed. If there are very few zeros in the data, a transformation, $e.g.$, $Y^* = \log(1 + Y)$, may solve this problem and allow sensible use of the standard HLM. However, in the cases mentioned above, there will typically be many zeros (many persons will not commit a crime during a given year and many children will not raise a question during a one-hour class). When there are many zeros, the normality assumption cannot be approximated by a transformation. Also, as in the case of the binary outcome, the variance of the level-1 random effects will depend on the predicted value (higher predicted values will be associated with larger variance). Similarly, the predicted values ought to be constrained to be positive.

Another example involves multi-category (≥ 2) data, where the outcome comprises teachers' responses about their commitment to their career choice. Teachers are asked if they would choose the teaching profession if they could go back to college and start over again. The three response categories are:

1. yes, I would choose teaching again
2. not sure
3. no, I would not choose teaching again

Such outcomes can be studied using a multinomial model. Thus, as discussed previously for models with binary outcomes, the use of the standard level-1 model would be inappropriate. Another model one may use is an ordinal model, which treats the categories as ordered.

Within HLM, the user can specify a nonlinear analysis appropriate for counts and binary, multinomial, or ordinal data. The approach is a direct extension of the generalized linear model of McCullagh & Nelder (1989) to the case of hierarchical data. We, therefore, refer to this approach as a "hierarchical generalized linear model" (HGLM). The execution of these analyses is in many ways similar to that in HLM but there are also important differences.

5.1 The two-level HLM as a special case of HGLM

The level-1 model in the HGLM may be viewed as consisting of three parts: a sampling model, a link function, and a structural model. In fact, the standard HLM can be viewed as a special case of the HGLM where the sampling model is normal and the link function is the identity link.

5.1.1 Level-1 sampling model

The sampling model for a two-level HLM might be written as

$$Y_{ij}|\mu_{ij} \sim NID(\mu_{ij}, \sigma^2) , \tag{5.1}$$

meaning that the level-one outcome Y_{ij}, given the predicted value, μ_{ij}, is normally and independently distributed with an expected value of μ_{ij} and a constant variance, σ^2. The level-1 expected value and mean may alternatively be written as

$$E(Y_{ij}|\mu_{ij}) = \mu_{ij} \qquad Var(Y_{ij}|\mu_{ij}) = \sigma^2 . \tag{5.2}$$

5.1.2 Level-1 link function

In general it is possible to transform the level-1 predicted value, μ_{ij}, to η_{ij} to insure that the predictions are constrained to lie within a given interval. Such a transformation is called a link function. In the normal case, no transformation is necessary. However, this decision not to transform may be made explicit by writing

$$\eta_{ij} = \mu_{ij} \ . \tag{5.3}$$

The *link function* in this case is viewed as the "identity link function."

5.1.3 Level-1 structural model

The transformed predicted value is now related to the predictors of the model through the linear model or "structural model"

$$\eta_{ij} = \beta_{0j} + \beta_{1j} X_{1ij} + \beta_{2j} X_{2ij} + \cdots + \beta_{Qj} X_{Qij} \ . \tag{5.4}$$

It is clear that, combining the level-1 sampling model (5.1), the level-1 link function (5.3), and the level-1 structural model (5.4) reproduces the level-1 model of HLM (1.1). In the context of a standard HLM, it seems silly to write three equations where only one is needed, but the value of the extra equations becomes apparent in the case of binary, count, and multi-category data.

5.2 Two- and three-level models for binary outcomes

While the standard HLM uses a normal sampling model and an identity link function, the binary outcome model uses a binomial sampling model and a logit link. Only the level-1 models differ from the linear case.

5.2.1 Level-1 sampling model

Let Y_{ij} be the number of "successes" in n_{ij} trials. Then we write that

$$Y_{ij}|\phi_{ij} \sim B(n_{ij}, \phi_{ij}) \ , \tag{5.5}$$

to denote that Y_{ij} has a binomial distribution with n_{ij} trials and probability of success ϕ_{ij}. According to the binomial distribution, the expected value and variance of Y_{ij} are then

$$E(Y_{ij}|\phi_{ij}) = n_{ij}\phi_{ij} \qquad Var(Y_{ij}|\phi_{ij}) = n_{ij}\phi_{ij}(1 - \phi_{ij}) \, . \qquad (5.6)$$

When $n_{ij} = 1$, Y_{ij} may take on values of either zero or unity. This is a special case of the binomial distribution known as the Bernoulli distribution. HGLM allows estimation of models in which $n_{ij} = 1$ (Bernoulli case) or $n_{ij} > 1$ (other binomial cases). The case with $n_{ij} > 1$ will be treated later.

For the Bernoulli case, the predicted value of the binary Y_{ij} is equal to the probability of a success, ϕ_{ij}.

5.2.2 Level-1 link function

When the level-1 sampling model is binomial, HGLM uses the logit link function

$$\eta_{ij} = \log\Big(\frac{\phi_{ij}}{1 - \phi_{ij}}\Big) \, . \qquad (5.7)$$

In words, η_{ij} is the log of the odds of success. Thus if the probability of success, ϕ_{ij}, is 0.5, the odds of success is 1.0 and the log-odds or "logit" is zero. When the probability of success is less than 0.5, the odds are less than one and the logit is negative; when the probability is greater than 0.5, the odds are greater than unity and the logit is positive. Thus, while ϕ_{ij} is constrained to be in the interval $(0, 1)$, η_{ij} can take on any real value.

5.2.3 Level-1 structural model

This will have exactly the same form as (5.4). Note that estimates of the β's in (5.4) make it possible to generate a predicted log-odds (η_{ij}) for any case. Such a predicted log-odds can be converted to an odds by computing $odds = \exp(\eta_{ij})$. Similarly, predicted log-odds can be converted to a *predicted probability* by computing

$$\phi_{ij} = \frac{1}{1 + \exp(-\eta_{ij})} \, . \tag{5.8}$$

Clearly, whatever the value of η_{ij}, applying (5.8) will produce a ϕ_{ij} between zero and unity.

5.2.4 Level-2 and level-3 models

In the case of a two-level analysis, the level-2 model has the same form as used in a standard two-level HLM (equations 1.2, 1.3, and 1.4). In the case of a three-level analysis, the level-2 and level-3 models are also the same as in a standard three-level HLM.

5.3 The model for count data

For count data, we use a Poisson sampling model and a log link function.

5.3.1 Level-1 sampling model

Let Y_{ij} be the number of events occurring during an interval time having length n_{ij}. For example, Y_{ij} could be the number of crimes a person i in group j commits during five years, so that $n_{ij} = 5$. The time-interval of n_{ij} units may be termed the "exposure." Then we write that

$$Y_{ij}|\lambda_{ij} \sim P(n_{ij}, \lambda_{ij}) \tag{5.9}$$

to denote that Y_{ij} has a Poisson distribution with exposure n_{ij} and event rate λ_{ij}. According to the Poisson distribution, the expected value and variance of Y_{ij} are then

$$E(Y_{ij}|\lambda_{ij}) = n_{ij}\lambda_{ij} \qquad Var(Y_{ij}|\lambda_{ij}) = n_{ij}\lambda_{ij} \; . \qquad (5.10)$$

The exposure n_{ij} need not be a measure of time. For example, if Y_{ij} is the number of bombs dropping on neighborhood i of city j during a war, n_{ij} could be the area of that neighborhood. A common case arises when for every i and j the exposure is the same (*e.g.*, Y_{ij} is the number of crimes committed during one year for each person i within each neighborhood j). In this case, we set $n_{ij} = 1$ for simplicity. HGLM allows estimation of models in which $n_{ij} = 1$ or $n_{ij} > 1$. (The case with $n_{ij} > 1$ will be treated later.)

According to our level-1 model, the predicted value of Y_{ij} when $n_{ij} = 1$ will be the event rate λ_{ij}.

Level-1 link function. HGLM uses the log link function when the level-1 sampling model is Poisson, that is

$$\eta_{ij} = \log(\lambda_{ij}) \; , \qquad (5.11)$$

In words, η_{ij} is the log of the event rate. Thus, if the event rate, λ_{ij}, is one, the log is zero. When the event rate is less than one, the log is negative; when the event rate is greater than one, the log is positive. Thus, while λ_{ij} is constrained to be non-negative, η_{ij} can take on any real value.

5.3.2 Level-1 structural model

This will have exactly the same form as (5.4). Note that estimates of the β's in (5.4) make it possible to generate a predicted log-event rate (η_{ij}) for any case. Such a predicted log-event rate can be converted to an event rate by computing

$$\lambda_{ij} = \text{event rate} = \exp(\eta_{ij}) \; .$$

Clearly, whatever the value of η_{ij}, λ_{ij} will be non-negative.

5.3.3 Level-2 and level-3 models

The level-2 model has the same form as the level-2 model for HLM2 (equations 1.2, 1.3, and 1.4); and the level-2 and level-3 models have the same form in the three-level case as in HLM3.

5.4 The model for multinomial data

For multi-category nominal data, we use a multinomial model and a logit link function. This is an extension of the Bernoulli model with more than two possible outcomes.

5.4.1 Level-1 sampling model

Let

$$\text{Prob}(R_{ij} = m) = \phi_{ij} \, ,$$

that is, the probability that person i in group j lands in category m is ϕ_{ij}, for categories $m = 1, \ldots, M$, there being M possible categories.

For example, $R_{ij} = 1$ if high school student i in school j goes on to college; $R_{ij} = 2$ if that student goes on to a job; $R_{ij} = 3$ if that student becomes unemployed. Here $M = 3$. The analysis is facilitated by constructing dummy variables $Y_1, \ldots, Y_M$, where $Y_{mij} = 1$ if $R_{ij} = m$, 0 otherwise, $m = 1, \ldots, M$. For example, if student ij goes to college, $R_{ij} = 1$, so $Y_{1ij} = 1, Y_{2ij} = 0, Y_{3ij} = 0$; if student ij goes to work, $R_{ij} = 2$, so $Y_{1ij} = 0, Y_{2ij} = 1, Y_{3ij} = 0$; if that student becomes unemployed, $R_{ij} = 3$, so $Y_{1ij} = 0, Y_{2ij} = 0, Y_{3ij} = 1$. This leads to a definition of the probabilities as $\text{Prob}(Y_{mij} = 1) = \phi_{mij}$. For example, for $M = 3$,

$$
\begin{aligned}
\text{Prob}(Y_{1ij} = 1) &= \phi_{1ij} \\
\text{Prob}(Y_{2ij} = 1) &= \phi_{2ij} \\
\text{Prob}(Y_{3ij} = 1) &= \phi_{3ij} = 1 - \phi_{1ij} - \phi_{2ij}
\end{aligned}
\tag{5.12}
$$

Note that because $Y_{3ij} = 1 - Y_{1ij} - Y_{2ij}$, Y_{3ij} is redundant.

According to the multinomial distribution, the expected value and variance of Y_{mij} given ϕ_{mij}, are then

$$\mathsf{E}(Y_{mij}|\phi_{mij}) = n_{ij}\phi_{mij} \qquad \mathsf{Var}(Y_{mij}|\phi_{mij}) = n_{ij}\phi_{mij}(1 - \phi_{mij}) \ . \tag{5.13}$$

The covariance between outcomes Y_{mij}, and $Y_{m'ij}$ is

$$\mathsf{Cov}(Y_{mij}, Y_{m'ij}) = -n_{ij}\phi_{mij}\phi_{m'ij} \ . \tag{5.14}$$

5.4.2 Level-1 link function

HGLM uses the logit link function when the level-1 sampling model is multinomial. Define η_{mij} as the log-odds of falling into category m relative to that of falling into category M. Specifically

$$\eta_{mij} = \log\left(\frac{\phi_{mij}}{\phi_{Mij}}\right) \tag{5.15}$$

where

$$\phi_{Mij} = 1 - \sum_{m=1}^{M-1} \phi_{mij} \ . \tag{5.16}$$

In words, η_{mij} is the log-odds of the m-th category relative to the M-th category, which is known as the "reference category."

5.4.3 Level-1 structural model

At level-1, we have

$$\eta_{mij} = \beta_{0j(m)} + \sum_{q=1}^{Q} \beta_{qj(m)} X_{qij} \,, \tag{5.17}$$

for $m = 1, \ldots, (M - 1)$. For example, with $M = 3$, there would be two level-1 equations, for η_{1ij} and η_{2ij}.

5.4.4 Level-2 model

The level-2 model has a parallel form

$$\beta_{qj(m)} = \gamma_{q0(m)} + \sum_{s=1}^{S_q} \gamma_{qs(m)} W_{sj} + u_{qj(m)} \,. \tag{5.18}$$

Thus, for $M = 3$, there would be two sets of level-2 equations.

5.5 The model for ordinal data

5.5.1 Level-1 sampling model

Again a person falls into category m and there are M possible categories ($m = 1, \ldots, M$). But now the categories are ordered. Given the ordered nature of the data, we derive the $M - 1$ dummy variables $Y_{1ij}, \ldots, Y_{(M-1)ij}$ for case i in unit j as

$$Y_{mij} = 1 \quad \text{if} \quad R_{ij} \le m \,, \quad 0 \ \text{otherwise} \,. \tag{5.19}$$

For example, with $M = 3$, we have

$$\begin{aligned} Y_{1ij} &= 1 \quad \text{if} \quad R_{ij} = 1 \\ Y_{2ij} &= 1 \quad \text{if} \quad R_{ij} \le 2 \end{aligned} \tag{5.20}$$

The probabilities $\text{Prob}(Y_{mij} = 1)$ are thus cumulative probabilities. For example, with $M = 3$,

$$
\begin{aligned}
\text{Prob}(Y_{1ij} = 1) &= \text{Prob}(R_{ij} = 1) = \phi_{1ij} \\
\text{Prob}(Y_{2ij} = 1) &= \text{Prob}(R_{ij} = 1) + \text{Prob}(R_{ij} = 2) = \phi_{2ij} \\
\text{Prob}(Y_{3ij} = 1) &= \text{Prob}(R_{ij} = 1) + \text{Prob}(R_{ij} = 2) + \text{Prob}(R_{ij} = 3) = 1
\end{aligned}
\tag{5.21}
$$

Since $Y_{3ij} = 1 - Y_{2ij}$, Y_{3ij} is redundant. We actually need only $M - 1$ dummy variables.

Associated with the cumulative probabilities are the cumulative logits

$$
\eta_{mij} = \log\left(\frac{\text{Prob}(R_{ij} \leq m)}{\text{Prob}(R_{ij} > m)}\right) = \log\left(\frac{\phi_{mij}}{1 - \phi_{mij}}\right) .
\tag{5.22}
$$

5.5.2 Level-1 structural model

The level-1 structural model assumes "proportional odds,"

$$
\eta_{mij} = \beta_{0j} + \sum_{q=1}^{Q} \beta_{qi} X_{qij} + \sum_{m=2}^{M} \delta_m .
\tag{5.23}
$$

Under the proportional odds assumption, the relative odds that $R_{ij} \leq m$ associated with a unit increase in the predictor does not depend on m.

Here δ_m is a "threshold" separating categories $m-1$ amd m. For example, when $M = 4$,

$$
\begin{aligned}
\eta_{1ij} &= \beta_{0j} + \sum_{q=1}^{Q} \beta_{qj} X_{qij} \\
\eta_{2ij} &= \beta_{0j} + \sum_{q=1}^{Q} \beta_{qj} X_{qij} + \delta_2
\end{aligned}
\tag{5.24}
$$

$$\eta_{3ij} = \beta_{0j} + \sum_{q=1}^{Q} \beta_{qj} X_{qij} + \delta_2 + \delta_3$$

5.6 Parameter estimation

HGLM uses two approaches to estimation. The first method bases inference on the joint posterior modes of the level-1 and level-2 (and level-3) regression coefficients given the variance-covariance estimates. The variance-covariance estimates are based on a normal approximation to the restricted likelihood. Stiratelli, Laird, & Ware (1984) and Wong & Mason (1985) developed this approach for the binary case. Schall (1991) discusses the extension of this approach to the wider class of generalized linear models. Breslow & Clayton (1993) refer to this estimation approach as "penalized quasi-likelihood" or PQL. Extending HLM to HGLM requires a doubly-iterative algorithm, significantly increasing computational time. Related approaches are described by Goldstein (1991), Longford (1993), and Hedeker & Gibbons (1994).

The second method of estimation ("Laplace6") involves a somewhat more computationally intensive algorithm but provides accurate approximation to maximum likelihood (ML). This approach is currently available for two-level Bernoulli models. We consider PQL below in some detail followed by a brief discussion of Laplace6.

5.6.1 Estimation via PQL

The approach can be presented heuristically by computing a "linearized dependent variable" as in the generalized linear model of McCullagh & Nelder (1989). Basically, the analysis involves use of a standard HLM model with the introduction of a special weighting at level-1. However, after this standard HLM analysis has converged, the linearized dependent variable and the weights must be recomputed. Then, the standard HLM analysis is re-computed. This iterative process of HLM analyses and re-computing weights and linearized dependent variable continues until estimates converge.

We term the standard HLM iterations "micro-iterations." The recomputation of the linearized dependent variable and the weights constitute a "macro iteration." The approach is outlined below for four cases: Bernoulli (binomial with $n_{ij} = 1$), Poisson with $n_{ij} = 1$, binomial with $n_{ij} > 1$, and Poisson with $n_{ij} > 1$.

5.6.1.1 Bernoulli (binomial with $n_{ij} = 1$)

Consider the model

$$Y_{ij} = \phi_{ij} + \epsilon_{ij} \tag{5.25}$$

with ϕ_{ij} defined as in Equation 5.8 and

$$\mathsf{E}(\epsilon_{ij}) = 0 \qquad \mathsf{Var}(\epsilon_{ij}) = w_{ij} = \phi_{ij}(1 - \phi_{ij}) . \tag{5.26}$$

We now substitute for ϕ_{ij} its linear approximation

$$\phi_{ij} \approx \phi_{ij}^{(0)} + \frac{\partial \phi_{ij}^{(i)}}{\partial \eta_{ij}^{(i)}} (\eta_{ij} - \eta_{ij}^{(0)}) \tag{5.27}$$

with

$$\eta_{ij}^{(0)} = \log \left(\frac{\phi_{ij}^{(0)}}{1 - \phi_{ij}^{(0)}} \right) , \tag{5.28}$$

where $\phi_{ij}^{(0)}$ is an initial estimate and

$$\frac{\partial \phi_{ij}}{\partial \eta_{ij}} = w_{ij} = \phi_{ij}(1 - \phi_{ij}) . \tag{5.29}$$

If we evaluate w_{ij} at its initial estimates

$$w_{ij}^{(0)} = \phi_{ij}^{(0)}(1 - \phi_{ij}^{(0)}) , \tag{5.30}$$

(5.25) can be written as

$$Y_{ij} = \phi_{ij}^{(0)} + w_{ij}^{(0)}(\eta_{ij} - \eta_{ij}^{(0)}) + \epsilon_{ij} . \tag{5.31}$$

Algebraically rearranging the equation so that all observables are on the left-hand side yields

$$\begin{aligned} Z_{ij}^{(0)} &= \eta_{ij} + \frac{\epsilon_{ij}}{w_{ij}^{(0)}} \\ &= \beta_{0j} + \beta_{1j}X_{1ij} + \beta_{2ij}X_{2ij} + \cdots + \beta_{Qij}X_{Qij} + e_{ij} , \end{aligned} \tag{5.32}$$

where

$$Z_{ij}^{(0)} = \frac{Y_{ij} - \phi_{ij}^{(0)}}{w_{ij}^{(0)}} + \eta_{ij}^{(0)} \tag{5.33}$$

is the linearized dependent variable and

$$\mathsf{Var}(e_{ij}) = \mathsf{Var}\left(\frac{\epsilon_{ij}}{w_{ij}^{(0)}}\right) \approx \frac{1}{w_{ij}^{(0)}} . \tag{5.34}$$

Thus, (5.32) is a standard HLM level-1 model with outcome $Z_{ij}^{(0)}$ and level-1 weighting variable $w_{ij}^{(0)}$.

The algorithm works as follows.

1. Given initial estimates of the predicted value, ϕ_{ij}, and therefore of the linearized dependent variable, Z_{ij}, and the weight, w_{ij}, compute a weighted HLM analysis with (5.32) as the level-1 model.

2. The HLM analysis from step 1 will produce new predicted values and thus new linearized dependent variables and weights. HLM will now compute a new, re-weighted SSM file with the appropriate linearized dependent variable and weights.

3. Based on the new linearized dependent variable and weights, re-compute step 1.

This process goes on until the linearized dependent variable, the weights, and therefore, the parameter estimates, converge to a prespecified tolerance. The program then stops.

5.6.1.2 Poisson with $n_{ij} = 1$

The procedure is exactly the same as in the binomial case with $n_{ij} = 1$ except that

$$\text{Var}(\epsilon_{ij}) = w_{ij} = \frac{\partial \lambda_{ij}}{\partial \eta_{ij}} = \lambda_{ij} \, . \tag{5.35}$$

5.6.1.3 Binomial with $n_{ij} > 1$

In the previous example, Y_{ij} was formally the number of successes in one trial and therefore could take on a value of 0 or 1. We now consider the case where Y_{ij} is the number of successes in n_{ij} trials, where Y_{ij} and n_{ij} are non-negative integers, $Y_{ij} \leq n_{ij}$.

Suppose that a researcher is interested in examining the relationship between pre-school experience (yes or no) and grade retention and wonders whether this relationship is similar for males and females. The design involves students at level 1 nested within schools at level 2. In this case, each school would have four "cell counts" (boys with and without pre-school and girls with and without pre-school). Thus, the data could be organized so that every school had four observations (except possibly for schools without variation on pre-school or sex), where each observation was a cell having a cell size n_{ij} and a cell count Y_{ij} of students in that cell who were, in fact, retained. One could then re-conceptualize the study as having up to four level-1 units (cells); the outcome Y_{ij}, given the cell probability ϕ_{ij} would be distributed as $\mathsf{B}(n_{ij}, \phi_{ij})$. There would be three level-1 predictors (a contrast for pre-school experience, a contrast for sex, and an interaction contrast). This problem then has the structure of a $2 \times 2 \times J$ contingency table (pre-school experience by sex by school) with the last factor viewed as random.

The structure of a level-1 file for group 2 might appear as follows.

Group	ID	n_{ij}	Y_{ij}	X_{1ij}	X_{2ij}	X_{3ij}
Girls with pre-school	2	n_{12}	Y_{12}	.5	.5	.25
Girls without pre-school	2	n_{22}	Y_{22}	.5	−.5	−.25
Boys with pre-school	2	n_{32}	Y_{32}	−.5	.5	−.25
Boys without pre-school	2	n_{42}	Y_{42}	−.5	−.5	.25

For example, n_{12} is the number of girls in school 2 with pre-school and Y_{12} is the number of those girls who were retained. The predictor X_{1ij} is a contrast coefficient to assess the effect of sex (.5 if female, −.5 if male); X_{2ij} is a contrast for pre-school experience (.5 if yes, −.5 if no), and $X_{3ij} = X_{1ij} * X_{2ij}$ is the interaction contrast.

Estimation works the same in this case as in the binomial case except that

$$Z_{ij} = \frac{Y_{ij} - n_{ij}\phi_{ij}}{w_{ij}} + \eta_{ij} \tag{5.36}$$

with

$$w_{ij} = n_{ij}\phi_{ij}(1 - \phi_{ij}) . \tag{5.37}$$

5.6.1.4 Poisson with $n_{ij} > 1$

Consider now a study of the number of homicides committed within each of j neighborhoods in a large city. Many neighborhoods will have no homicides. The expected number of homicides in a neighborhood will depend not only on the homicide rate for that neighborhood, but also on the size of that neighborhood as indexed by its number of residents, n_{ij}. Level-1 variables might include characteristics of the homicide (*e.g.*, whether the homicide involved a domestic dispute, whether it involved use of a gun). Each cell (*e.g.*, the four types of homicide as defined by the cross-classification of domestic — yes or no — and use of a gun — yes or no) would be a level-1 unit.

Estimation in this case is the same as in the Poisson case with $n_{ij} = 1$ except that

$$Z_{ij} = \frac{Y_{ij} - n_{ij}\lambda_{ij}}{w_{ij}} + \eta_{ij} \tag{5.38}$$

and

$$w_{ij} = n_{ij}\lambda_{ij} . \tag{5.39}$$

5.6.2 Properties of the estimators

Using PQL, HGLM produces approximate empirical Bayes estimates of the randomly-varying level-1 coefficients, generalized least squares estimators of the level-2 (and level-3) coefficients, and approximate restricted maximum-likelihood estimators of the variance and covariance parameters. Yang (1995) has conducted a simulation study of these estimators in comparison with an alternative approach used by some programs that sets the level-2 random coefficients to zero in computing the linearized dependent variables. Breslow & Clayton (1993) refer to this alternative approach as "marginalized quasi-likelihood" or MQL. Rodriquez & Goldman (1995) had found that MQL produced biased estimates of the level-2 variance and the level-2 regression coefficients. Yang's results showed a substantial improvement (reduction in bias and mean squared error) in using the approach of HGLM. In particular, the bias in estimation of the level-2 coefficients was never more than 10 percent for HGLM, while the MQL approach commonly produced a bias between 10 and 20 percent. HGLM performed better than the alternative approach in estimating a level-2 variance component as well. However, a negative bias was found in estimating this variance component, ranging between two percent and 21 percent. The bias was most severe when the true variance was very large and the typical "probability of success" was very small (or, equivalently, very large). Initial simulation results under the Poisson model appear somewhat more favorable than this. Breslow & Clayton (1993) suggest that the estimation will be more efficient as n_{ij} increases.

5.6.3 Parameter estimation: A high-order Laplace approximation of maximum likelihood

For two-level Bernoulli models, HGLM provides an alternative to estimation via PQL. The alternative uses a sixth order approximation to the likelihood based on a Laplace transform and is therefore called "Laplace6." Simulations by Yang (1998) and Raudenbush, Yang, & Yosef (in press) show that this approach produced remarkably accurate approximation to maximum likelihood (ML), and therefore provides efficient (or nearly efficient) estimates of all parameters. We refer the interested readers to Yang's (1998) dissertation and to Raudenbush, Yang, & Yosef (in press) for details.

5.7 Unit-specific and population-average models

The models described above have been termed "unit-specific." They model the expected outcome for a level-2 unit conditional on a given set of random effects. For example, in the Bernoulli case ($n_{ij} = 1$), we might have a level-1 (within-school) model

$$\eta_{ij} = \beta_{0j} + \beta_{1j} X_{ij} \ , \tag{5.40}$$

and a level-2 (between-school) model

$$\begin{aligned} \beta_{0j} &= \gamma_{00} + \gamma_{01} W_j + u_{0j} \\ \beta_{1j} &= \gamma_{10} \end{aligned} \tag{5.41}$$

leading to the combined model

$$\eta_{ij} = \gamma_{00} + \gamma_{01}W_j + \gamma_{10}X_{ij} + u_{0j} \,. \tag{5.42}$$

Under this model, the predicted probability for case ij, given u_{0j} would be

$$\mathsf{E}(Y_{ij}|u_{0j}) = \frac{1}{1 + \exp\{-(\gamma_{00} + \gamma_{01}W_j + \gamma_{10}X_{ij} + u_{0j})\}} \,. \tag{5.43}$$

In this model, γ_{10} is the expected difference in the log-odds of "success" between two students who differ by one unit on X (holding W_j and u_{0j} constant); γ_{01} is the expected difference in the log-odds of success between two students who have the same value on X but attend schools differing by one unit on W (holding u_{0j} constant). These definitions parallel definitions used in a standard HLM for continuous outcomes.

However, one might also want to know the average difference between log-odds of success of students having the same X but attending schools differing by one unit on W, that is, the difference of interest *averaging over all possible values of* u_{0j}. In this case, the unit-specific model would not be appropriate. The model that would be appropriate would be a "population-average" model (Zeger, Liang, & Albert, 1988). The distinction is tricky in part because it does not arise in the standard HLM (with an identity link function). It arises only in the case of a nonlinear link function.

Using the same example as above, the population average model would be

$$\mathsf{E}(Y_{ij}) = \frac{1}{1 + \exp\{-(\gamma_{00}^* + \gamma_{01}^*W_j + \gamma_{10}^*X_{ij})\}} \,. \tag{5.44}$$

Notice that (5.44) does not condition on (or "hold constant") the random effect u_{0j}. Thus, γ_{01}^* gives the expected difference in log-odds of success between two students with the same X who attend schools differing by one unit on W — without respect to the random effect, u_{0j}. If one had a nationally representative sample and could validly assign a causal inference to W, γ_{01}^* would be the average change in the log-odds of success in the whole society associated with boosting W by one unit while γ_{01} would be the average change in log-odds associated with boosting W one unit for those schools sharing the same value of u_{0j}.

HGLM produces estimates for both the unit-specific and population-average models. The population-average results are based on generalized least squares given the variance-covariance estimates from the unit-specific model. Moreover, HGLM produces robust standard error estimates for the population-average model (Zeger, *et al.*, 1988). These standard errors are relatively insensitive to misspecification of the variances and covariances at the two levels and to the distributional assumptions at each level. The method of estimation used in HGLM for the population-average model is equivalent to the "generalized estimating equation" (GEE) approach popularized by Zeger, *et al.* (1988).

The following differences between unit-specific and population-average results are to be expected:

- ❑ If all predictors are held constant at their means, and if their means are zero, the population-average intercept can be used to estimate the average probability of success across the entire population, that is

$$\hat{\phi}_{ij} = \frac{1}{1 + \exp\{-\gamma_{00}^*\}} \, . \tag{5.45}$$

  This will not be true of unit-specific intercepts unless the average probability of success is very close to .5.

- ❑ Coefficient estimates (other than the intercept) based on the population-average model will often tend to be similar to those based on the unit-specific model but will tend to be smaller in absolute value.

Users will need to take care in choosing unit-specific versus population-average results for their research. The choice will depend on the specific research questions that are of interest. In the previous example, if one were primarily interested in how a change in W can be expected to affect a particular individual school's mean, one would use the unit-specific model. If one were interested in how a change in W can be expected to affect the overall population mean, one would use the population-average model.

5.8 Over-dispersion and under-dispersion

As mentioned earlier, if the data follow the assumed level-1 sampling model, the level-1 variance of the Y_{ij} will be $1/w_{ij}$ where

$$
\begin{aligned}
w_{ij} &= n_{ij}\phi_{ij}(1 - \phi_{ij}) , \qquad \text{Binomial case, or} \qquad (5.46)\\
w_{ij} &= n_{ij}\lambda_{ij} , \qquad\qquad\quad \text{Poisson case .}
\end{aligned}
$$

However, if the level-1 data do not follow this model, the actual level-1 variance may be larger than that assumed (over-dispersion) or smaller than that assumed (under-dispersion). For example, if undetected clustering exists within level-1 units or if the level-1 model is under-specified, extra-binomial or extra-Poisson dispersion may arise. This problem can be handled in a variety of ways; HGLM allows estimation of a scalar variance so that the level-1 variance will be σ^2.

5.9 Restricted versus full PQL versus full ML

The default method of estimation for the two-level HGLM is restricted PQL, while full PQL is an option. For the three-level HGLM, PQL estimation is by means of full PQL only. All Laplace6 estimates involve full ML.

5.10 Hypothesis testing

The logic of hypothesis testing with HGLM is quite similar to that used in the case of HLM. Thus, for the fixed effects (the γ's), a table of approximate t-values is routinely printed for univariate tests; multivariate tests for the fixed effects are available using the approach described earlier in Chapter 2. Similarly, univariate test for variance components (approximate chi-squares) are also routinely printed out. The one exception is that multivariate tests based on comparing model deviances ($-2 * $ *log-likelihood at convergence*) are not available using PQL, because PQL is based on quasi-likelihood rather than maximum-likelihood estimation. These are available using Laplace.

6 Working with HGLM

Both HGLM ("nonlinear analysis") and HLM ("linear analysis") use the same process for the construction of the SSM file. The same SSM file can be used for both nonlinear and linear analyses.

6.1 Executing nonlinear analyses based on the SSM file

Model specification for nonlinear analyses, as in the case of linear analyses, can be achieved via Windows (PC implementation only), through interactive execution, or batch execution. The mechanics of model specification are generally the same as in linear analyses with the following differences:

1. In the case of nonlinear analysis, the level-1 data file **must remain in the directory in which it was located when the SSM file was made, and it must keep the same filename.** This is because nonlinear analysis, unlike linear analysis, requires access to the raw level-1 data (these data are read anew at each macro iteration).

2. The user has an option of six types of nonlinear analysis. With the Windows version, these options are displayed in the **Nonlinear Specification** dialog box (see Fig. 6.1). There are two choices for dichotomous outcomes, two for count outcomes, one for multinomial outcomes, and one for ordinal outcomes.

3. Highly accurate Laplace approximation to maximum likelihood is available for two-level Bernoulli models.

4. The user may wish to allow extra-binomial or extra-Poisson dispersion (not available for Laplace).

5. As mentioned, the nonlinear analysis is doubly iterative so the maximum number of macro iterations must be specified as well as the maximum number of micro iterations.

   Similarly, convergence criteria can be reset for macro iterations as well as micro iterations.[1]

Below we provide two detailed examples of nonlinear analyses: the first uses the Bernoulli model, that is, a binomial model with the number of trials, n_{ij}, equal to one. The second example uses a binomial model with $n_{ij} > 1$. The analogs of these two analyses for count data are, respectively, the Poisson model with equal exposure and the Poisson case with variable exposure (some brief notes about these two applications are also included). Finally, we furnish two brief examples for multi-category outcomes, one for multinomial data and one for ordinal data. Windows mode specification is illustrated. See Appendix refch:appdxc for interactive and batch specification.

6.2 Case 1: a Bernoulli model

Data are from a national survey of primary education in Thailand (see Raudenbush & Bhumirat, 1992, for details), conducted in 1988, and yielding, for our analysis, complete data on 7,516 sixth graders nested within 356 primary schools. Of interest is the probability that a child will repeat a grade during the primary years (REP1 = 1 if yes, 0 if no). It is hypothesized that the sex of the child (MALE = 1 if male, 0 of female), the child's pre-primary experience (PPED = 1 if yes, 0 if no), and the school mean SES (MSESC) will be associated with the probability of repetition. Every

---

[1]The overall accuracy of the parameter estimates is determined by the convergence criterion for macro iterations. The convergence criterion for micro iterations will influence the number of micro iterations per macro iteration. The default specifications stop macro iterations when the largest parameter estimate change is less than 10^{-4}; micro iterations within macro iterations stop when the conditional log likelihood (conditional on the current weights and values of the linearized dependent variable) changes by less than 10^{-6}.

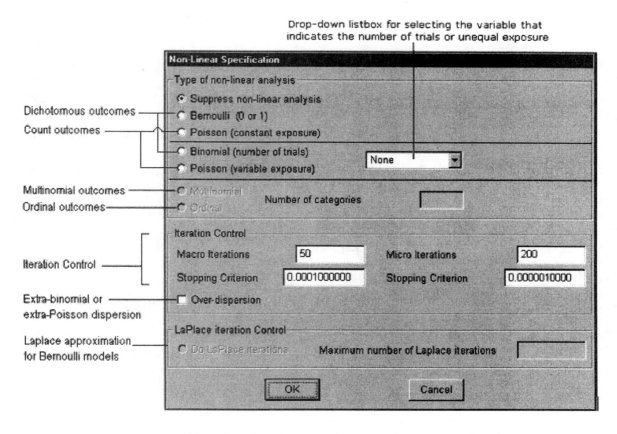

Figure 6.1   Nonlinear Specification dialog box

level-1 record corresponds to a student, with a single binary outcome per student, so the model type is Bernoulli.

These data[2] are provided along with the HLM software so that users may replicate our results in order to assure that the program is operating correctly.

Below are the steps for specifying a Bernoulli model in a Windows mode session.

To specify a Bernoulli model

1. After specifying the outcome in the model specification window (REP1 in our example), open the **Optional Specifications** menu.
2. Choose **Setup Nonlinear Model** to open the **Nonlinear Specification** dialog box (see Fig. 6.1).
3. Select **Bernoulli (0 or 1)** as there is one binary outcome per level-1 unit.
4. (Optional) Specify the maximum number of macro and micro iterations.
5. (Optional) Select **Laplace approximation** (see Sections 6.8.2 and 5.6.3).
6. Click **OK**.

The model described above is displayed in Fig. 6.2. The command file for the model is THAIU1.HLM.

Below we provide a transcript of the messages that HLM2 sent to the iteration screen during computation of the results (using example THAIU1.HLM).

```
                      MACRO ITERATION 1

Starting values computed.  Iterations begun.
Should you wish to terminate the iterations prior to convergence, enter cntl-c
The value of the likelihood function at iteration 1 = -2.400265E+003
The value of the likelihood function at iteration 2 = -2.399651E+003
The value of the likelihood function at iteration 3 = -2.399620E+003
The value of the likelihood function at iteration 4 = -2.399614E+003
The value of the likelihood function at iteration 5 = -2.399612E+003
The value of the likelihood function at iteration 6 = -2.399612E+003
The value of the likelihood function at iteration 7 = -2.399612E+003
```

[2]The specific data files are: UTHAI1.SAV (level-1 data), THAI2.SAV (level-2 data), and THAIUGRP.SSM (SSM file)

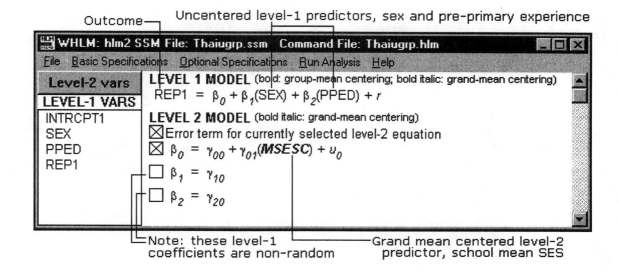

Figure 6.2   Model specification window for the Bernoulli model

Macro iteration number 1 has converged after seven micro iterations. This macro iteration actually computes the linear-model estimates (using the identity link function as if the level-1 errors were assumed normal). These results are then transformed and input to start macro iteration 2, which is, in fact, the first nonlinear iteration.

```
                    MACRO ITERATION 2

Starting values computed.  Iterations begun.
Should you wish to terminate the iterations prior to convergence, enter cntl-c
The value of the likelihood function at iteration 1 = -1.067218E+004
The value of the likelihood function at iteration 2 = -1.013726E+004
 . . .
 . . .
 . . .
The value of the likelihood function at iteration 10 = -1.010187E+004
The value of the likelihood function at iteration 11 = -1.010187E+004
The value of the likelihood function at iteration 12 = -1.010187E+004
```

Macro iteration 2, the first nonlinear macro iteration, converged after 12 micro iterations.

```
. . .
. . .
                       MACRO ITERATION 8

Starting values computed.  Iterations begun.
Should you wish to terminate the iterations prior to convergence, enter cntl-c
The value of the likelihood function at iteration 1 = -1.000374E+004
The value of the likelihood function at iteration 2 = -1.000374E+004
```

Note that macro iteration 8 converged with just 2 micro iterations. Macro iteration 8 was the final "unit-specific" macro iteration. One final "population-average" iteration is computed. Its output is given below.

```
MACRO ITERATION 9

Starting values computed.  Iterations begun.
Should you wish to terminate the iterations prior to convergence, enter cntl-c
The value of the likelihood function at iteration 1 = -1.011638E+004
The value of the likelihood function at iteration 2 = -1.010710E+004
The value of the likelihood function at iteration 3 = -1.010710E+004
```

Next, we examine the output file.

```
Program:            HLM 5 Hierarchical Linear and Nonlinear Modeling
Authors:            Stephen Raudenbush, Tony Bryk, & Richard Congdon
Publisher:          Scientific Software International, Inc. (c) 2000
-------------------------------------------------------------------------
Module:     HLM2.EXE (5.01.2040.2)
Date:       9 February 2000, Wednesday
Time:          12:43:40

-------------------------------------------------------------------------
```

The first page of the output has a program header and the specifics for this analysis, including the date and time the problem ran. If you need to contact technical support at SSI, be sure to include the version number, given in parentheses right after the module name.

```
SPECIFICATIONS FOR THIS NON-LINEAR HLM2 RUN

 Problem Title: Bernoulli output, Thailand data
 The data source for this run  = THAIUGRP.SSM
 The command file for this run = THAIU1.HLM
 Output file name              = THAIUGRP.OUT
 The maximum number of level-2 units = 356
 The maximum number of micro iterations = 50
 Method of estimation: restricted PQL
 Maximum number of macro iterations = 50
```

6 WORKING WITH HGLM

```
Distribution at Level-1: Bernoulli

The outcome variable is      REP1

The model specified for the fixed effects was:
----------------------------------------------------
    Level-1                 Level-2
    Coefficients            Predictors
    --------------------    ---------------
         INTRCPT1, B0       INTRCPT2, G00
$                             MSESC, G01
#       MALE slope, B1      INTRCPT2, G10
#       PPED slope, B2      INTRCPT2, G20

'#' - The residual parameter variance for this level-1 coefficient has been set
      to zero.
'$' - This level-2 predictor has been centered around its grand mean.

The model specified for the covariance components was:
----------------------------------------------------------
          Tau dimensions
              INTRCPT1

Summary of the model specified (in equation format)
---------------------------------------------------
Level-1 Model

        Prob(Y=1|B) = P
```

This is the program's way of saying that the level-1 sampling model is Bernoulli; the above equation, written with subscripts and Greek letters, is

$$\mathsf{Prob}(Y_{ij} = 1|\beta_j) = \phi_{ij} \ .$$

```
        log[P/(1-P)] = B0 + B1*(MALE) + B2*(PPED)
```

Thus, the level-1 structural model is:

$$\eta_{ij} = \log\left[\frac{\phi_{ij}}{1 - \phi_{ij}}\right] = \beta_{0j} + \beta_{1j}(\mathsf{MALE})_{ij} + \beta_{2j}(\mathsf{PPED})_{ij} \ .$$

```
Level-2 Model

        B0 = G00 + G01*(MSESC) + U0
        B1 = G10
        B2 = G20
```

And the level-2 structural model is:

$$\beta_{0j} = \gamma_{00} + \gamma_{01}(MSESC)_j + u_{0j}$$
$$\beta_{1j} = \gamma_{10}$$
$$\beta_{2j} = \gamma_{20}.$$

```
Level-1 variance = 1/[P(1-P)]
```

In the metric of the linearized dependent variable, the level-1 variance is the reciprocal of the Bernoulli variance, $\phi_{ij}(1-\phi_{ij})$. Note that the variance is heteroscedastic — it varies across level-1 units. Thus there is no single "level-1 variance" in this or other nonlinear models.

Three sets of output results appear below: those for the normal linear model with identity link function, those for the unit-specific model with logit link function, and those for the population-average model with logit link. Typically, only the latter two sets of results will be relevant for drawing conclusions. The linear model with identity link is estimated simply to obtain starting values for the estimation of the models with logit-link.

```
RESULTS FOR LINEAR MODEL WITH THE IDENTITY LINK FUNCTION

Sigma—squared =        0.12181

Tau
INTRCPT1,B0        0.01880

Standard Errors of Tau
INTRCPT1,B0        0.00188

Tau (as correlations)
INTRCPT1,B0   1.000


----------------------------------------------------
 Random level-1 coefficient   Reliability estimate
----------------------------------------------------
  INTRCPT1, B0                       0.747
----------------------------------------------------
```

```
The value of the likelihood function at iteration 7 = -2.399612E+003

 The outcome variable is     REP1
```

Estimation of fixed effects: (linear model with identity link function)

```
-------------------------------------------------------------------------------
                                      Standard           Approx.
       Fixed Effect       Coefficient Error     T-ratio  d.f.     P-value
-------------------------------------------------------------------------------
For       INTRCPT1, B0
   INTRCPT2, G00           0.153743   0.010789  14.251   354      0.000
       MSESC, G01         -0.033394   0.022393  -1.491   354      0.136
For       MALE slope, B1
   INTRCPT2, G10           0.054125   0.008329   6.498   7512     0.000
For       PPED slope, B2
   INTRCPT2, G20          -0.064614   0.010918  -5.918   7512     0.000
-------------------------------------------------------------------------------
```

RESULTS FOR NON-LINEAR MODEL WITH THE LOGIT LINK FUNCTION: Unit-Specific Model (macro iteration 8)

```
Tau
INTRCPT1,B0     1.28157

Standard Errors of Tau
INTRCPT1,B0     0.13841

Tau (as correlations)
INTRCPT1,B0  1.000
```

```
----------------------------------------------------------
 Random level-1 coefficient   Reliability estimate
----------------------------------------------------------
 INTRCPT1, B0                        0.680
----------------------------------------------------------
```

The value of the likelihood function at iteration 2 = -1.000374E+004

The outcome variable is   REP1

Final estimation of fixed effects: (Unit-specific model)

```
-------------------------------------------------------------------------------
                                      Standard           Approx.
       Fixed Effect       Coefficient Error     T-ratio  d.f.     P-value
-------------------------------------------------------------------------------
For       INTRCPT1, B0
   INTRCPT2, G00          -2.045281   0.093716 -21.824   354      0.000
       MSESC, G01         -0.254151   0.192517  -1.320   354      0.187
For       MALE slope, B1
   INTRCPT2, G10           0.508195   0.073907   6.876   7512     0.000
For       PPED slope, B2
   INTRCPT2, G20          -0.594100   0.095855  -6.198   7512     0.000
-------------------------------------------------------------------------------
```

```
Final estimation of variance components:
-------------------------------------------------------------------------
Random Effect          Standard    Variance     df   Chi-square  P-value
                       Deviation   Component
-------------------------------------------------------------------------
INTRCPT1,        U0     1.13206     1.28157     354  1430.37736   0.000
-------------------------------------------------------------------------
```

RESULTS FOR NON-LINEAR MODEL WITH THE LOGIT LINK FUNCTION:
Population Average Model

```
Tau
INTRCPT1,B0      1.28157

Standard Errors of Tau
INTRCPT1,B0      0.12598

Tau (as correlations)
INTRCPT1,B0   1.000
```

The value of the likelihood function at iteration 3 = -1.010710E+004

The outcome variable is   REP1

```
Final estimation of fixed effects: (Population-average model)
-------------------------------------------------------------------------
                                    Standard           Approx.
      Fixed Effect      Coefficient Error     T-ratio  d.f.     P-value
-------------------------------------------------------------------------
For        INTRCPT1, B0
    INTRCPT2, G00       -1.748596   0.087746  -19.928     354    0.000
        MSESC, G01      -0.283515   0.184452   -1.537     354    0.124
For        MALE slope, B1
    INTRCPT2, G10        0.446558   0.067024    6.663    7512    0.000
For        PPED slope, B2
    INTRCPT2, G20       -0.536527   0.088442   -6.066    7512    0.000
-------------------------------------------------------------------------
```

Notice that the results for the population-average model are quite similar to the results for the unit-specific model except in the case of the intercept. The intercept in the population-average model in this case is the expected log-odds of repetition for a person with values of zero on the predictors (and therefore, for a female without pre-primary experience attending a school of average SES). In this case, this expected log-odds corresponds to a probability of $1/(1 + \exp\{1.748596\}) = .148$, which is "population-average" repetition rate for this group. In contrast, the unit-specific intercept is the expected log-odds of repetition rate for the same kind of student, but one who attends a school that not only has a mean SES of 0, but also has a random effect of zero (that is, a school with a "typical" repetition rate for *the school of its type). This conditional expected log-odds is* -2.045281, *corresponding to a probability of* $1/(1 + \exp\{2.045281\}) = .114$. *Thus the probability of repetition is lower in a school with a random effect of zero than the average in the population of schools having mean SES of zero taken as a whole. This is a typical result. Population-average probabilities will be closer to .50 (than will the corresponding unit-specific probabilities). One final set of results is printed out: population-average results with robust standard errors (below). Note that the robust standard errors in this case are very similar to the model-based standard errors, with a slight increase for the level-2 predictor and slight decreases for level-1 predictors. Results for other data may not follow this pattern.*

```
The outcome variable is      REP1

Final estimation of fixed effects
(Population-average model with robust standard errors)
-------------------------------------------------------------------------
                                    Standard            Approx.
    Fixed Effect       Coefficient  Error     T-ratio   d.f.    P-value
-------------------------------------------------------------------------
For         INTRCPT1, B0
    INTRCPT2, G00       -1.748596   0.082243  -21.261    354    0.000
       MSESC, G01       -0.283515   0.196226   -1.445    354    0.148
For       MALE slope, B1
    INTRCPT2, G10        0.446558   0.062859    7.104   7512    0.000
For       PPED slope, B2
    INTRCPT2, G20       -0.536527   0.082355   -6.515   7512    0.000
-------------------------------------------------------------------------
```

6.3   Case 2: a binomial model (number of trials, $n_{ij} > 1$)

A familiar example of two-level binomial data is the number of hits, Y_{ij}, in game i for baseball player j based on n_{ij} at bats. In an experimental setting, a subject j under condition i might produce Y_{ij} successes in n_{ij} trials.

A common use of a binomial model is when analysts do not have access to the raw data at level 1. For example, one might know the proportion of children passing a criterion-referenced test within each of many schools. This proportion might be broken down within schools by sex and grade. A binomial model could be used to analyze such data. The cases would be sex-by-age "cells" within each school where Y_{ij} is the number passing within cell i of school j and n_{ij} is the number of "trials," that is, the number of children in that cell. Sex and grade would be level-1 predictors.

Indeed, in the previous example, although raw level-1 data were available, the two level-1 predictors, gender MALE and pre-primary experience PPED, were categorical. For illustration, we reorganized these data so that each school had, potentially, four cells defined by the cross-classification of gender and pre-primary experience:

- Females without pre-primary experience
- Females with pre-primary experience
- Males without pre-primary experience
- Males with pre-primary experience

Level-1 predictors were the same as before: MALE $= 1$ if male, 0 if female; PPED $= 1$ if pre-primary experience, 0 if not. The outcome is the number of children retained in a particular cell, and we created a variable TRIAL, which is the number of children in each cell. In some schools there were no children of a certain type (*e.g.*, no females with pre-primary experience). Such schools would have fewer than four cells. The necessary steps for executing the analysis in a Windows session are given below.

To specify a Binomial model

1. After specifying the outcome in the model specification screen (REP1 in our example), open the **Optional Specifications** pull-down menu.
2. Choose **Setup Nonlinear Model** to open the **Nonlinear Specification** dialog box (see Fig. 6.1).
3. Select **Binomial (number of trials)**.
4. Select the variable from the drop-down listbox in the dialog box that indicates number of trials (TRIAL in our example). (See Fig. 6.1).
5. (Optional) Specify the maximum number of macro and micro iterations.
6. (Optional) Select the **Over-dispersion** option if appropriate (see Section 6.8 (*Additional Features*).
7. Click **OK**.

The model described above uses the same predictors at level-1 and level-2 as those in the Bernoulli example (see Fig. 6.2). The command file for the example is THAIBNML.HLM.

```
Module:       HLM2.EXE (5.01.2040.2)
Date:         9 February 2000, Wednesday
Time:         12:43:33
--------------------------------------------------------------------------------

SPECIFICATIONS FOR THIS NON-LINEAR HLM2 RUN

 Problem Title: BINOMIAL ANALYSIS, THAILAND DATA

 The data source for this run  = THAIGRP.SSM
 The command file for this run = THAIBNML.HLM
 Output file name              = THAIBNML.OUT
 The maximum number of level-2 units = 356
 The maximum number of micro iterations = 50
 Method of estimation: restricted PQL
 Maximum number of macro iterations = 50


 Distribution at Level-1: Binomial

 The outcome variable is     REP1

The model specified for the fixed effects was:
-------------------------------------------------------


    Level-1                  Level-2
    Coefficients             Predictors
    ----------------------   ---------------
         INTRCPT1, B0        INTRCPT2, G00
$                            MSESC, G01
#       MALE slope, B1       INTRCPT2, G10
#       PPED slope, B2       INTRCPT2, G20

'#' - The residual parameter variance for this level-1 coefficient has been set
      to zero.
'$' - This level-2 predictor has been centered around its grand mean.

The model specified for the covariance components was:
----------------------------------------------------------
         Tau dimensions
            INTRCPT1

 Summary of the model specified (in equation format)
 -----------------------------------------------------

Level-1 Model

        E(Y|B) = TRIAL*P
        V(Y|B) = TRIAL*P(1-P)
```

This is the program's way of saying that the level-1 sampling model is binomial with TRIAL indicating the number of trials, so that the above equation, written with subscripts and Greek letters, is:

$$E(Y_{ij}|\beta_j) = n_{ij}\phi_{ij}$$
$$\text{Var}(Y_{ij}|\beta_j) = n_{ij}\phi_{ij}(1 - \phi_{ij}) \,,$$

where $n_{ij} = $ TRIAL.

```
    log[P/(1-P)] = B0 + B1*(MALE) + B2*(PPED)

Level-2 Model
    B0 = G00 + G01*(MSESC) + U0
    B1 = G10
    B2 = G20
```

Notice that the level-1 and level-2 structural models are identical to those in Case 1.

```
Level-1 variance = 1/[TRIAL*P(1-P)]
```

In the metric of the linearized dependent variable, the level-1 variance is the reciprocal of the binomial variance,

$$n_{ij}\phi_{ij}(1 - \phi_{ij}) \,.$$

Results for the unit-specific model, population-average model, and population-average model with robust standard errors, are not printed below. They are essentially identical to the results using the Bernoulli model.

6.4 Case 3: a Poisson model with equal exposure

Suppose that the outcome variable in Case 1 had been the number of days absent during the previous year rather than grade repetition. This outcome would be a non-negative integer, that is, a count rather than a dichotomy. Thus, the Poisson model with a log link would be a reasonable choice for the model. Notice that the time interval during which the absences could accumulate, that is, one year, would be the same for each student. We call this a case of "equal exposure," meaning that each level-1 case had an "equal opportunity" to accumulate absences. (Case 4 describes an example where exposure varies across level-1 cases.)

This model has exactly the same logic as in Case 1 except that the type of model and therefore the corresponding link function will be different.

To specify a Poisson model with equal exposure

1. After specifying the outcome in the model specification screen (REP1 in our example), open the **Optional Specifications** drop-down menu.
2. Choose **Setup Nonlinear Model** to open the **Nonlinear Specification** dialog box (See Fig. 6.1).
3. Select **Poisson (constant exposure)** to tell HLM that the level-1 sampling model is Poisson with equal exposure per level-1 case.
4. (Optional) Specify the maximum number of macro and micro iterations.
5. (Optional) Select the **Over-dispersion** option if appropriate (see Section 6.8 (*Additional Features*).
6. Click **OK**.

The HLM output would describe the model as follows

```
Level-1 Model

    E(Y|B) = L
    E(Y|B) = L
```

The above equation, written with subscripts and Greek letters, is:

$$E(Y_{ij}|\beta_j) = \lambda_{ij}$$
$$\text{Var}(Y_{ij}|\beta_j) = \lambda_{ij} ,$$

where λ_{ij} is the "true" rate of absence for child ij.

```
    log(L) = B0 + B1*(MALE) + B2*(PPED)
```

Notice that the log link replaces the logit link when we have count data. In the example above, β_2 is the expected difference in log-absenteeism between two children of the same sex attending the same school. To translate back to the rate of absenteeism, we would expect a child with pre-primary *experience to have* $\exp\{\beta_2\}$ *times the absenteeism rate of a child attending the same school who did not have pre-primary experience (holding sex constant). In this particular case, the estimated effect for β_2 is most plausibly negative; their $\exp\{\beta_2\}$ is less than 1.0 so that pre-primary experience would reduce the rate of absenteeism.*

```
Level-2 Model

    B0 = G00 + G01*(MSESC) + U0
    B1 = G10
    B2 = G20
```

Notice that the level-2 structural models are identical to those in Case 1.

```
Level-1 variance = 1/L
```

In the metric of the linearized dependent variable, the level-1 variance is the reciprocal of the Poisson variance, λ_{ij}.

6.5   Case 4: a Poisson model with variable exposure

Suppose that the frequency of a given kind of cancer were tabulated for each of many counties. For example, with five age-groups, the data could be organized so that each county had five counts, with Y_{ij} being the number of cancers in age-group i of county j and n_{ij} being the population size of that age group in that county. A Poisson model with variable exposure would be appropriate, with n_{ij} the variable measuring exposure.

Thus, the model choice would be specified as follows.

To specify a Poisson model with variable exposure

1. After specifying the outcome in the model specification screen, open the **Optional Specifications** menu.
2. Choose **Setup Nonlinear Model** to open the **Nonlinear Specification** dialog box (see Fig. 6.1).
3. Select **Poisson (variable exposure)** to tell HLM that the level-1 sampling model is Poisson with variable exposure per level-1 case.

4. Select the variable that indicates variable exposure from the drop-down listbox (see Fig. 6.1).

   (In the illustration below, we use SIZE as the variable to indicate variable exposure, n_{ij}, for age group i in county j).

5. (Optional) Specify the maximum number of macro and micro iterations.

6. (Optional) Select the **Over-dispersion** option if appropriate (See Section 6.8 (*Additional Features*).

7. Click **OK**.

The HLM output would describe the model as follows:

```
Level-1 Model

    E(Y|B) = SIZE*L
    E(Y|B) = SIZE*L
```

This is the program's way of saying that the level-1 sampling model is Poisson with variable exposure per level-1 case, so that the above equation, written with subscripts and Greek letters, is:

$$
\begin{aligned}
\mathsf{E}(Y_{ij}|\beta_j) &= n_{ij}\lambda_{ij} \\
\mathsf{Var}(Y_{ij}|\beta_j) &= n_{ij}\lambda_{ij} \, ,
\end{aligned}
$$

Notice that the log link replaces the logit link when we have count data.

```
Level-2 Model

    B0 = G00 + G01*(MSESC) + U0
    B1 = G10
    B2 = G20
```

Notice that the level-1 and level-2 structural models are identical to those in Case 1.

```
Level-1 variance = 1/L
```

In the metric of the linearized dependent variable, the level-1 variance is the reciprocal of the Poisson variance, $n_{ij}\lambda_{ij}$.

6.6 Case 5: a multinomial model

Data are from a 1990 survey of teachers in 16 high schools in California and Michigan. In the SSM file[3] is a sample of data from 650 teachers. An outcome with three response categories is derived from teachers' responses to the hypothetical question of whether they would become a teacher if they could go back to college and start over again. The possible responses are:

1. yes, I would choose teaching again
2. not sure
3. no, I would not choose teaching again

At the teacher level, it is hypothesized that teachers' perception of task variety is positively associated with the odds of the first category relative to the third category, and with odds of the second category relative to the third category. The perception is measured by a task variety scale that assessed the extent to which teachers followed the same teaching routines each day, performed the same tasks each day, had something new happening in their job each day, and liked the variety present in their work (Rowan, Raudenbush, & Cheong, 1993).

At the school level, it is postulated that the extent of teacher control has an effect. The teacher control scale is constructed by aggregating nine-item scale scores of teachers within a school. This scale indicates teacher control over school policy issues such as student behavior codes, content of in-service programs, student grouping, school curriculum, and text selection; and control over classroom issues such as teaching content and techniques, and amount of homework assigned (Rowan, Raudenbush, & Kang, 1991).

As a previous analysis showed that there is little between-school variability in their log-odds of choosing the second category relative to the third category, the level-1 coefficient associated with it is fixed. Furthermore, the effects associated with perception of task variety are constrained to be the same across schools for the sake of parsimony.

---

[3]TCHR.SSM, included with the software. The level-1 SPSS input file is TCHR1.SAV, and the level-2 file is TCHR2.SAV.

The general procedure to specify a multinomial logit model is given below.

Note: The multinomial and ordinal analyses provide unit-specific estimates only. They do not currently produce population-average estimates.

To specify a multinomial model (Fig. 6.3 displays the model discussed.)

1. After specifying the outcome, open the **Optional Specifications** menu.
2. Choose **Setup Nonlinear Model** to open the **Nonlinear Specification** dialog box (see Fig. 6.1).
3. Select **Multinomial** to tell HLM that the level-1 sampling model is multinomial.
4. Enter the correct number into the **Number of Categories** edit box.
5. (Optional) Specify the maximum number of macro and micro iterations.
6. Click **OK**.

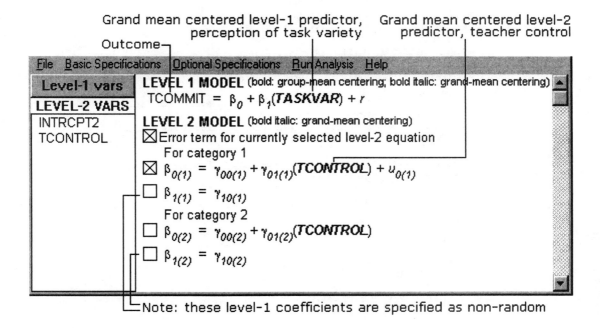

Figure 6.3   Model specification window for the multinomial model

```
Module:     HLM2.EXE (5.01.2040.2)
Date:       9 February 2000, Wednesday
Time:       16:13:50
```

SPECIFICATIONS FOR THIS MULTINOMIAL HLM2 RUN

  Problem Title: MULTINOMIAL OUTPUT, HIGH SCHOOL CONTEXT DATA

  The data source for this run = TCHR.SSM
  The command file for this run = TCHR1.HLM
  Output file name   = TCHR1.OUT
  The maximum number of level-2 units = 16
  The maximum number of iterations = 50
  Number of categories = 3
  Method of estimation: restricted maximum likelihood

  The outcome variable is TCOMMIT

  The model specified for the fixed effects was:

    Level-1   Level-2
    Coefficients   Predictors
  ----------------------   ---------------
For category 1:
          INTRCPT1, B0(1)   INTRCPT2, G00(1)
$ TCONTROL, G01(1)
#% TASKVAR slope, B1(1)   INTRCPT2, G10(1)
For category 2:
INTRCPT1, B0(2)   INTRCPT2, G00(2)
$ TCONTROL, G01(2)
#% TASKVAR slope, B1(2)   INTRCPT2, G10(2)

'#' - The residual parameter variance for this level-1 coefficient has been set
      to zero.
'%' - This level-1 predictor has been centered around its grand mean.
'$' - This level-2 predictor has been centered around its grand mean.

  The model specified for the covariance components was:

          Sigma squared (constant across level-2 units)

          Tau dimensions
              INTRCPT1(1)

Summary of the model specified (in equation format)

Level-1 Model

        Prob[Y(1) = 1|B] = P(1)
        Prob[Y(2) = 1|B] = P(2)
        Prob[Y(3) = 1|B] = P(3) = 1 - P(1) - P(2)
```

*6 WORKING WITH HGLM*
```

This is the program's way of saying that the level-1 sampling model is multinomial; the above equations, written with subscripts and Greek letters, are:

$$\text{Prob}(Y_{ij(1)} = 1|\beta_j) = \phi_{ij(1)}$$
$$\text{Prob}(Y_{ij(2)} = 1|\beta_j) = \phi_{ij(2)}$$
$$\text{Prob}(Y_{ij(3)} = 1|\beta_j) = \phi_{ij(3)} = 1 - \phi_{ij(1)} - \phi_{ij(2)}$$

```
log[P(1)/P(3)] =B0(1) + B1(1)*(TASKVAR)
log[P(2)/P(3)] =B0(2) + B1(2)*(TASKVAR)
```

Thus, the level-1 structural models are:

$$\eta_{ij(1)} = \log\left[\frac{\phi_{ij(1)}}{\phi_{ij(3)}}\right] = \beta_{0j(1)} + \beta_{1j(1)}(\text{TASKVAR})_{ij}$$

$$\eta_{ij(2)} = \log\left[\frac{\phi_{ij(2)}}{\phi_{ij(3)}}\right] = \beta_{0j(2)} + \beta_{1j(2)}(\text{TASKVAR})_{ij}$$

```
Level-2 Model

    B0(1) = G00(1) + G01(1)*(TCONTROL) + U0(1)
    B1(1) = G10(1)

    B0(2) = G00(2) + G01(2)*(TCONTROL)
    B1(2) = G10(2)
```

The level-2 structural models are:

$$\beta_{0j(1)} = \gamma_{00(1)} + \gamma_{01(1)}(\text{TCONTROL})_{ij} + u_{0j(1)}$$
$$\beta_{1j(1)} = \gamma_{10(1)}$$

$$\beta_{0j(2)} = \gamma_{00(2)} + \gamma_{01(2)}(\text{TCONTROL})_{ij}$$
$$\beta_{1j(2)} = \gamma_{10(2)}$$

```
RESULTS FOR MULTINOMIAL ITERATION 132

Tau
  INTRCPT1(1)      0.00986

Tau (as correlations)
  INTRCPT1(1),BO  1.000
```

```
-------------------------------------------------------
Random level-1 coefficient    Reliability estimate
-------------------------------------------------------
INTRCPT1(1), B0(1)                    0.082
-------------------------------------------------------
```

The value of the likelihood function at iteration 2 = -1.246207E+003

The outcome variable is TCOMMIT

Final estimation of fixed effects:

Fixed Effect	Coefficient	Standard Error	T-ratio	Approx. d.f.	P-value
For Category 1					
For INTRCPT1, B0(1)					
INTRCPT2, G00(1)	1.079276	0.123371	8.748	14	0.000
TCONTROL, G01(1)	2.090138	0.508149	4.113	14	0.001
For TASKVAR slope, B1(1)					
INTRCPT2, G10(1)	0.398348	0.113648	3.505	644	0.001
For Category 2					
For INTRCPT1, B0(2)					
INTRCPT2, G00(2)	0.091931	0.141642	0.649	644	0.516
TCONTROL, G01(2)	1.057291	0.577668	1.830	644	0.067
For TASKVAR slope, B1(2)					
INTRCPT2, G10(2)	0.030695	0.130029	0.236	644	0.814

G00(1) is the expected log-odds of an affirmative response relative to a negative response for a teacher with mean perception of task variety and working in a school with average teacher control and a random effect of zero. It is adjusted for the between-school heterogeneity in the likelihood of an affirmative response relative to a negative response. The estimated conditional expected log-odds, is 1.079276.

The predicted probability that the same teacher responses affirmatively (Category 1), is undecided (Category 2), or gives a negative response (Category 3), is, respectively:

$$\exp\{1.079276\}/(1 + \exp\{1.079276\} + \exp\{0.091931\}) = .584$$
$$\exp\{0.091931\}/(1 + \exp\{1.079276\} + \exp\{0.091931\}) = .218$$
$$1 - .584 - .218 = .198$$

The sets of G01 and G10 give the estimates of the change in the respective log-odds given one-unit change in the predictors, holding all other vari-

ables constant. For example, all else being equal, a standard deviation in-crease in TCONTROL (.32; calculated from the raw data) will nearly double the odds of an affirmative response to a negative response ($\exp\{2.090207 * .32\} = 1.952$). *Note that the partial effect associated with perception of task variety is statistically significant for the logit of affirmative versus negative responses but not for the logit of undecided versus negative re-sponses.*

Below is a table for the results for the fixed effects with robust standard errors.

```
The outcome variable is  TCOMMIT

Final estimation of fixed effects
(with robust standard errors)
-----------------------------------------------------------------------
                                      Standard           Approx.
      Fixed Effect       Coefficient  Error     T-ratio  d.f.    P-value
-----------------------------------------------------------------------
For Category 1
For       INTRCPT1,  B0(1)
     INTRCPT2, G00(1)      1.079276   0.128244   8.416     14    0.000
     TCONTROL, G01(1)      2.090138   0.409618   5.103     14    0.000
For   TASKVAR slope,  B1(1)
     INTRCPT2, G10(1)      0.398348   0.127504   3.124    644    0.002

For Category 2
For       INTRCPT1,  B0(2)
     INTRCPT2, G00(2)      0.091931   0.139643   0.658    644    0.510
     TCONTROL, G01(2)      1.057291   0.529624   1.996    644    0.046
For   TASKVAR slope,  B1(2)
     INTRCPT2, G10(2)      0.030695   0.126447   0.243    644    0.808
-----------------------------------------------------------------------
```

The robust standard errors are appropriate for data sets having a moderate to large number of level 2 units. These data do not meet this criterion.

```
Final estimation of variance components:
-----------------------------------------------------------------------
Random Effect         Standard     Variance    df   Chi-square  P-value
                      Deviation    Component
-----------------------------------------------------------------------
INTRCPT1(1),    U0(1)   0.09839      0.00968    14   17.87545    0.212
-----------------------------------------------------------------------
```

Note that the residual variance of $\beta_{00(1)}$ is not statistically different from zero. The user may set the coefficient to be non-random and re-run the model.

6.7 Case 6: an ordinal model

The same dataset, multi-category outcome, and predictors as in Case 5 are used here. The procedure for specifying an ordinal model is very similar to that of a multinomial model. The user selects the **Ordinal** instead of the **Multinomial** option in the **Nonlinear Specification** dialog box (See Fig. 6.1). Fig. 6.4 displays the model specified for the example (TCHR2.HLM).

Note: The multinomial and ordinal analyses currently produce unit-specific results only. They do not provide population-average results.

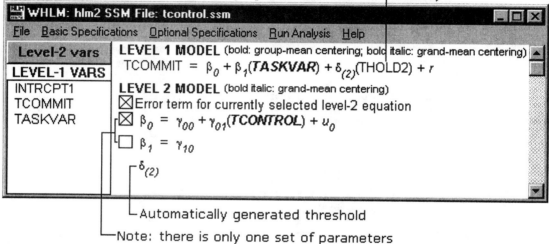

The threshold that separates the two cumulative logits—
(automatically generated by the program when "ordinal" is selected)

Figure 6.4   Model specification window for the ordinal model

```
SPECIFICATIONS FOR THIS ORDINAL HLM2 RUN

Problem Title: ORDINAL OUTPUT, HIGH SCHOOL CONTEXT DATA

The data source for this run  = TCHR.SSM
The command file for this run = TCHR2.HLM
Output file name              = TCHR2.OUT
The maximum number of level-2 units = 16
The maximum number of iterations = 50
Number of categories = 3
Method of estimation: restricted maximum likelihood
```

```
The outcome variable is  TCOMMIT

The model specified for the fixed effects was:
-------------------------------------------------------
   Level-1                  Level-2
   Coefficients             Predictors
   ----------------------   ----------------
   INTRCPT1 slope, B0       INTRCPT2, G00
$                           TCONTROL, G01
#%  TASKVAR slope, B1       INTRCPT2, G10
              THOLD2,            d(2)

'#' - The residual parameter variance for this level-1 coefficient has been set
      to zero.
'%' - This level-1 predictor has been centered around its grand mean.
'$' - This level-2 predictor has been centered around its grand mean.

The model specified for the covariance components was:
-------------------------------------------------------------
         Sigma squared (constant across level-2 units)

         Tau dimensions
             INTRCPT1

Summary of the model specified (in equation format)
-------------------------------------------------------
Level-1 Model

        Prob[R = 1|B] = P'(1) = P(1)
        Prob[R <= 2|B] = P'(2) = P(1) + P(2)
        Prob[R <= 3|B] = 1.0

    where

        P(1) = Prob[Y(1) = 1|B]
        P(2) = Prob[Y(2) = 1|B]
```

This is the program's way of saying that the level-1 sampling model is ordinal; the equations, written with subscripts and Greek letters, are:

$$\text{Prob}_{ij}(R_{ij} = 1|\beta_j) = \phi'_{ij(1)} = \phi_{ij(1)}$$
$$\text{Prob}_{ij}(R_{ij} \leq 2|\beta_j) = \phi'_{ij(2)} = \phi_{ij(1)} + \phi_{ij(2)}$$
$$\text{Prob}_{ij}(R_{ij} \leq 3|\beta_j) = 1$$

where

$$\phi_{ij(1)} = \text{Prob}(R_{ij} = 1|\beta_j)$$
$$\phi_{ij(2)} = \text{Prob}(R_{ij} = 2|\beta_j)$$

```
log[P'(1)/(1 - P'(1)] = B0 + B1*(TASKVAR)
log[P'(2)/(1 - P'(2)] = B0 + B1*(TASKVAR) + d(2)
```

Thus, the level-1 structural models are:

$$\eta'_{ij(1)} \;\;=\;\; \log\left[\frac{\phi'_{ij(1)}}{1 - \phi'_{ij(1)}}\right] = \beta_{0j} + \beta_{1j}(\text{TASKVAR})_{ij}$$

$$\eta'_{ij(2)} \;\;=\;\; \log\left[\frac{\phi'_{ij(2)}}{1 - \phi'_{ij(2)}}\right] = \beta_{0j} + \beta_{1j}(\text{TASKVAR})_{ij} + \delta_{(2)} \;.$$

```
Level-2 Model

    B0 = G00 + G01*(TCONTROL) + U0
    B1 = G10
```

The level-2 structural model is:

$$\beta_{0j} \;\;=\;\; \gamma_{00} + \gamma_{01}(\text{TCONTROL})_{ij} + u_{0j}$$
$$\beta_{1j} \;\;=\;\; \gamma_{10}$$

```
RESULTS FOR ORDINAL ITERATION 9152
```

The extremely large number of iterations reflects the fact that the final estimate of the between-school variance, τ_{00}, is zero, after adjusting for TCONTROL.

```
Tau
INTRCPT1,B0        0.00010

Tau (as correlations)
INTRCPT1,B0   1.000
```

```
----------------------------------------------------
 Random level-1 coefficient   Reliability estimate
----------------------------------------------------
 INTRCPT1, B0                       0.001
----------------------------------------------------
```

```
The value of the likelihood function at iteration 2 = -1.249070E+003

The outcome variable is  TCOMMIT
```

6 WORKING WITH HGLM

```
Final estimation of fixed effects:
--------------------------------------------------------------------------------
                                       Standard           Approx.
        Fixed Effect       Coefficient   Error   T-ratio   d.f.   P-value
--------------------------------------------------------------------------------
For INTRCPT1 slope, B0
    INTRCPT2, G00          0.333918    0.089735    3.721     14    0.003
    TCONTROL, G01          1.541051    0.365624    4.215     14    0.001
For   TASKVAR slope, B1
    INTRCPT2, G10          0.348801    0.087280    3.996    646    0.000
For         THOLD2
        d(2)               1.054888    0.080868   13.045    646    0.000
--------------------------------------------------------------------------------
```

G00 is the expected log-odds of an affirmative response relative to an undecided or negative response for a teacher with mean perception of task variety and working in a school with average teacher control and a random effect of zero. It is adjusted for the between-school heterogeneity in the likelihood of an affirmative response relative to a negative response. This conditional expected log-odds, is 0.333918. The expected log-odds for a teacher to give an affirmative or undecided response relative to a negative response is 0.333918 + 1.054888 = 1.388806. G01 and G10 give the estimates of the change in the respective cumulative logits, holding all other variables constant. For example, all else being equal, a standard deviation increase in TCONTROL (.32) will increase the odds of an affirmative response relative to an undecided or negative response as well as the odds of an affirmative or undecided response relative to a negative response by a factor of $1.637(\exp\{1.541051 * .32\} = 1.637)$. The threshold is estimated as 1.055. This is the difference in the log-odds of category 2 versus 1, holding constant the explanatory variables and the random effects.

Below is a table of the results for the fixed effects with robust standard errors.

```
The outcome variable is  TCOMMIT

Final estimation of fixed effects
(with robust standard errors)
--------------------------------------------------------------------------------
                                       Standard           Approx.
        Fixed Effect       Coefficient   Error   T-ratio   d.f.   P-value
--------------------------------------------------------------------------------
For INTRCPT1 slope, B0
    INTRCPT2, G00          0.333918    0.092707    3.602     14    0.003
    TCONTROL, G01          1.541051    0.340944    4.520     14    0.000
```

```
For  TASKVAR slope, B1
     INTRCPT2, G10              0.348801    0.092285    3.780      646    0.000
For          THOLD2,
         d(2)                   1.054888    0.080353   13.128      646    0.000
---------------------------------------------------------------------------
```

The robust standard errors are appropriate for datasets having a moderate to large number of level 2 units. These data do not meet this criterion.

Final estimation of variance components:

Random Effect		Standard Deviation	Variance Component	df	Chi-square	P-value
INTRCPT1,	U0	0.01016	0.00010	14	14.57034	0.408

Note that the residual variance of β_0 is not statistically different from zero. In fact, it is zero, which accounts for the large number of iterations required to achieve convergence. The user may set the coefficient to be non-random and re-run the model.

6.8 Additional Features

6.8.1 Over-dispersion

For binomial models with $n_{ij} > 1$ and for all Poisson models, the user has the option to estimate a level-1 dispersion parameter σ^2 (see Fig. 6.1). If the assumption of no dispersion holds, $\sigma^2 = 1.0$. If the data are over-dispersed, $\sigma^2 > 1.0$; if the data are under-dispersed, $\sigma^2 < 1.0$. This applies to all Poisson models too.

6.8.2 Laplace approximation for binary outcome models

For two-level binary outcome models, the user can select the highly accurate Laplace approximation to maximum likelihood (see Fig. 6.1). When estimating the model parameters, the program will send messages similar to the following to the iteration screen during computation of the results.

```
.The Laplace-6 likelihood is -9.631409E+003
.The Laplace-6 likelihood is -9.627559E+003
.The Laplace-6 likelihood is -9.627231E+003
.The Laplace-6 likelihood is -9.627213E+003
.The Laplace-6 likelihood is -9.627211E+003
.The Laplace-6 likelihood is -9.627211E+003
.The Laplace-6 likelihood is -9.627211E+003
```

The following is an example of output for Laplace6 iterations.

```
RESULTS FOR LAPLACE-6 ITERATION 7

    Tau
    INTRCPT1      1.66300

    Standard Errors of Tau
    INTRCPT1      0.21066

Tau (as correlations)
    INTRCPT1  1.000


    ------------------------------------------------------
     Random level-1 coefficient   Reliability estimate
    ------------------------------------------------------
      INTRCPT1, B0                       0.730
    ------------------------------------------------------
The Laplace-6 likelihood is -9.627211E+003

The outcome variable is     REP1

    Final estimation of fixed effects
    (Laplace)
    --------------------------------------------------------------------------
                                      Standard            Approx.
        Fixed Effect      Coefficient  Error     T-ratio   d.f.    P-value
    --------------------------------------------------------------------------
    For        INTRCPT1, B0
        INTRCPT2, G00      -2.234464   0.101893  -21.930     354    0.000
          MSESC, G01       -0.289988   0.205878   -1.409     354    0.159
    For       MALE slope, B1
        INTRCPT2, G10       0.535565   0.072653    7.372    7512    0.000
    For      PPED slope, B2
        INTRCPT2, G20      -0.626382   0.100351   -6.242    7512    0.000
    --------------------------------------------------------------------------
```

6.8.3 Printing variance-covariance matrices for fixed effects

Users may request files containing variance-covariances for the fixed effects for the unit-specific, population-averaged, and Laplace6 estimates. See Section A.5 in Appendix refch:appdxa for more details.

6.9 Fitting HGLMs with three levels

For simplicity of exposition, all of the examples above have used the two-level HGLM. These procedures generalize directly to three-level applications of the binomial and Poisson model. Again, the user must specify the type of nonlinear model desired at level-1. There are now, however, structural models at both levels 2 and 3 as in the case of HLM3. Any user familiar with HLM3 will find the extension to nonlinear analyses straightforward.

Estimation of multinomial and ordinal models is currently available only for two-level data.

7

Conceptual and Statistical Background for Hierarchical Multivariate Linear Models (HMLM)

One of the most frequent applications of hierarchical models involves repeated observations (level 1) nested within persons (level 2). These are described in Chapter 6 of *Hierarchical Linear Models*. In these models, the outcome Y_{ij} for occasion i within person j is conceived as a univariate outcome, observed under different conditions or at different times. An advantage of viewing the repeated observations as nested within the person is that it allows each person to have a different repeated measures design. For example, in a longitudinal study, the number of time points may vary across persons, and the spacing between time points may be different for different persons. Such unbalanced designs would pose problems for standard methods of analysis such as the analysis of variance.

Suppose, however, that the aim of the study is to observe every participant according to a fixed design with, say, T observations per person. The design might involve T observation times or T different outcome variables or even T different experimental conditions. Given the fixed design, the analysis can be reconceived as a multivariate repeated measures analysis. The multivariate model is flexible in allowing a wide variety of assumptions about the variation and covariation of the T repeated measures (Bock, 1985). In the standard application of multivariate repeated measures, a key limitation is that there can be no missing outcomes: every participant must have a full complement of T repeated observations.

Advances in statistical computation, beginning with the EM algorithm (Dempster, Laird, & Rubin, 1977; see also Jennrich & Schluchter, 1986), allow the estimation of multivariate normal models from incomplete data. In this case, the aim of the study was to collect T observations per person, but only n_j observations were collected ($n_j \leq T$). These n_j observations are indeed collected according to a fixed design, but $T - n_j$ data points are missing at random.

HMLM builds on this theory to allow estimation of multivariate normal models from incomplete data; HMLM2 builds on this theory to allow for study of multivariate outcomes for persons who are, in turn, nested within higher-level units. Within the framework of HMLM, it is possible to estimate models having:

1. An unrestricted covariance structure, that is a full $T \times T$ covariance matrix.

2. A model with homogeneous level-1 variance and random intercepts and/or slopes at level 2.

3. A model with heterogeneous variance at level 1 (a different variance for each occasion) and random intercepts and/or slopes at level 2.

4. A model that includes a log-linear structure for the level-1 variance and random intercepts and/or slopes at level 2.

5. A model with first-order auto-regressive level-1 random errors and random intercepts and/or slopes at level 2.

We note that applications 2–4 are available within the standard HLM2. However, within HMLM, models 2–4 can be compared to the unrestricted model (model 1), using a likelihood ratio test. No "unrestricted model" can be meaningfully defined within the standard HLM2: Such a model is definable only within the confines of a fixed design with T measurements.

HMLM2 allows the five models listed above to be embedded within a nested structure, *e.g.*, the persons who are repeatedly observed may be nested within schools.

7.1 Unrestricted Model

This model is appropriate when the aim of the study is to collect T observations per participant according to a fixed design. However, one or more observations may be missing at random. We assume a constant but otherwise arbitrary $T \times T$ covariance matrix for each person's "complete data."

7.1.1 Level-1 model

The level-1 model relates the observed data, Y, to the complete data, Y^*:

$$Y_{ij} = \sum_{t=1}^{T} m_{tij} Y_{ij}^* \tag{7.1}$$

(7.1) where Y_{ij} is the outcome for person j associated with time i. Here Y_{ij}^* is the value that person j would have displayed if that person had been observed at time t, and m_{tij} is an indicator variable taking on a value of unity if Y_{ij} was observed at time t and zero otherwise. Thus, Y_{ij}^*, $t = 1, \ldots, T$, represents the complete data for person j while Y_{ij}, $i = 1, \ldots, n_j$ represents the observed data, and the indicator variables m_{tij} tell us the pattern of missing data for person j.

To make this clear, consider $T = 5$ and a person who has data at occasions 1, 2, and 4, but not at occasions 3 and 5. Then Equation 7.1 expands to

$$\begin{pmatrix} Y_{1j} \\ Y_{2j} \\ Y_{3j} \end{pmatrix} = \begin{pmatrix} 1 & 0 & 0 & 0 & 0 \\ 0 & 1 & 0 & 0 & 0 \\ 0 & 0 & 0 & 1 & 0 \end{pmatrix} \begin{pmatrix} Y_{1j}^* \\ Y_{2j}^* \\ Y_{3j}^* \\ Y_{4j}^* \\ Y_{5j}^* \end{pmatrix} \tag{7.2}$$

or, in matrix notation,

$$Y_j = M_j Y_j^* . \tag{7.3}$$

This model says simply that the three observed data points for person j were observed at times 1, 2, and 4, so that data were missing at times 3 and 5. Although these data were missing, they do exist, in principle. Thus, every participant has a full 5×1 vector of "complete data" even though the $n_j \times 1$ vector of observed data will vary in length across persons.

We now pose a structural model for the within-person variation in Y^*:

$$Y_{tj}^* = \beta_{0j} + \sum_{q=1}^{Q_j} \beta_{qj} X_{qjt} + r_{tj} \qquad (7.4)$$

or, in matrix notation

$$Y_j^* = X_j \boldsymbol{\beta}_j + r_j \, , \qquad (7.5)$$

where we assume that r_j is multivariate normal in distribution with a mean vector of 0 and an arbitrary $T \times T$ covariance matrix $\boldsymbol{\Delta}$. In fact, while X_j varies over t and thus accounts for within-person variation, $\boldsymbol{\Delta}$ is not a "within-person" covariance matrix. Rather, it captures all variation and covariation among the T repeated observations.

7.1.2 Level-2 model

The level-2 model includes covariates, W_j that vary between persons:

$$\beta_{qj} = \gamma_{q0} + \sum_{s=1}^{S_q} W_{qsj} \gamma_{qsj} \, . \qquad (7.6)$$

Note there is no random variation between persons in the regression coefficients β_{qj} because all random variation has been absorbed into $\boldsymbol{\Delta}$ (see text below Equation 7.5).

7.1.3 Combined model

Substituting the level-2 model into the level-1 model gives the combined model for the complete data, in matrix form:

$$Y_j^* = X_j W_j \gamma + r_j , \qquad r_j \sim N(\mathbf{0}, \boldsymbol{\Delta}) . \tag{7.7}$$

Here the design matrix captures main effects of within-person covariates (the Xs), main effects of person-level covariates (Ws), and two-way interaction effects between them ($X * W$ terms).

In sum, our reformulation poses a "multiple measures" model (Equation 7.3) that relates the observed data Y_j to the "complete data" Y_j^*, that is, the data that would have been observed if the users were successful in obtaining outcome data at every time point. Our combined model is a standard multivariate normal regression model for the complete data. Algebraically substituting the combined model expression for Y_j^* into the model for the observed data (Equation 7.3) yields the combined model

$$Y_j = M_j X_j W_j \gamma + M_j r_j . \tag{7.8}$$

Under the unrestricted model, the number of parameters estimated is $f + T(T+1)/2$, where f is the number of fixed effects and T is the number of observations intended for each person. Models below impose constraints on the unrestricted model, and therefore include fewer parameters. The fit of these simpler models to the data can be compared to the fit of the unrestricted model using a likelihood ratio test.

7.2 Standard HLM with homogeneous level-1 variance

Under the special case in which the within-person design is fixed,[1] with T observations per person and randomly missing time points, the two-level HLM can be derived from the unrestricted model by imposing restrictions on the covariance matrix, $\boldsymbol{\Delta}$. (Note: Regressors X_j having varying designs may be included in the level-1 model, but coefficients associated with such X_j values must not have random effects at level 2.) The most frequently used assumption in the standard HLM is that the within-person residuals are independent with a constant variance, σ^2.

---

[1]That is, $X_j = X$ for all j.

7.2.1 Level-1 model

The level-1 model remains the same as in the unrestricted model. However, we now assume that the level-1 residuals, r_j are independent with constant variance:

$$\mathsf{Var}(r_j) = \boldsymbol{\Sigma} = \boldsymbol{\sigma}^2 I \; . \tag{7.9}$$

7.2.2 Level-2 model

The level-2 model includes covariates, W_j that vary between persons. Degrees of freedom are now available to estimate randomly varying intercepts and slopes across people:

$$\boldsymbol{\beta}_{qj} = \boldsymbol{\gamma}_{q0} + \sum_{s=1}^{S_q} W_{qj} \boldsymbol{\gamma}_{qsj} + \mathbf{u}_{qj} \; . \tag{7.10}$$

All of the usual forms are now available for the intercepts and slopes (fixed, randomly varying, non-randomly varying), provided T is large enough.

7.2.3 Combined model

Substituting the level-2 model into the level-1 model gives the combined model for the complete data, in matrix form:

$$\begin{aligned} Y_j^* &= X W_j \boldsymbol{\gamma} + X_j \mathbf{u}_j + r_j \\ &= X W_j \boldsymbol{\gamma} + \boldsymbol{\epsilon}_j \; , \end{aligned} \tag{7.11}$$

where $\boldsymbol{\epsilon}_j = X_j \mathbf{u}_j + r_j$ has variance-covariance matrix

$$\begin{aligned} \mathsf{Var}(\boldsymbol{\epsilon}_j) &= \boldsymbol{\Delta} = \mathsf{Var}(X \mathbf{u}_j + r_j) \\ &= X \boldsymbol{\tau} X' + \boldsymbol{\Sigma} \; , \end{aligned} \tag{7.12}$$

7 HMLM: CONCEPTUAL AND STATISTICAL BACKGROUND

where $\Sigma = \sigma^2 I_T$. Note that Δ_j will equal a common Δ for all j (that is, for all persons) only if X_j is equal to a common X for all persons. This occurs only when the within-subject design is constant across all people, since X_j is the within-subjects design matrix.

Under the HLM with homogeneous level-1 variance, the number of parameters estimated is $f + r(r+1)/2 + 1$, where r is the dimension of τ. Thus, r must be less than T.

7.3 HLM with varying level-1 variance

One can model heterogeneity of level-1 variance as a function of the occasion of measurement. Such a model is suitable when we suspect that the level-1 residual variance varies across occasions. The models that can be estimated are a subset of the models that can be estimated within the standard HLM2 (see Section 2.9.5 on the option for heterogeneity of level-1 variance). The level-1 model is the same as in the case of homogeneous variances (Equations 7.11 and 7.12), except that now

$$\Sigma = \mathrm{diag}\{\sigma_t^2\} \, , \tag{7.13}$$

that is, Σ is now diagonal with elements σ_t^2, the variance associated with occasion t, $t = 1, \ldots, T$.

The number of parameters estimated is $f + r(r+1)/2 + T$. Now r must be no larger than $T - 1$. When $r = T - 1$, the results will duplicate those based on the unrestricted model.

7.4 HLM with a log-linear model for the level-1 variance

The model with varying level-1 variance, described above, assumes a unique level-1 variance for every occasion. A more parsimonious model would specify a functional relationship between aspects of the occasion (*e.g.*, time or age) and the variance. We would again have $\Sigma = \mathrm{diag}\{\sigma_t^2\}$, but now

$$\log(\sigma_t^2) = \alpha_0 + \sum_{h=1}^{H} \alpha_h C_{ht} . \qquad (7.14)$$

Thus, the natural log of the level-1 variance may be, for example, a linear or quadratic function of age. If the explanatory variables c_h are $T-1$ dummy variables, each indicating the occasion of measurement, the results will duplicate those of the previous section.

The number of parameters estimated is now $f + r(r+1)/2 + H + 1$. Again, r must be no larger than $T-1$ and H must be no larger than $T-1$.

7.5 First-order auto-regressive model at level-1

This model allows the level-1 residuals to be correlated under Markov assumptions (a level-1 residual is a function of the immediately preceding level-1 residual). The model for the residuals is

$$
\begin{aligned}
r_{tj} &= e_{tj} , & (t=1) \\
r_{tj} &= \rho e_{(t-1)j} + (1-\rho)e_{tj} , & (t>1) \\
e_{tj} &\sim \text{ independently } N(0, \sigma^2) .
\end{aligned}
\qquad (7.15)
$$

This leads to the level-1 covariance structure

$$\text{Cov}(r_{tj}, r_{t'j}) = \sigma^2 \rho^{|t-t'|} . \qquad (7.16)$$

Thus, the variance at each time point is σ^2 and each correlation between pairs of residuals diminishes with the distance between time points, so that the correlations are $\rho, \rho^2, \rho^3, \ldots$ as the distance between occasions is $1, 2, 3, \ldots$

The number of parameters estimated is now $f + r(r+1)/2 + 2$. Again, r must be no larger than $T-1$.

7.6 HMLM2: A multilevel, multivariate model

Suppose now that the persons with repeated measures are nested within higher-level units such as schools. We can embed the multivariate model for incomplete data within this multilevel structure.

7.6.1 Level-1 model

The level-1 model again relates the observed data, Y, to the complete data, Y^*. We simply add a subscript to the HMLM model to create the HMLM equation for the observed data:

$$Y_{ijk} = \sum_{t=1}^{T} m_{tijk} Y_{tjk}^* \ . \tag{7.17}$$

Here individual j is nested within unit k $(k = 1, \ldots, K)$. Again, we pose a structural model for the within-person variation in Y^*:

$$Y_{tjk}^* = \pi_{0jk} + \sum_{p=1}^{P} \pi_{pjk} a_{pt} + e_{tjk} \ , \tag{7.18}$$

or, in matrix notation,

$$Y_{jk}^* = A\pi_{jk} + e_{jk} \ , \tag{7.19}$$

where we assume that e_{jk} is multivariate normal in distribution with a mean vector of 0 and an arbitrary $T \times T$ covariance matrix Σ.

7.6.2 Level-2 model

The level-2 model includes covariates, X_{jk}, that vary between persons within groups:

$$\pi_{pjk} = \beta_{p0k} + \sum_{s=1}^{S_p} \beta_{psk} X_{sjk} + r_{pjk} . \qquad (7.20)$$

Here we assume that the vector $\mathbf{r}_{jk}$, composed of elements r_{pjk}, is multivariate normal in distribution with a mean vector of 0 and variance-covariance matrix τ_π.

7.6.3 Level-3 model

Now the coefficients defined on persons (in the level-2 model) are specified as possibly varying at level-3 over groups:

$$\beta_{psk} = \gamma_{ps0} + \sum_{q=1}^{Q_{ps}} \gamma_{psq} W_{qsk} + u_{psk} . \qquad (7.21)$$

Here the vector $\mathbf{u}_k$, composed of elements u_{psk} is multivariate normal in distribution with a zero mean vector and covariance matrix τ_β.

7.6.4 The combined model

The combined model can then be written in matrix notation as

$$Y_{jk} = AX_{jk}W_k\gamma + AX_{jk}u_k + \epsilon_{jk} , \qquad (7.22)$$

where

$$\epsilon_{jk} = Ar_{jk} + e_{jk} \qquad (7.23)$$

has variance

$$\mathsf{Var}(\epsilon_{jk}) = \Delta , \qquad (7.24)$$

where

$$\Delta = A\tau_{\pi}A' + \Sigma \, , \qquad\qquad (7.25)$$

and Σ is modeled just as in the case of HMLM, depending on which sub-model is of interest. The next chapter provides an illustration.

Note that level-1 predictors a_{pt} are assumed to have the same values for all level-2 units of the complete data. This assumption can be relaxed. However, if the design for a_{ptjk} varies over j or k, the coefficient for a_{ptjk}, that is π_{pjk}, must have no random effect at level 2. In this regard, the standard three-level model (see Chapters 3 and 4) is more flexible than is HMLM2.

8 Working with HMLM and HMLM2

HMLM and HMLM2 execute analyses using MDM (multivariate data matrix) files, which consist of the combined level-1 and level-2 data files.

The procedures for constructing the MDM file are similar to the ones for HLM2 and HLM3 with one major difference: the user has to create and input indicator variables for the outcome(s) while constructing the MDM file. Model specification for HMLM and HMLM2 involves the same mechanics as in HLM2 and HLM3 with an extra step of modeling the covariance structure selection.

Below we provide two examples. The first, using HMLM, involves the National Youth Survey (Elliot, Huizinga, & Menard, 1989, Raudenbush, 1999). The second, using HMLM2, is based on time-series observations on students nested within public primary schools in Chicago as described in Chapter 6. Windows mode execution is illustrated. See Appendix D for details about interactive and batch mode execution.

8.1 An HMLM analysis using Windows mode

8.1.1 Constructing the MDM file from raw data

The user has the same range of options for data input as with HLM2 and HLM3. We will use SPSS file input in our example.

8.1.1.1 Level-1 file

The level-1 file, NYS1.SAV, has 1,079 observations collected from interviewing annually eleven-year-old youths beginning at 1976 for five consecutive years. Therefore, $T = 5$. The variables and the T indicator variables are:

ATTIT   A nine-item scale assessing attitudes favorable to deviant behavior

         Subjects were asked how wrong (very wrong, wrong, a little bit wrong, not wrong at all) they believe it is for someone their age, for example, to damage and destroy property, use marijuana, use alcohol, sell hard drugs, or steal.

         The measure was positively skewed; so a logarithmic transformation was performed to reduce the skewness.

EXPO   Exposure to deviant peers

         Subjects were asked how many of their friends engaged in the nine deviant behaviors surveyed in the ATTIT scale.

AGE   Age of the participant

AGE11   Age of participant at a specific time minus 11

AGE13   Age of participant at a specific time minus 13

AGE11S   AGE11 * AGE11

AGE13S   AGE13 * AGE13

IND1   Indicator for measure at time 1

IND2   Indicator for measure at time 2

IND3   Indicator for measure at time 3

IND4   Indicator for measure at time 4

IND5   Indicator for measure at time 5

The five indicators were created to facilitate use of HMLM. Data for the first two children are shown in Fig. 8.1.

Child 15 had data for all five years. Child 33, however, did not have data for the fourth year.

Indicators for the repeated measures ⌐

	id	attit	expo	age	age11	age13	age11s	age13s	ind1	ind2	ind3	ind4	ind5
16	15	.44	.07	11	0	-2	0	4	1	0	0	0	0
17	15	.44	.32	12	1	-1	1	1	0	1	0	0	0
18	15	.89	.47	13	2	0	4	0	0	0	1	0	0
19	15	.75	.26	14	3	1	9	1	0	0	0	1	0
20	15	.80	.47	15	4	2	16	4	0	0	0	0	1
21	33	.20	-.27	11	0	-2	0	4	1	0	0	0	0
22	33	.64	-.27	12	1	-1	1	1	0	1	0	0	0
23	33	.69	-.27	13	2	0	4	0	0	0	1	0	0
24	33	.11	.07	15	4	2	16	4	0	0	0	0	1

Figure 8.1   Two children in the NYS1.SAV dataset

8.1.1.2   Level-2 file

The level-2 data file, NYS2.SAV, consists of three variables on 241 youths. The file has the same structure as that for HLM2. The variables are:

FEMALE   An indicator for gender (1 = female, 0 = male)

MINORITY An indicator for ethnicity (1 = minority, 0 = other)

INCOME   Income

The construction of the MDM involves three major steps:

1. Select type of input data.
2. Supply the program with the appropriate data-defining information.
3. Check whether the data have been properly read into the program.

The steps are very similar to the ones described in Section 2.5.1. The user will select HMLM in the **Select SSM/MDM type** dialog box (see Fig. 2.4) and specify the type of data input in the next dialog box.

While the structure of input files for HMLM is almost the same as in HLM2, there is one important difference: the indicator variables. In order to create these, one first needs to know the maximum number of level-1 records per level-2 group; this determines the number of indicators. We shall call them the number of "occasions." (This is the number of time points in a repeated measures study or the number of outcome variables in a cross-sectional multivariate study. Also note that each group does not need to have this number of cases.) Then create the indicator variables so that a given variable takes on the value of 1.0 if the given case is at a given occasion, 0.0 otherwise. Looking at Fig. 8.1, we see that IND1 is 1 if AGE11 is 0, IND2 is 1 if AGE11 is 1, IND3 is 1 if AGE11 is 2, and so on.

Fig. 8.2 shows the **Choose variables – HMLM** dialog box where the indicator variables are checked before the MDM file is created. This dialog box can be opened from the **Level-1 Specification** section in the **Make MDM – HMLM** dialog box.

8.2 Executing analyses based on the MDM file

The steps involved are similar to the ones for HLM2 as described in Section 2.2. The user specifies:

1. the level-1 model,
2. the level-2 structural model, and
3. the level-1 coefficients as random or non-random.

Under HMLM, level-1 predictors having random effects must have the same value for all participants at a given occasion. If the user specifies a predictor not fullfilling this condition to have a random effect, such coefficients will be automatically set as non-random by the program. Furthermore, an extra step for selecting the covariance structure for the models to be estimated is needed. Fig. 8.3 displays the model specified for our example. Fig. 8.4 shows the dialog box where the user selects the covariance structure.

8.3 An Annotated Example of HMLM

In the example below (see NYS1.MLM), we specify AGE13 and AGE13S as predictors at level 1. At level 2, the model is unconditional. This is dis-

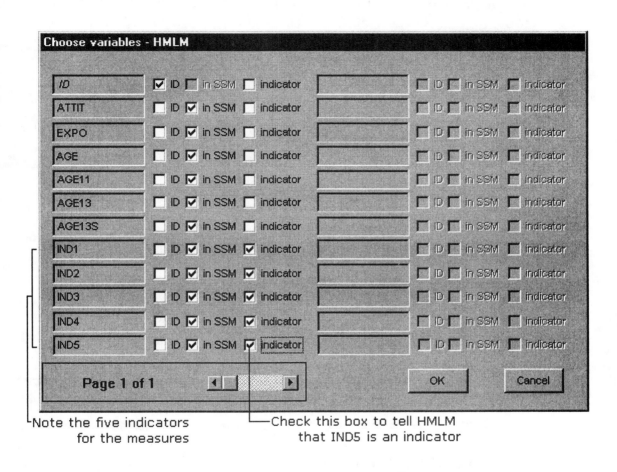

Figure 8.2 Choose variables – HMLM dialog box

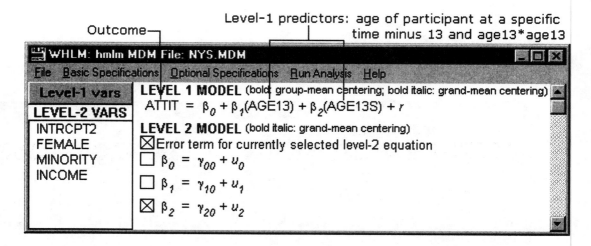

Figure 8.3   Model specification window for the NYS example

played in Figure 8.3. We shall compare three alternative covariance structures:

- an unrestricted model,
- the homogeneous model, $\sigma_t^2 = \sigma^2$ for all t, and
- the heterogeneous model, which allows σ_t^2 to vary over t.

These three models are requested simply by checking the **Heterogeneous** button in the **Basic Model Specifications** dialog box, as shown in Fig. 8.4.

Similarly, checking the **Log-linear** button would produce output on:

- the unrestricted model,
- the homogeneous model, and
- the log-linear model for σ_t^2.

And, again similarly, choosing the **1st order auto-regressive** button would produce unrestricted and homogeneous results in addition to first-order auto-regressive results.

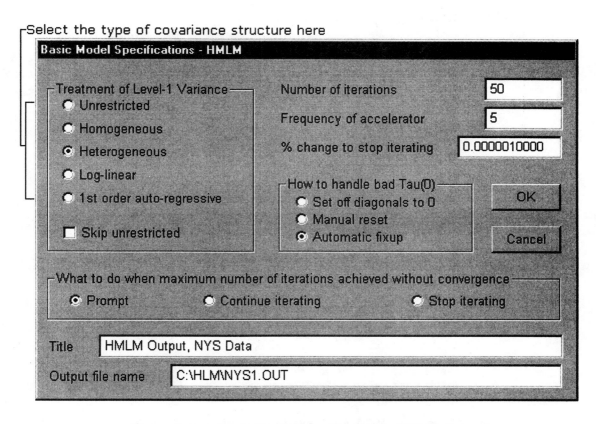

Select the type of covariance structure here

Figure 8.4   Basic Model Specifications - HMLM dialog box

```
Program:          HLM 5 Hierarchical Linear and Nonlinear Modeling
Authors:          Stephen Raudenbush, Tony Bryk, & Richard Congdon
Publisher:        Scientific Software International, Inc. (c) 2000
                                            techsupport@ssicentral.com
                                                     www.ssicentral.com
-------------------------------------------------------------------
Module:    HMLM.EXE (5.01.2040.2)
Date:      9 February 2000, Wednesday
Time:      12:24: 6
-------------------------------------------------------------------
```

The first page of the output lists, after a program header, the specifics for this analysis, including the date and time the problem ran. If you need to contact technical support at SSI, be sure to include the version number, given in parentheses right after the module name.

```
SPECIFICATIONS FOR THIS HMLM RUN

  Problem Title: HMLM OUTPUT, NYS DATA

  The data source for this run  = NYS.MDM
  The command file for this run = NYS1.MLM
  Output file name              = NYS1.OUT
  The maximum number of level-2 units = 239
  The maximum number of iterations = 50


  The outcome variable is    ATTIT


  The model specified for the fixed effects was:
------------------------------------------------------


    Level-1                Level-2
    Coefficients           Predictors
  ----------------------   ---------------

        INTRCPT1, B0       INTRCPT2, G00
     AGE13 slope, B1       INTRCPT2, G10
     AGE13S slope, B2      INTRCPT2, G20
```

The results for the unrestricted model are printed first.

```
OUTPUT FOR UNRESTRICTED MODEL

Summary of the model specified (in equation format)
----------------------------------------------------

Level-1 Model

      Y = IND1*Y1* + IND2*Y2* + IND3*Y3* + IND4*Y4* + IND5*Y5*
```

The level-1 model relates the observed data, Y, to the complete data, Y^*.

```
Y* = B0 + B1*(AGE13) + B2*(AGE13S) + R
```

Level-2 Model

```
B0 = G00
B1 = G10
B2 = G20
```

For the unrestricted model, there is no random variation between persons in regression coefficient B0, B1, and B2 because all random variation has been absorbed into D.

```
VAR(Y*) = D
```

D(0)

IND1	0.02911	0.01118	0.01397	0.01471	0.01716
IND2	0.01118	0.03921	0.02487	0.02105	0.02243
IND3	0.01397	0.02487	0.06978	0.04719	0.04451
IND4	0.01471	0.02105	0.04719	0.07734	0.05879
IND5	0.01716	0.02243	0.04451	0.05879	0.08209

```
The value of the likelihood function at iteration 1 = 1.852563E+002
The value of the likelihood function at iteration 2 = 1.889909E+002
The value of the likelihood function at iteration 3 = 1.891217E+002
The value of the likelihood function at iteration 4 = 1.891322E+002
The value of the likelihood function at iteration 5 = 1.891333E+002
The value of the likelihood function at iteration 6 = 1.891335E+002
The value of the likelihood function at iteration 7 = 1.891335E+002

Iterations stopped due to small change in likelihood function


******* ITERATION 8 *******
```

D

IND1	0.03507	0.01671	0.01889	0.02149	0.02486
IND2	0.01671	0.04458	0.02779	0.02468	0.02714
IND3	0.01889	0.02779	0.07272	0.05303	0.04801
IND4	0.02149	0.02468	0.05303	0.08574	0.06636
IND5	0.02486	0.02714	0.04801	0.06636	0.08985

The 5-by-5 matrix "D" contains the maximum likelihood estimates of the five variances (one for each time point) and ten covariances (one for each pair of time points). The associated correlation matrix is printed below.

```
D (as correlations)
      IND1  1.000  0.423  0.374  0.392  0.443
      IND2  0.423  1.000  0.488  0.399  0.429
      IND3  0.374  0.488  1.000  0.672  0.594
      IND4  0.392  0.399  0.672  1.000  0.756
      IND5  0.443  0.429  0.594  0.756  1.000

Standard Errors of D
      IND1     0.00347      0.00304      0.00375      0.00413      0.00429
      IND2     0.00304      0.00434      0.00430      0.00457      0.00473
      IND3     0.00375      0.00430      0.00678      0.00631      0.00625
      IND4     0.00413      0.00457      0.00631      0.00811      0.00736
      IND5     0.00429      0.00473      0.00625      0.00736      0.00853
```

The 5-by-5 matrix above contains estimated standard errors for each element of D.

```
The value of the likelihood function at iteration 8 = 1.891335E+002

The outcome variable is    ATTIT

Final estimation of fixed effects:
--------------------------------------------------------------------------
    Fixed Effect       Coefficient   Standard Error   T-ratio   P-value
--------------------------------------------------------------------------
For       INTRCPT1, B0
    INTRCPT2, G00       0.320244       0.014981       21.377     0.000
For     AGE13 slope, B1
    INTRCPT2, G10       0.059335       0.004710       12.598     0.000
For    AGE13S slope, B2
    INTRCPT2, G20       0.000330       0.003146        0.105     0.917
```

The expected log attitude at age 13 is 0.320244. The mean linear growth rate of increase is estimated to be 0.059335, $t = 12.598$, indicating that the average rate of increase in deviant attitudes at age 13 is highly significant. The quadratic rate is not statistically significant.

```
Statistics for current covariance components model
---------------------------------------------------
Deviance =   -378.26695
Number of estimated parameters =   18
```

There are 3 fixed effects ($f = 3$) and five observations in the "complete data" for each person ($T = 5$). Thus, there are a total of $f + T(T+1)/2 = 3 + 5(5+1)/2 = 18$ parameters. This is the end of the unrestricted model output.

Next follow the results for the homogeneous level-1 variance.

OUTPUT FOR RANDOM EFFECTS MODEL WITH HOMOGENEOUS LEVEL-1 VARIANCE

Summary of the model specified (in equation format)

Level-1 Model

$\qquad$ Y = IND1*Y1* + IND2*Y2* + IND3*Y3* + IND4*Y4* + IND5*Y5*

$\qquad$ Y* = B0 + B1*(AGE13) + B2*(AGE13S) + R

Level-2 Model

$\qquad$ B0 = G00 + U0
$\qquad$ B1 = G10 + U1
$\qquad$ B2 = G20 + U2

VAR(Y*) = D = X*Tau*X' + S where S = sigma_squared*I

The above equation, written with subscripts and Greek letters, is:

$$\text{Var}(Y^*) = \Delta = \mathbf{XTX'} + \Sigma \, ,$$

where $\Sigma = \sigma^2 \mathbf{I}$.

X

IND1	1.00000	-2.00000	4.00000
IND2	1.00000	-1.00000	1.00000
IND3	1.00000	0.00000	0.00000
IND4	1.00000	1.00000	1.00000
IND5	1.00000	2.00000	4.00000

The above matrix describes the design matrix on occasions one through five.

The value of the likelihood function at iteration 1 = 1.541423E+002
The value of the likelihood function at iteration 2 = 1.741023E+002
The value of the likelihood function at iteration 3 = 1.741132E+002
The value of the likelihood function at iteration 4 = 1.741132E+002

Iterations stopped due to small change in likelihood function

Note: The results below duplicate exactly the results produced by a standard HLM2 run using homogeneous level-1 variance.

```
******* ITERATION 5 *******

                    Parameter      Standard Error
                  ------------     ----------------
  sigma_squared =    0.02421          0.001672

Tau
  INTRCPT1      0.04200      0.00808      -0.00242
     AGE13      0.00808      0.00277      -0.00012
    AGE13S     -0.00242     -0.00012       0.00049

Tau (as correlations)
  INTRCPT1   1.000   0.749  -0.532
     AGE13   0.749   1.000  -0.101
    AGE13S  -0.532  -0.101   1.000

Standard Errors of Tau
  INTRCPT1      0.00513      0.00127       0.00089
     AGE13      0.00127      0.00054       0.00024
    AGE13S      0.00089      0.00024       0.00025

D
     IND1      0.03536      0.01388      0.01616      0.01801      0.01943
     IND2      0.01388      0.04870      0.03150      0.03488      0.03464
     IND3      0.01616      0.03150      0.06620      0.04766      0.04849
     IND4      0.01801      0.03488      0.04766      0.08056      0.06095
     IND5      0.01943      0.03464      0.04849      0.06095      0.09625
```

The 5-by-5 matrix above contains the five variance and ten covariance estimates implied by the "homogeneous level-1 variance" model.

```
D (as correlations)
     IND1   1.000   0.334   0.334   0.338   0.333
     IND2   0.334   1.000   0.555   0.557   0.506
     IND3   0.334   0.555   1.000   0.653   0.607
     IND4   0.338   0.557   0.653   1.000   0.692
     IND5   0.333   0.506   0.607   0.692   1.000
```

The value of the likelihood function at iteration 5 = 1.741132E+002

The outcome variable is   ATTIT

Final estimation of fixed effects:
```
--------------------------------------------------------------------------
  Fixed Effect     Coefficient   Standard Error   T-ratio   P-value
--------------------------------------------------------------------------
For          INTRCPT1, B0
   INTRCPT2, G00      0.327231      0.015306       21.379     0.000
For      AGE13 slope, B1
   INTRCPT2, G10      0.064704      0.004926       13.135     0.000
For     AGE13S slope, B2
   INTRCPT2, G20      0.000171      0.003218        0.053     0.958
```

```
Statistics for current covariance components model
----------------------------------------------------
Deviance =   -348.22643
Number of estimated parameters =   10
```

There are 3 fixed effects ($f = 3$); the dimension of $\mathbf{T}$ is 3; and a common σ^2 is estimated at level 1. Thus, there are a total of $f + r(r + 1)/2 + 1 = 3 + 3(3 + 1)/2 + 1 = 10$ parameters.

This is the end of the output for the "homogeneous level-1 variance" model.

Finally, the heterogeneous level-1 variance solution is listed.

```
OUTPUT FOR RANDOM EFFECTS MODEL WITH HETEROGENEOUS LEVEL-1 VARIANCE

Summary of the model specified (in equation format)
----------------------------------------------------

Level-1 Model

      Y = IND1*Y1* + IND2*Y2* + IND3*Y3* + IND4*Y4* + IND5*Y5*

      Y* = B0 + B1*(AGE13) + B2*(AGE13S) + R

Level-2 Model

        B0 = G00 + U0
        B1 = G10 + U1
        B2 = G20 + U2

VAR(Y*) = D = X*Tau*X' + S,
where S = diag(sigma_squared(1),...,sigma_squared(5))
```

The above equation, written with subscripts and Greek letters, is:

$$\mathrm{Var}(Y^*) = \mathbf{XTX'} + \mathbf{\Sigma} \ ,$$

where $\mathbf{\Sigma} = \mathrm{diag}\{\sigma_t^2\}$, i.e., $\mathbf{\Sigma}$ is now a diagonal matrix with diagonal elements σ_t^2, the variance associated with occasion t, $t = 1, \ldots, T$.

```
X
      IND1      1.00000      -2.00000      4.00000
      IND2      1.00000      -1.00000      1.00000
      IND3      1.00000       0.00000      0.00000
      IND4      1.00000       1.00000      1.00000
      IND5      1.00000       2.00000      4.00000
```

```
The value of the likelihood function at iteration 1 = 1.741132E+002
The value of the likelihood function at iteration 2 = 1.814278E+002
The value of the likelihood function at iteration 3 = 1.815978E+002
The value of the likelihood function at iteration 4 = 1.816068E+002
The value of the likelihood function at iteration 5 = 1.816074E+002
The value of the likelihood function at iteration 6 = 1.816074E+002
The value of the likelihood function at iteration 7 = 1.816074E+002

Iterations stopped due to small change in likelihood function

******* ITERATION 8 *******

                    sigma_
                    squared        Standard Error
                 ------------     ----------------
        IND1        0.01373           0.005672
        IND2        0.02600           0.003296
        IND3        0.02685           0.003658
        IND4        0.02602           0.003633
        IND5        0.00275           0.007377
```

The five estimates above are the estimates of the level-1 variance for each time point.

```
Tau
   INTRCPT1      0.04079        0.00736       -0.00241
      AGE13      0.00736        0.00382        0.00025
     AGE13S     -0.00241        0.00025        0.00106

Tau (as correlations)
   INTRCPT1   1.000   0.590  -0.366
      AGE13   0.590   1.000   0.124
     AGE13S  -0.366   0.124   1.000

Standard Errors of Tau
   INTRCPT1      0.00512        0.00124        0.00088
      AGE13      0.00124        0.00066        0.00042
     AGE13S      0.00088        0.00042        0.00030

D
       IND1      0.03410        0.01707        0.01646        0.01851        0.02325
       IND2      0.01707        0.05165        0.03103        0.03322        0.03223
       IND3      0.01646        0.03103        0.06764        0.04574        0.04588
       IND4      0.01851        0.03322        0.04574        0.08208        0.06421
       IND5      0.02325        0.03223        0.04588        0.06421        0.08996
```

The 5-by-5 matrix above contains the estimates of five variances and ten covariances implied by the "heterogeneous level-1 variance" model.

```
D (as correlations)
    IND1  1.000  0.407  0.343  0.350  0.420
    IND2  0.407  1.000  0.525  0.510  0.473
    IND3  0.343  0.525  1.000  0.614  0.588
    IND4  0.350  0.510  0.614  1.000  0.747
    IND5  0.420  0.473  0.588  0.747  1.000

The value of the likelihood function at iteration 8 = 1.816074E+002

The outcome variable is     ATTIT

Final estimation of fixed effects:
-------------------------------------------------------------------------------
    Fixed Effect      Coefficient   Standard Error   T-ratio   P-value
-------------------------------------------------------------------------------
For       INTRCPT1, B0
    INTRCPT2, G00      0.327646       0.015252       21.482     0.000
For    AGE13 slope, B1
    INTRCPT2, G10      0.060864       0.004737       12.849     0.000
For    AGE13S slope, B2
    INTRCPT2, G20     -0.000541       0.003178       -0.170     0.865


Statistics for current covariance components model
--------------------------------------------------------
Deviance =    -363.21489
Number of estimated parameters =   14
```

There are 3 fixed effects $(f = 3)$, the dimension of $\mathbf{T}$ is 3, and there are five observations intended for each person, each associated with a unique level-1 variance. Thus, there are a total of $f + r(r+1)/2 + T = 3 + 3(3+1)/2 + 5 = 14$ parameters.

```
Summary of Model Fit
--------------------------------------------------------------------
Model                              Number of          Deviance
                                   Parameters
--------------------------------------------------------------------
1. Unrestricted                       18             -378.26695
2. Homogeneous sigma_squared          10             -348.22643
3. Heterogeneous sigma_squared        14             -363.21489


--------------------------------------------------------------------
Model Comparison               Chi-square     df     P-value
--------------------------------------------------------------------
Model 1 vs Model 2              30.04052        8     0.000
Model 1 vs Model 3              15.05206        4     0.005
Model 2 vs Model 3              14.98846        4     0.005
```

The model deviances are employed to evaluate the fits of the three models (homogeneous sigma_squared, heterogeneous sigma_squared, and unrestricted). Differences between deviances are distributed asymptotically as chi-square variates under the null hypothesis that the simpler model fits the data as well as the more complex model does. The results show that Model 1 fits better than does the homogeneous sigma_squared model $\chi^2 = 30.04052$, df $= 8$; it also fits better than does the heterogeneous sigma_squared model $\chi^2 = 15.05206$, df $= 4$.

In addition to the evaluation of models based on their fit to the data, users could use the above results to check the sensitivity of key inferences to alternative specifications of the variance-covariance structure. For example, one could compare the mean and variance in the rate of change at age 13 obtained in Model 2 and Model 3 to assess how robust the results are to alternative plausible covariance specifications. The mean rate, G10, for Model 2 is 0.064704(s.e. $= 0.004926$), and the variance, τ_{22}, is 0.00277(s.e. $= 0.00054$). The mean rate, G10, for Model 3 is 0.060864(s.e. $= 0.004737$), and the variance, τ_{22}, is 0.00382(s.e. $= 0.00066$). The results are quite similar. See Raudenbush (in press) for a more detailed analysis of alternative covariance structures for polynomial models of individual growth and change using the same NYS data sets employed here for the illustrations.

Below are partial outputs for two other random effect models

First, results of the log-linear model for σ^2. (Example NYS3.MLM.)

```
OUTPUT FOR RANDOM EFFECTS MODEL FOR LOG-LINEAR MODEL FOR LEVEL-1 VARIANCE

Summary of the model specified (in equation format)
-----------------------------------------------------
Level-1 Model

      Y = IND1*Y1* + IND2*Y2* + IND3*Y3* + IND4*Y4* + IND5*Y5*

      Y* = B0 + B1*(AGE13) + B2*(AGE13S) + R

Level-2 Model

      B0 = G00 + U0
      B1 = G10 + U1
      B2 = G20 + U2

VAR(Y*) = D = X*Tau*X' + S,
where S = diag(sigma_squared(1),...,sigma_squared(5)),
and log(sigma_squared(t)) = alpha0 + alpha1(EXPO)
```

Note the log-linear model for the level-1 variance.

The above equation, written with subscripts and Greek letters, is:

$$\text{Var}(Y^*) = \mathbf{XTX'} + \mathbf{\Sigma} \, ,$$

where $\mathbf{\Sigma} = \text{diag}\{\sigma_t^2\}$, *and*

$$\log(\sigma_t^2) = \alpha_0 + \alpha_1 \text{EXPO}_t \, .$$

```
X
    IND1      1.00000      -2.00000       4.00000
    IND2      1.00000      -1.00000       1.00000
    IND3      1.00000       0.00000       0.00000
    IND4      1.00000       1.00000       1.00000
    IND5      1.00000       2.00000       4.00000

The value of the likelihood function at iteration 1 = 1.741132E+002
The value of the likelihood function at iteration 2 = 1.749203E+002
The value of the likelihood function at iteration 3 = 1.749567E+002
The value of the likelihood function at iteration 4 = 1.749582E+002
The value of the likelihood function at iteration 5 = 1.749582E+002
The value of the likelihood function at iteration 6 = 1.749582E+002

Iterations stopped due to small change in likelihood function

******* ITERATION 7 *******

                    Parameter      Standard Error
                   ------------    ---------------
    alpha0    =     -3.72883          0.069238
    alpha1    =     -1.43639          1.053241
```

The results suggest no linear association between AGE *and the* $\log \sigma_t^2$, $Z = -1.436/1.053 = -1.36$.

```
                    sigma_
                    squared
                   ------------
    IND1             0.02690
    IND2             0.02677
    IND3             0.02419
    IND4             0.02188
    IND5             0.02136

Tau
  INTRCPT1    0.04255       0.00831      -0.00257
     AGE13    0.00831       0.00277      -0.00005
    AGE13S   -0.00257      -0.00005       0.00051
```

```
Tau (as correlations)
  INTRCPT1  1.000  0.766 -0.549
     AGE13  0.766  1.000 -0.042
    AGE13S -0.549 -0.042  1.000

Standard Errors of Tau
  INTRCPT1      0.00517      0.00128      0.00089
     AGE13      0.00128      0.00054      0.00025
    AGE13S      0.00089      0.00025      0.00025

D
      IND1      0.03576      0.01267      0.01566      0.01782      0.01917
      IND2      0.01267      0.05095      0.03168      0.03516      0.03464
      IND3      0.01566      0.03168      0.06674      0.04829      0.04889
      IND4      0.01782      0.03516      0.04829      0.07909      0.06192
      IND5      0.01917      0.03464      0.04889      0.06192      0.09510
```

The 5-by-5 matrix above contains the variance and covariance estimates implied by the "log-linear" model for the level-1 variance.

```
D (as correlations)
      IND1  1.000  0.297  0.320  0.335  0.329
      IND2  0.297  1.000  0.543  0.554  0.498
      IND3  0.320  0.543  1.000  0.665  0.614
      IND4  0.335  0.554  0.665  1.000  0.714
      IND5  0.329  0.498  0.614  0.714  1.000
```

The value of the likelihood function at iteration 7 = 1.749583E+002

The outcome variable is   ATTIT

Final estimation of fixed effects:

Fixed Effect	Coefficient	Standard Error	T-ratio	P-value
For INTRCPT1, B0				
INTRCPT2, G00	0.328946	0.015379	21.390	0.000
For AGE13 slope, B1				
INTRCPT2, G10	0.064661	0.004923	13.135	0.000
For AGE13S slope, B2				
INTRCPT2, G20	-0.000535	0.003222	-0.166	0.869

Statistics for current covariance components model

Deviance =   -349.91650
Number of estimated parameters =   11

There are 3 fixed effects ($f = 3$), the dimension of $\mathbf{T}$ is 3 ($r = 3$), and there is one intercept and one explanatory ($H = 1$) variable. Thus, there

8 WORKING WITH HMLM AND HMLM2

are a total of $f + r(r+1)/2 + 1 + H = 3 + 3(3+1)/2 + 1 + 1 = 11$ parameters.

Next are the results for the first-order auto-regressive model. (Example NYS4.MLM.)

```
OUTPUT FOR RANDOM EFFECTS MODEL FIRST-ORDER AUTOREGRESSIVE MODEL
FOR LEVEL-1 VARIANCE

Summary of the model specified (in equation format)
------------------------------------------------------

Level-1 Model

        Y = IND1*Y1* + IND2*Y2* + IND3*Y3* + IND4*Y4* + IND5*Y5*

        Y* = B0 + B1*(AGE13) + B2*(AGE13S) + R

Level-2 Model

        B0 = G00 + U0
        B1 = G10
        B2 = G20
```

Note that B1 and B2 are specified as non-random due to the fact that the time-series is relatively short and therefore the data do not allow the estimation of a 3×3 **T** plus an auto-correlation at level 1.

```
VAR(Y*) = D = X*Tau*X' + S, where S = {sigma_squared*rho**|t - t'|}
```

The above equation, written with subscripts and Greek letters, is:

$$\mathrm{Var}(Y^*) = \mathbf{XTX'} + \boldsymbol{\Sigma},$$

where $\boldsymbol{\Sigma} = \sigma^2 \rho^{|t-t'|}$.

```
X
        IND1        1.00000
        IND2        1.00000
        IND3        1.00000
        IND4        1.00000
        IND5        1.00000


The value of the likelihood function at iteration 1 = 1.145082E+002
The value of the likelihood function at iteration 2 = 1.447774E+002
```

```
The value of the likelihood function at iteration 3 = 1.471597E+002
The value of the likelihood function at iteration 4 = 1.471600E+002
The value of the likelihood function at iteration 5 = 1.471600E+002

Iterations stopped due to small change in likelihood function


******* ITERATION 6 *******

                        Parameter     Standard Error
                        ------------   ----------------
    rho            =      0.39675         0.053849
    sigma_squared  =      0.04158         0.003582
```

Note that the maximum-likelihood estimate of $\hat{\rho} = 0.397$ is much larger than its standard error (0.054), suggesting a significantly positive auto-correlation.

```
Tau
  INTRCPT1       0.02427

Tau (as correlations)
  INTRCPT1  1.000

Standard Errors of Tau
  INTRCPT1       0.00450

D
    IND1    0.06585    0.04077    0.03081    0.02686    0.02530
    IND2    0.04077    0.06585    0.04077    0.03081    0.02686
    IND3    0.03081    0.04077    0.06585    0.04077    0.03081
    IND4    0.02686    0.03081    0.04077    0.06585    0.04077
    IND5    0.02530    0.02686    0.03081    0.04077    0.06585
```

The 5-by-5 matrix above contains the variance and covariance estimates implied by the "auto-correlation" model for the level-1 variance.

```
D (as correlations)
    IND1  1.000  0.619  0.468  0.408  0.384
    IND2  0.619  1.000  0.619  0.468  0.408
    IND3  0.468  0.619  1.000  0.619  0.468
    IND4  0.408  0.468  0.619  1.000  0.619
    IND5  0.384  0.408  0.468  0.619  1.000

The value of the likelihood function at iteration 6 = 1.471600E+002

The outcome variable is    ATTIT
```

```
Final estimation of fixed effects:
--------------------------------------------------------------------------------
    Fixed Effect       Coefficient   Standard Error   T-ratio   P-value
--------------------------------------------------------------------------------
For         INTRCPT1, B0
    INTRCPT2, G00        0.327579        0.015265       21.459    0.000
For     AGE13 slope, B1
    INTRCPT2, G10        0.061428        0.004836       12.703    0.000
For     AGE13S slope, B2
    INTRCPT2, G20        0.000211        0.003373        0.062    0.951

Statistics for current covariance components model
--------------------------------------------------
Deviance =   -294.31992
Number of estimated parameters =    6
```

8.4   An HMLM2 analysis using Windows mode

To illustrate how to use HMLM2, we use the data files from the public school example described in Section 4.1.1.1. We prepared six indicators for the measures of mathematics proficiency collected over the six years and put them in the level-1 file, EG1.SAV. The new level-1 file is called EG1HMLM2.SAV. The same level-2 and level-3 files, EG2.SAV and EG3.SAV, respectively, are used. The MDM file created is EGHMLM2.MDM. As in the case with HMLM, users need to tell the program what the indicator variables are while creating the MDM file (see Fig. 8.2).

8.5   Executing analyses based on the MDM file

The steps involved are similar to the ones for HMLM outlined previously and for HLM3 as described in Section 4.2. The user specifies:

1. the level-1 model,
2. the level-2 structural model, and
3. the level-1 coefficients as random or non-random.

In addition, the user selects the covariance structure for the models to be estimated. Below is the output for the same linear growth model specified in Section 4.2. As in the case for HMLM, the results allow us to compare model fit and assess sensitivity of inferences with alternative specification of variance-covariance structures.

The example below (EGHMLM1.MLM) estimates

- ☐ the unrestricted model,
- ☐ a model with homogeneous level-1 variance, and
- ☐ a model with heterogeneous variance.

In each case, between-school variance components are also estimated.

```
Module:      HMLM2.EXE (5.01.2040.2)
Date:        9 February 2000, Wednesday
Time:        12:28:36
--------------------------------------------------------------------------------

SPECIFICATIONS FOR THIS HMLM2 RUN

 Problem Title: HMLM2 OUTPUT, PUBLIC SCHOOL DATA

 The data source for this run  = EGHMLM2.MDM
 The command file for this run = EGHMLM1.MLM
 Output file name              = EGHMLM2.OUT
 The maximum number of level-2 units = 1721
 The maximum number of level-3 units = 60
 The maximum number of iterations = 50

 The outcome variable is      MATH

 The model specified for the fixed effects was:
 ----------------------------------------------------

   Level-1            Level-2           Level-3
 ------------------- ---------------   ----------------
      INTRCPT1, P0       INTRCPT2, B00    INTRCPT3, G000
      YEAR slope, P1     INTRCPT2, B10    INTRCPT3, G100
```

Results for the unrestricted model follow.

OUTPUT FOR UNRESTRICTED MODEL

Summary of the model specified (in equation format)

Level-1 Model

     Y = IND1*Y1* + IND2*Y2* + IND3*Y3* + IND4*Y4* + IND5*Y5* + IND6*Y6*
     Y* = P0 + P1*(YEAR) + E

Level-2 Model

     P0 = B00
     P1 = B10

Level-3 Model

     B00 = G000 + U0
     B10 = G100 + U1

VAR(Y*|u) = D

The outcome variable is   MATH

Estimation of fixed effects
(Based on starting values of covariance components)

Fixed Effect	Coefficient	Standard Error	T-ratio	P-value
For INTRCPT1, P0				
For INTRCPT2, B00				
INTRCPT3, G000	-0.827685	0.012189	-67.906	0.000
For YEAR slope, P1				
For INTRCPT2, B10				
INTRCPT3, G100	0.765828	0.008433	90.812	0.000

D(0)

IND1,P0	0.04268	0.01233	0.01919	0.01968	0.01506	0.00898
IND2,P1	0.01233	0.60634	0.35457	0.42101	0.31132	0.24927
IND3,P2	0.01919	0.35457	0.76957	0.62363	0.42394	0.35205
IND4,P3	0.01968	0.42101	0.62363	1.15453	0.67302	0.52773
IND5,P4	0.01506	0.31132	0.42394	0.67302	0.81870	0.55086
IND6,P5	0.00898	0.24927	0.35205	0.52773	0.55086	0.65701

Tau(beta)(0)
 INTRCPT1   YEAR
 INTRCPT2,B00 INTRCPT2,B10
   0.20128   0.01542
   0.01542   0.01608

The value of the likelihood function at iteration 1 = -8.445655E+003
The value of the likelihood function at iteration 2 = -8.228973E+003
The value of the likelihood function at iteration 3 = -8.166659E+003
The value of the likelihood function at iteration 4 = -8.126574E+003

```
. . .
. . .
. . .
The value of the likelihood function at iteration 30 = -7.980255E+003
The value of the likelihood function at iteration 31 = -7.980254E+003

Iterations stopped due to small change in likelihood function

******* ITERATION 32 *******

D
    IND1,P0    0.67340    0.31616    0.38755    0.52412    0.53030    0.38971
    IND2,P1    0.31616    0.77832    0.47127    0.56726    0.54171    0.50187
    IND3,P2    0.38755    0.47127    0.91072    0.76829    0.66199    0.64640
    IND4,P3    0.52412    0.56726    0.76829    1.24542    0.88364    0.81782
    IND5,P4    0.53030    0.54171    0.66199    0.88364    1.05646    0.84356
    IND6,P5    0.38971    0.50187    0.64640    0.81782    0.84356    0.98722
```

The 5-by-5 matrix above contains estimates of five variances and ten co-variances of time-series observations within schools.

```
Standard Errors of D
    IND1,P0    0.08003    0.05328    0.07256    0.02999    0.02811    0.04341
    IND2,P1    0.05328    0.05757    0.06998    0.02542    0.03289    0.03656
    IND3,P2    0.07256    0.06998    0.07252    0.02966    0.03284    0.03565
    IND4,P3    0.02999    0.02542    0.02966    0.02844    0.03044    0.03913
    IND5,P4    0.02811    0.03289    0.03284    0.03044    0.03030    0.03518
    IND6,P5    0.04341    0.03656    0.03565    0.03913    0.03518    0.03859

D (as correlations)
    IND1,P0   1.000   0.437   0.495   0.572   0.629   0.478
    IND2,P1   0.437   1.000   0.560   0.576   0.597   0.573
    IND3,P2   0.495   0.560   1.000   0.721   0.675   0.682
    IND4,P3   0.572   0.576   0.721   1.000   0.770   0.738
    IND5,P4   0.629   0.597   0.675   0.770   1.000   0.826
    IND6,P5   0.478   0.573   0.682   0.738   0.826   1.000

Tau(beta)
 INTRCPT1         YEAR
 INTRCPT2,B00 INTRCPT2,B10
    0.14824       0.01268
    0.01268       0.00935


Standard Errors of Tau(beta)
 INTRCPT1         YEAR
 INTRCPT2,B00 INTRCPT2,B10
    0.03286       0.00626
    0.00626       0.00218

Tau(beta) (as correlations)
 INTRCPT1/INTRCPT2,B00   1.000   0.341
     YEAR/INTRCPT2,B10   0.341   1.000
```

"Tau(beta)" describes the between-school covariance structure of the intercept β_0 and the YEAR slope, β_1.

```
The value of the likelihood function at iteration 32 = -7.980254E+003

The outcome variable is    MATH

Final estimation of fixed effects:
-------------------------------------------------------------------------------
    Fixed Effect        Coefficient   Standard Error   T-ratio   P-value
-------------------------------------------------------------------------------
For        INTRCPT1, P0
   For INTRCPT2, B00
      INTRCPT3, G000      -0.824938       0.054960      -15.010    0.000
For      YEAR slope, P1
   For INTRCPT2, B10
      INTRCPT3, G100       0.755026       0.014229       53.062    0.000

Statistics for current covariance components model
----------------------------------------------------
Deviance =  15960.50740
Number of estimated parameters =   26
```

Results for the homogeneous level-1 variance model.

```
OUTPUT FOR RANDOM EFFECTS MODEL WITH HOMOGENEOUS LEVEL-1 VARIANCE

Summary of the model specified (in equation format)
------------------------------------------------------

Level-1 Model

          Y = IND1*Y1* + IND2*Y2* + IND3*Y3* + IND4*Y4* + IND5*Y5* + IND6*Y6*
          Y* = P0 + P1*(YEAR) + E

Level-2 Model       P0 = B00 + R0
                    P1 = B10 + R1

Level-3 Model       B00 = G000 + U0
                    B10 = G100 + U1

VAR(Y*|u) = D = A*Tau(pi)*A' + S where S = sigma_squared*I

A
      IND1,P0    1.00000    -2.50000
      IND2,P1    1.00000    -1.50000
      IND3,P2    1.00000    -0.50000
      IND4,P3    1.00000     0.50000
      IND5,P4    1.00000     1.50000
      IND6,P5    1.00000     2.50000
```

```
The value of the likelihood function at iteration 1 = -7.980254E+003
The value of the likelihood function at iteration 2 = -8.271230E+003
The value of the likelihood function at iteration 3 = -8.163134E+003
The value of the likelihood function at iteration 4 = -8.163116E+003
```

Iterations stopped due to small change in likelihood function

******* ITERATION 5 *******

	Parameter	Standard Error
sigma_squared =	0.30144	0.00660

Tau(pi)

INTRCPT1,P0	0.64046	0.04679
YEAR,P1	0.04679	0.01126

Tau(pi) (as correlations)

INTRCPT1	1.000	0.551
YEAR	0.551	1.000

Standard Errors of Tau(pi)

INTRCPT1,P0	0.02515	0.00499
YEAR,P1	0.00499	0.00197

D

IND1,P0	0.77832	0.49553	0.51417	0.53282	0.55146	0.57011
IND2,P1	0.49553	0.82687	0.55533	0.58523	0.61513	0.64503
IND3,P2	0.51417	0.55533	0.89793	0.63765	0.67880	0.71996
IND4,P3	0.53282	0.58523	0.63765	0.99150	0.74247	0.79489
IND5,P4	0.55146	0.61513	0.67880	0.74247	1.10758	0.86981
IND6,P5	0.57011	0.64503	0.71996	0.79489	0.86981	1.24618

The 5-by-5 matrix above contains estimates of the within-school variances and covariances implied by the "homogeneous level-1 variance" model.

D (as correlations)

IND1,P0	1.000	0.618	0.615	0.607	0.594	0.579
IND2,P1	0.618	1.000	0.644	0.646	0.643	0.635
IND3,P2	0.615	0.644	1.000	0.676	0.681	0.681
IND4,P3	0.607	0.646	0.676	1.000	0.709	0.715
IND5,P4	0.594	0.643	0.681	0.709	1.000	0.740
IND6,P5	0.579	0.635	0.681	0.715	0.740	1.000

Tau(beta)

INTRCPT1	YEAR
INTRCPT2,B00	INTRCPT2,B10
0.16532	0.01705
0.01705	0.01102

8 WORKING WITH HMLM AND HMLM2

```
Standard Errors of Tau(beta)
 INTRCPT1         YEAR
 INTRCPT2,B00  INTRCPT2,B10
     0.03641       0.00720
     0.00720       0.00252


Tau(beta) (as correlations)
 INTRCPT1/INTRCPT2,B00  1.000  0.399
     YEAR/INTRCPT2,B10  0.399  1.000
```

The value of the likelihood function at iteration 5 = -8.163116E+003

The outcome variable is   MATH

Final estimation of fixed effects:

Fixed Effect	Coefficient	Standard Error	T-ratio	P-value
For INTRCPT1, P0				
For INTRCPT2, B00				
INTRCPT3, G000	-0.779305	0.057829	-13.476	0.000
For YEAR slope, P1				
For INTRCPT2, B10				
INTRCPT3, G100	0.763028	0.015262	49.996	0.000

Statistics for current covariance components model

Deviance = 16326.23120
Number of estimated parameters =   9

Results for the heterogeneous level-1 variance model.

OUTPUT FOR RANDOM EFFECTS MODEL WITH HETEROGENEOUS LEVEL-1 VARIANCE

Summary of the model specified (in equation format)

Level-1 Model

$$Y = IND1*Y1* + IND2*Y2* + IND3*Y3* + IND4*Y4* + IND5*Y5* + IND6*Y6*$$
$$Y* = P0 + P1*(YEAR) + E$$

Level-2 Model

$$P0 = B00 + R0$$
$$P1 = B10 + R1$$

Level-3 Model

$$B00 = G000 + U0$$
$$B10 = G100 + U1$$

```
VAR(Y*|u) = D = A*Tau(pi)*A' + S,
where S = diag(sigma_squared(1),...,sigma_squared(6))

A
      IND1,P0     1.00000     -2.50000
      IND2,P1     1.00000     -1.50000
      IND3,P2     1.00000     -0.50000
      IND4,P3     1.00000      0.50000
      IND5,P4     1.00000      1.50000
      IND6,P5     1.00000      2.50000
```

```
The value of the likelihood function at iteration 1 = -8.163116E+003
The value of the likelihood function at iteration 2 = -8.072346E+003
The value of the likelihood function at iteration 3 = -8.070198E+003
The value of the likelihood function at iteration 4 = -8.070087E+003
The value of the likelihood function at iteration 5 = -8.070080E+003
The value of the likelihood function at iteration 6 = -8.070080E+003
```

Iterations stopped due to small change in likelihood function

******* ITERATION 7 *******

	sigma_squared	Standard Error
IND1	0.34891	0.05960
IND2	0.38314	0.02056
IND3	0.31846	0.01491
IND4	0.37849	0.01584
IND5	0.20344	0.01147
IND6	0.15546	0.01422

```
Tau(pi)
  INTRCPT1,P0    0.62722     0.04769
      YEAR,P1    0.04769     0.01386

Tau(pi) (as correlations)
  INTRCPT1    1.000   0.511
      YEAR    0.511   1.000

Standard Errors of Tau(pi)
  INTRCPT1,P0    0.02499     0.00495
      YEAR,P1    0.00495     0.00205
```

```
D
      IND1,P0    0.82432   0.48844   0.50148   0.51451   0.52755   0.54058
      IND2,P1    0.48844   0.89848   0.54224   0.56913   0.59603   0.62293
      IND3,P2    0.50148   0.54224   0.90146   0.62376   0.66452   0.70528
      IND4,P3    0.51451   0.56913   0.62376   1.05687   0.73300   0.78762
      IND5,P4    0.52755   0.59603   0.66452   0.73300   1.00493   0.86997
      IND6,P5    0.54058   0.62293   0.70528   0.78762   0.86997   1.10778
```

The 5-by-5 matrix above contains estimates of the within-school covariance structure implied by the "heterogeneous level-1 variance" model.

```
D (as correlations)
     IND1,P0  1.000  0.568  0.582  0.551  0.580  0.566
     IND2,P1  0.568  1.000  0.603  0.584  0.627  0.624
     IND3,P2  0.582  0.603  1.000  0.639  0.698  0.706
     IND4,P3  0.551  0.584  0.639  1.000  0.711  0.728
     IND5,P4  0.580  0.627  0.698  0.711  1.000  0.825
     IND6,P5  0.566  0.624  0.706  0.728  0.825  1.000


Tau(beta)
 INTRCPT1        YEAR
 INTRCPT2,B00 INTRCPT2,B10
    0.16531       0.01552
    0.01552       0.00971

Standard Errors of Tau(beta)
 INTRCPT1        YEAR
 INTRCPT2,B00 INTRCPT2,B10
    0.03637       0.00677
    0.00677       0.00225

Tau(beta) (as correlations)
 INTRCPT1/INTRCPT2,B00  1.000  0.387
     YEAR/INTRCPT2,B10  0.387  1.000


The value of the likelihood function at iteration 7 = -8.070079E+003

The outcome variable is    MATH


Final estimation of fixed effects:
-------------------------------------------------------------------------
    Fixed Effect       Coefficient  Standard Error  T-ratio   P-value
-------------------------------------------------------------------------
For       INTRCPT1, P0
   For INTRCPT2, B00
      INTRCPT3, G000    -0.781960      0.057792     -13.531    0.000
For     YEAR slope, P1
   For INTRCPT2, B10
      INTRCPT3, G100     0.751231      0.014452      51.983    0.000

Statistics for current covariance components model
--------------------------------------------------------
Deviance =  16140.15899
Number of estimated parameters =   14
```

Summary of Model Fit

```
-----------------------------------------------------------------
Model                         Number of         Deviance
                              Parameters
-----------------------------------------------------------------
1. Unrestricted                   26           15960.50740
2. Homogeneous sigma_squared       9           16326.23120
3. Heterogeneous sigma_squared    14           16140.15899


-----------------------------------------------------------------
Model Comparison              Chi-square     df     P-value
-----------------------------------------------------------------
Model 1 vs Model 2            365.72380      17     0.000
Model 1 vs Model 3            179.65159      12     0.000
Model 2 vs Model 3            186.07221       5     0.000
```

9 Special Features

9.1 Latent variable analysis

Researchers may be interested in studying the randomly varying coefficients not only as outcomes, but as predictors as well. For instance, in a two-level repeated measures study of adolescents' tolerance of deviant behaviors, a user may choose to use the level-1 coefficient capturing the level of tolerance at the beginning of the study to predict the coefficient tapping the linear growth rate.

Treating these coefficients as latent variables, the HLM2, HLM3, and HMLM modules allow the users to study direct as well as indirect effects among them, and to assess their impacts on coefficients associated with observed covariates in the model. Furthermore, using HMLM with unrestricted covariance structures, one may use latent variable analysis to run regression with missing data.

Below are two examples of latent variable analysis via Windows mode. See Appendix E for batch and interactive mode.

9.1.1 A latent variable analysis using HMLM: Example 1

The first example employs the National Youth Survey data sets described in Section 8.1. The MDM file is NYS.MDM, the level-1 data file is NYS1.SAV, and the level-2 file is NYS2.SAV. Fig. 9.1 displays a linear growth model at level 1 with gender as a covariate at level 2. The command file that contains the model specification information is NYS2.MLM.

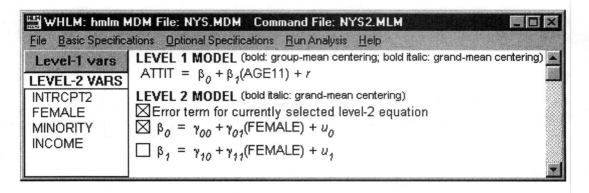

Figure 9.1   Model screen for the NYS example

We shall use β_0, the level of tolerance at age 11, to predict β_1, the linear growth rate, controlling for gender. Note that FEMALE must be in the model for both β_0 and β_1 to control for gender fully. Note also that β_0 and β_1 are latent variables, that is, they are free of measurement error, which is contained in r. Furthermore, we assess whether the effect of gender on the linear growth rate may change after controlling for the initial status at age 11. We select the homogeneous level-1 variance option for this model. Thus, using HLM2 will yield identical results in this case.

Below are the steps for setting up a latent variable analysis.

To set up a latent variable analysis

1. After specifying the model, open the **Optional Specifications** menu.
2. Choose **Latent Variable Regression** to open the **Latent Variable Regression** dialog box (see Fig. 9.2 for an illustration using the NYS example).
3. Select the predictor(s) and outcome(s) by clicking the radio buttons in front of them (for our example, select INTRCPT1, β_0, as the predictor and AGE11, β_1, as the outcome).

Select HMLM output to illustrate latent variable regression follows.

Check the radio buttons to select outcome and predictor

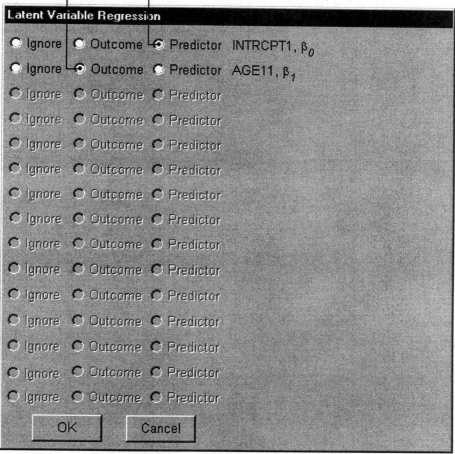

Figure 9.2   Latent Variable Regression dialog box for the NYS example

```
Final estimation of fixed effects:
-------------------------------------------------------------------------------
    Fixed Effect      Coefficient   Standard Error   T-ratio   P-value
-------------------------------------------------------------------------------
For        INTRCPT1, B0
    INTRCPT2, G00       0.221755       0.015961      13.894     0.000
      FEMALE, G01      -0.048274       0.022926      -2.106     0.035
For     AGE11 slope, B1
    INTRCPT2, G10       0.070432       0.006781      10.386     0.000
      FEMALE, G11      -0.012003       0.009826      -1.222     0.222
```

The results indicate that there is a significant linear growth rate in the attitude toward deviant behaviors (coefficient = 0.070432, s.e. = 0.006781) for males. Also, there is no gender effect on the linear growth rate.

```
Latent Variable Regression Results

The model specified (in equation format)

    B1 = G10* + G11*(FEMALE) + G12*(B0) + U1*

-------------------------------------------------------------------------------
  Outcome      Predictor       Estimated      Standard     T-ratio   P-value
                               Coefficient    Error
-------------------------------------------------------------------------------
  AGE11,B1   INTRCPT2,G10*      0.024765      0.024807      0.998     0.319
             FEMALE,G11*       -0.002062      0.013058     -0.158     0.875
             B0,G12*            0.205934      0.105410      1.954     0.050
-------------------------------------------------------------------------------
```

The results indicate that, controlling for gender, the initial status at AGE11 has a marginally significant effect on the linear growth rate (coefficient = 0.205934, s.e. = 0.105410). There is no statistically significant gender effect, however. Indeed, the gender effect on β_1 appears somewhat reduced after controlling β_0.

```
Latent Variable Regression: Comparison of Original and Adjusted Coefficients
-------------------------------------------------------------------------------
  Outcome      Predictor     Original      Adjusted    Difference   Standard
                             Coefficient   Coefficient              Error of
                                                                    Difference
-------------------------------------------------------------------------------
  AGE11,B1   INTRCPT2         0.07043       0.02477      0.04567     0.024311
             FEMALE          -0.01200      -0.00206     -0.00994     0.006941
-------------------------------------------------------------------------------
```

This table lists the original coefficients, the adjusted coefficients, and the difference between the two for the intercept and the gender effect. For the variable FEMALE, the "original coefficient" decribes the total association, the "adjusted coefficient" describes the direct association, and the "difference" is the indirect association between gender and the linear growth rate, respectively.

```
Var(u1*)
    AGE11       0.00196
```

An estimate of the variance of u1*, the residual variance in β_1, controlling both FEMALE and β_0, is also given.

As mentioned earlier, a latent variable analysis using *HLM2* will reproduce identical results. The same procedures generalize to three-level applications (HMLM2, HLM3, & HGLM) to model randomly varying level-2 coefficients as outcome variables. See Raudenbush & Sampson (1999) for an example that implemented a latent variable analysis with a three-level model. In the study, they investigated the extent to which neighborhood social control mediated the association between neighborhood social composition and violence in Chicago.

9.1.2 A latent variable analysis using HMLM: Example 2

In this example, we illustrate how to use latent variable analysis to run regression with missing data with an artificial data set. We are interested in estimating regression coefficients that relate two predictors to the outcome. There are three intended measures, an outcome (OUTCOME) and two predictors (PRED1 and PRED2) for 15 participants in the data. Some participants are missing one or two measures. To use HMLM to run regression with missing data, we first re-organize the data and re-conceive the three measures for each participant j as "occasions of measurement." If the data are complete, each case has $M = 3$ occasions. If participant j is missing one value, there will only be two occasions for that participant, and if participant j is missing two values, there will be only one occasion for that case. The measure is then re-conceived as MEASURE$_{ij}$, that is, the value of the datum collected at occasion i for participant j, with $i = 1, \ldots, n_j$, and with $n_j \leq M = 3$. If the data are complete for participant j, then:

$$MEASURE_{1j} = OUTCOME_j \, ,$$
$$MEASURE_{2j} = PRED_{1j} \, ,$$
$$MEASURE_{3j} = PRED_{2j} \, .$$

Three indicators IND_{1j}, IND_{2j}, and IND_{3j} indicating whether $MEASURE_{ij}$ is $OUTCOME_j$, $PRED_{1j}$, or $PRED_{2j}$ are added to the data set.

Data for the first three participants are shown in Fig. 9.3.

	id	measures	ind1	ind2	ind3
1	1	48.92	1.00	.00	.00
2	1	41.86	.00	1.00	.00
3	1	60.41	.00	.00	1.00
4	2	56.06	.00	1.00	.00
5	2	52.99	.00	.00	1.00
6	3	59.49	1.00	.00	.00

Figure 9.3   First three participants for Example 2

Note that participant 1 has complete data, participant 2 has data on PRED1 and PRED2 but not the outcome, and the participant 3 has data only on OUTCOME.

Data on the measures and the three indicators constitute the level-1 data file, MISSING1.SAV, for the example. The level-2 file, MISSING2.SAV, contains a dummy variable, DUMMY, which is not to be used in the analysis. An MDM file, MISSING.MDM, is created. Fig. 9.4 displays the model specified with unrestricted covariance structure for the missing data example. The file that contains the file specification information is MISSING1.MLM.

To regress OUTCOME (IND1) on PRED1 (IND2) and PRED2 (IND3) , the user selects IND1 as the outcome and IND2 and IND3 as predictors in the **Latent Variable Regression** dialog box.

The following selected output (example MISSING1.MLM) gives the latent variable regression results.

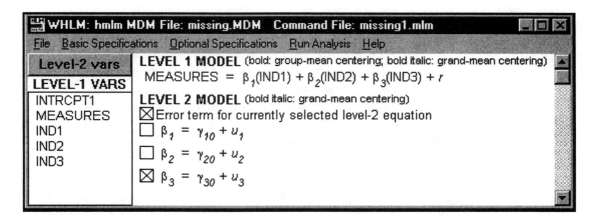

Figure 9.4   Model window for the missing data example

Latent Variable Regression Results

Outcome	Predictor	Estimated Coefficient	Standard Error	T-ratio	P-value
IND1,B1	INTRCPT2,G10*	-23.966161	14.173726	-1.691	0.116
	B2,G11*	0.879462	0.232665	3.780	0.003
	B3,G12*	0.544410	0.220194	2.472	0.030

Latent Variable Regression: Comparison of Original and Adjusted Coefficients

Outcome	Predictor	Original Coefficient	Adjusted Coefficient	Difference	Standard Error of Difference
IND1,B1	INTRCPT2	52.25565	-23.96616	76.22181	14.285875

Var(u1*)
IND1	33.51134

The results indicate that B2 (associated with IND2) and B3 (associated with IND3) have statistically significant effects on IND1 (OUTCOME).[1]

---

[1]Raudenbush & Bryk (forthcoming) have shown that using this approach with complete data replicated the results of SPSS regression analysis for the regression coefficients. As HMLM adopts the full maximum likelihood estimation approach and SPSS uses the re-

9.2 Applying HLM to multiply-imputed data

A useful analytic strategy when data are missing at random involves multiple, model-based imputation (Rubin, 1987, Little & Rubin, 1987, Schafer, 1997). A multiple imputation procedure produces M "complete" data sets. Users can apply HLM2 and HLM3 to these multiply-imputed data to produce appropriate estimates that incorporate the uncertainty resulting from imputation.

There can be multiply-imputed values for the outcome or one covariate or for the outcome and/or covariates.

HLM has two methods to analyze multiply-imputed data. They both use the same equations to compute the averages, so the method chosen depends on the data you are analyzing.

"Plausible Values" as described in Sections 9.2.1 and 9.2.3. This method is usually preferable for data sets that have only one variable (outcome or predictor) for which you have several plausible values. In this case, you need to make one SSM file containing *all* of the plausible values, plus any other variables of interest.

"Multiple Imputation" as described in Section 9.2.4. This method is necessary if you have more than one variable for which you have multiply-imputed data. This method also requires a different way of setting up SSM files. Here, you have to create as many SSMs as you have plausible values. When making these SSMs, you should use the same level-2 file (and level-3 file if using HLM3), but several level-1 files are needed. For those variables that are not multiply imputed, they should be the same in all these level-1 files. For those variables that *are* multiply-imputed, they should be separated into the separate level-1 files, but they *must* have the same variable names across these level-1 files, since the same model is run on each of these SSMs.

---

stricted maximum likelihood approach, the two sets of standard errors estimated differ by a factor of $\sqrt{\frac{J}{J-Q-1}}$, where $J = 15$ and $Q = 2$.

9.2.1 Data with multiply-imputed values for the outcome or one covariate

HLM2 and HLM3 enable users to produce correct HLM estimates when using data sets that contain two or more values or plausible values for the outcome variable or one covariate. One such data set is the National Assessment of Educational progress (NAEP), an U.S. Department of Education achievement test given to a national sample of fourth, eighth, and twelfth graders.

Due to the use of balanced incomplete block (BIB) spiraling in the administration of the NAEP assessment battery, special procedures and calculations are necessary when estimating any statistical parameters and their standard errors with data sets such as NAEP. Every student was not tested on the same items, so item response theory (IRT) was used to estimate proficiency scores for each individual student. This procedure estimated a range or distribution of plausible values for each student's proficiency rather than an individual observed score. NAEP drew five plausible values at random from the conditional distribution of proficiency scores for each student. The measurement error is due to the fact that these scores are estimated, rather than observed.

In general, these plausible values are used to produce parameter estimates in the following way.

1. Each parameter is estimated for each of the five plausible values, and the five estimates are averaged.
2. Then, the standard error for this average estimate is calculated using the approach recommended by Little & Schenker (1995).
3. This formula essentially combines the average of the sampling error variance from the five estimates with the variance between the five estimates.

In an HLM analysis, either a two- or three-level one, the parameter estimates are based on the average parameter estimates from separate HLM analyses of five plausible values. That is, a separate HLM analysis is conducted on each of the five plausible values.

Without HLM, these procedures could be performed by producing HLM estimates for each plausible value, and then averaging the estimates and calculating the standard errors using another computer program. These procedures are tedious and time-consuming, especially when performed on many models, grades, and dependent variables.

HLM takes the plausible values into account in generating the HLM estimates. For each HLM model, the program runs each of the five (or the number specified) plausible values internally, and produces their average value and the correct standard errors. The user seems to be producing one estimate, but the five HLM estimates from the five plausible values are produced and their average and measurement error calculated correctly, thus ensuring an accurate treatment of plausible value data. The output is similar to the standard HLM program output, except that all the components are averaged over estimates derived from the five plausible values. In addition, the output from the five plausible value runs is available in a separate output file.

9.2.2 Calculations performed

The program conducts a separate HLM analysis for each plausible value. The output of the separate HLM analyses is written to files with consecutive numbers, for example, OUT.1, OUT.2, OUT.3, etc. Then, HLM calculates the average of the parameter estimates from the separate analyses and computes the standard errors. The output of the average HLM parameter estimates and their standard errors is found in the output file with the extension AVG.

9.2.2.1 Average parameter estimates

The following parameter estimates are averaged by HLM:

- ❏ The gammas
- ❏ The reliabilities
- ❏ The parameter variances (tau) and its correlations
- ❏ The chi-square values to test whether the parameter variance is zero
- ❏ The standard errors for the variance-covariance components (full maximum likelihood estimates)
- ❏ Multivariate hypothesis testing for fixed effects

9.2.2.2 Standard error of the gammas

The standard error of the averaged gammas is estimated as described below. The Student's t-value is calculated by dividing the average gamma by its standard error, and the probability of the t-value is estimated from a standard t-distribution table.

The standard error of the gammas consists of two components — sampling error and measurement error. The following routine provided in the NAEP *Data Files User Guide* (Rogers, *et al.*, 1992) is used to approximate the component of error variance due to the error in measurement and to add it to the sampling error.

Let $\hat{\theta}_m$ $(m = 1, \ldots, M)$ represent the m-th plausible value. Let $\hat{t}_m$ represent the parameter estimate based on the m-th plausible value. Let U_m represent the variance of $\hat{t}_m$.

- Five HLM runs were conducted based on each plausible value $\hat{\theta}_m$. The parameter estimates from these runs were averaged:

$$t^* = \frac{\sum_{m=1}^{M} \hat{t}_m}{M}$$

- The variance of the parameters from these runs were averaged:

$$U^* = \frac{\sum_{m=1}^{M} U_m}{M}$$

- The variance of the m estimates, $\hat{t}_m$, was estimated:

$$B_m = \frac{\sum_{m=1}^{M} (\hat{t}_m - t^*)^2}{(M - 1)}$$

- The final estimate of the variance of the parameter estimate is the sum of the two components:

$$V = U^* + (1 + M^{-1}) B_m$$

The square root of this variance is the standard error of the gamma, and it is used in a standard Student's t formula to evaluate the statistical significance of each gamma.

9.2.3 Working with plausible values in HLM

Below is the procedure for running a plausible value analysis via Windows mode:

To run a plausible value analysis

1. After specifying the outcome, open the **Optional Specifications** menu.
2. Choose **Plausible Values** to open the **Select Plausible Value Outcome Variables** dialog box (see Fig. 9.5 for an example with three plausible values).
3. Select the first plausible value (either the outcome or a covariate) from the **Choose first variable from level-1 equation** drop-down listbox.
4. Double-click the other plausible values from the **Possible choices** listbox.
5. Click **OK**.

9.2.4 Data with multiply-imputed values for the outcome and covariates

There may be multiply-imputed values for both the outcome and the co-variates. To apply HLM to such data, users need to prepare as many SSM files as the number of imputed data sets. Thus, if there are five imputed data sets, five SSM files with identical variable labels need to be prepared. To run these models in batch mode, refer to Section E.3 in Appendix E.

Below are the commands for running an analysis with multiply-imputed data sets via Windows mode.

To run an analysis with multiply-imputed data sets

1. After specifying the outcome, open the **Optional Specifications** menu.
2. Choose **Multiple Imputation** to open the **Multiple Imputation SSM files** dialog box (see Fig. 9.6 for an example).
3. Enter the names for the SSM files that contain the multiply-imputed data either by typing into the **File #** edit boxes or clicking **Browse** to open them.
4. Click **OK**. Model specification follows the usual format.

The calculations involved are very similar to the ones mentioned in Section 9.2.2.

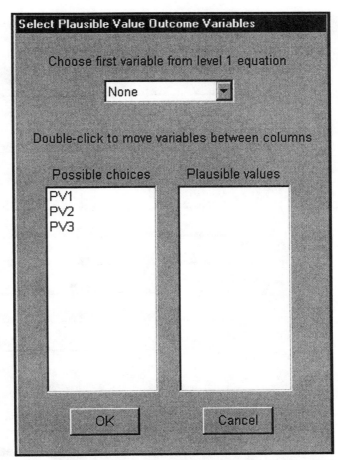

Figure 9.5   Select Plausible Value Outcome Variables dialog box

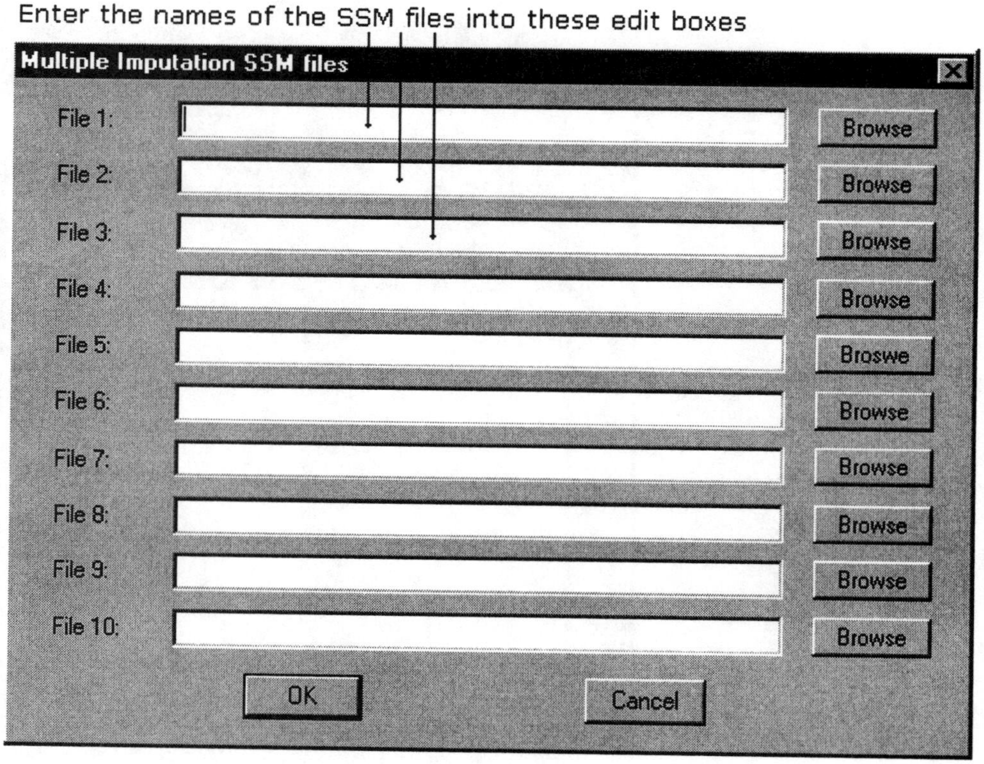

Enter the names of the SSM files into these edit boxes

Figure 9.6   Multiple Imputation SSM files dialog box

9 SPECIAL FEATURES

9.3 "V-Known" Models for HLM2

The V-known option of HLM2 is a general routine that can be used for applications where the level-1 variances (and covariances) are known. Included here are problems of meta-analysis (or research synthesis) and a wide range of other possible uses as discussed in Chapter 7 of *Hierarchical Linear Models*. The program input consists of Q random level-1 statistics for each group and their associated error variances and covariances.

We illustrate the use of the program with the data from the meta-analysis of teacher expectancy effects described on pp. 161–168 of *Hierarchical Linear Models*. Formulation and testing of V-known models can be done only via interactive mode. Also, users may construct the SSM file only from ASCII input. The input data for this application are displayed below.

1	0.030	0.016	2.000
2	0.120	0.022	3.000
3	−0.140	0.028	3.000
4	1.180	0.139	0.000
5	0.260	0.136	0.000
6	−0.060	0.011	3.000
7	−0.020	0.011	3.000
8	−0.320	0.048	3.000
9	0.270	0.027	0.000
10	0.800	0.063	1.000
11	0.540	0.091	0.000
12	0.180	0.050	0.000
13	−0.020	0.084	1.000
14	0.230	0.084	2.000
15	−0.180	0.025	3.000
16	−0.060	0.028	3.000
17	0.300	0.019	1.000
18	0.070	0.009	2.000
19	−0.070	0.030	3.000

9.3.1 Data input format

Unlike the standard HLM2 program, the V-known routine uses only a single data input file. It consists of the following information:

1. The first field is the unit ID in character format.

2. This is followed by the Q statistics from each unit. In the teacher expectancy effects meta-analysis Q equals one, the experiment effect size. (The effect size estimate appears in the third column of Table 7.1 in *Hierarchical Linear Models*.)

3. Next are the $Q(Q+1)/2$ error variances and covariances associated with the set of Q statistics. These variance-covariance elements must be specified in row-column sequence from the lower triangle of the matrix, *i.e.*, $V_{11}, V_{21}, V_{22}, \ldots, V_{Q,Q-1}, V_{Q,Q}$. For the meta-analysis application only a single error variance is needed. (Note the values in the third column above are the squares of the standard errors that appear in the fourth column of Table 7.1.)

4. Last are the potential level-2 predictor variables. In the teacher expectancy effects meta-analysis, there was only one predictor, the number of weeks of prior contact. (See column 2 of Table 7.1).

The Q statistics, their error variances and covariances, and the level-2 predictors must be ordered as described above and have a numeric format.

9.3.2 Creating the SSM file

The "V-known" program must be implemented in batch or interactive mode; it is not available in Windows mode.

We present below an example of an HLM2 session that creates a sufficient statistics file using the V-known routine on the teacher expectancy effects data.

```
Will you be starting with raw data? Y
Is the input file a v-known file? Y

How many level-1 statistics are there? 1
How many level-2 predictors are there? 1

Enter 8 character name for level-1 variable number 1: EFFSIZE
Enter 8 character name for level-2 variable number 1: WEEKS

Input format of raw data file (the first field must be the character ID)
format: (A2,3F12.3)
What file contains the data? EXPECT.DAT
Enter name of ssm file: EXPECT.SSM

19 groups have been processed
```

The file, EXPECT.DAT, contains the input data displayed above and the resulting sufficient statistics are saved in the EXPECT.SSM file. All subsequent analyses use EXPECT.SSM. Note that the input format has been specified for the character ID, the level-1 statistic, EFFSIZE, the associated variance, and the level-2 predictor, WEEKS.

9.3.3 Estimating a V-known model

Once the SSM file has been created, it can be used to specify and estimate a variety of models as in any other HLM2 application. The example below illustrates interactive use of the V-known program (example EXPECT.HLM).

```
HLM2 EXPECT.SSM

                      SPECIFYING AN HLM MODEL

Level-1 predictor variable specification

Which level-1 predictors do you wish to use?

The choices are:
 For  EFFSIZE enter  1

 level-1 predictor? (Enter 0 to end)  1

Level-2 predictor variable specification

Which level-2 variables do you wish to use?

The choices are:
 For    WEEKS enter  1

Which level-2 predictors to model  EFFSIZE?
 Level-2 predictor? (Enter 0 to end)  1

                    ADDITIONAL PROGRAM FEATURES

Select the level-2 variables that you might consider for
inclusion as predictors in subsequent models.

 The choices are:
 For    WEEKS enter  1

Which level-2 variables to model  EFFSIZE?
 Level-2 variable? (Enter 0 to end)   0

Do you want to run this analysis with a heterogeneous sigma2? N
Do you wish to use any of the optional hypothesis testing procedures? N
```

OUTPUT SPECIFICATION

Do you want a residual file? **N**
How many iterations do you want to do? **10000**
Do you want to see OLS estimates for all of the level-2 units? **N**
 Enter a problem title: **Teacher expectancy meta-analysis**
 Enter name of output file: **EXPECT.OUT**

Computing . . ., please wait

```
Program:          HLM 5 Hierarchical Linear and Nonlinear Modeling
Authors:          Stephen Raudenbush, Tony Bryk, & Richard Congdon
Publisher:        Scientific Software International, Inc. (c) 2000
                                                techsupport@ssicentral.com
                                                www.ssicentral.com
-------------------------------------------------------------------------
Module:    HLM2.EXE (5.01.2040.2)
Date:      9 February 2000, Wednesday
Time:      12:41:15
-------------------------------------------------------------------------
```

The first page of the output lists, after a program header, the specifics for this analysis. For your convenience, it has the date and time the problem ran. If you need to contact technical support at SSI, be sure to include the version number of the module you are using. It is given in parentheses right after the module name.

SPECIFICATIONS FOR THIS HLM2 RUN

  Problem Title: TEACHER EXPECTANCY META-ANALYSIS

  The data source for this run = EXPECT.SSM
  The command file for this run = EXPECT.HLM
  Output file name   = EXPECT.OUT
The maximum number of level-2 units = 19
The maximum number of iterations = 10000
Method of estimation: restricted maximum likelihood
Note: this is a v-known analysis

The outcome variable is EFFSIZE

The model specified for the fixed effects was:

  Level-1   Level-2
  Effects   Predictors
---------------------   ----------------
        EFFSIZE, B1   INTRCPT2, G10
                       WEEKS, G11

The model specified for the covariance components was:

        Variance(s and covariances) at level-1 externally specified
        Tau dimensions
            EFFSIZE slope

Summary of the model specified (in equation format)

Level-1 Model

        Y1 = B1 + E1

Level-2 Model

        B1 = G10 + G11*(WEEKS) + U1

STARTING VALUES

  Tau(0)
   EFFSIZE,B1   0.02004

  Estimation of fixed effects
  (Based on starting values of covariance components)

                                       Standard   Approx.
        Fixed Effect   Coefficient Error   T-ratio d.f.   P-value
    ----
    For   EFFSIZE, B1
       INTRCPT2, G10   0.433737   0.109700   3.954   17   0.001
          WEEKS, G11   -0.168572   0.046563   -3.620   17   0.002

The value of the likelihood function at iteration 1 = -3.414348E+001
The value of the likelihood function at iteration 2 = -3.350241E+001
The value of the likelihood function at iteration 3 = -3.301695E+001
The value of the likelihood function at iteration 4 = -3.263749E+001

                                        .
                                        .
                                        .

The value of the likelihood function at iteration 7849 = -2.979898E+001
The value of the likelihood function at iteration 7850 = -2.979898E+001
The value of the likelihood function at iteration 7851 = -2.979897E+001
The value of the likelihood function at iteration 7852 = -2.979897E+001

Iterations stopped due to small change in likelihood function

******* ITERATION 7853 *******

Tau
   EFFSIZE,B1   0.00001

Tau (as correlations)
   EFFSIZE,B1   1.000

```
------------------------------------------------------------
Random level-1 coefficient    Reliability estimate
------------------------------------------------------------
  EFFSIZE, B1                         0.000
------------------------------------------------------------
```

The value of the likelihood function at iteration 7853 = -2.979897E+001

Final estimation of fixed effects:

Fixed Effect	Coefficient	Standard Error	T-ratio	Approx. d.f.	P-value
For EFFSIZE, B1					
INTRCPT2, G10	0.408572	0.087146	4.688	17	0.000
WEEKS, G11	-0.157963	0.035943	-4.395	17	0.000

Final estimation of variance components:

Random Effect		Standard Deviation	Variance Component	df	Chi-square	P-value
EFFSIZE,	U1	0.00283	0.00001	17	16.53614	>.500

Statistics for current covariance components model
```
--------------------------------------------------------
Deviance =      59.59795
Number of estimated parameters =     2
```

In general, the HLM2 results for this example closely approximate the more traditional results that would be obtained from a graphical examination of the likelihood function. (For this particular model, the likelihood mode is at zero.) Note, the value of the likelihood was still changing after 7850 iterations. Often, HLM2 converges after a relatively small number of iterations. When the number of iterations required is large, as in this case, it indicates that the estimation is moving toward a boundary condition. (In this example it is a variance estimate of zero for Tau.) This can be seen by comparing the starting value estimate for Tau, 0.02004, with the final estimate of 0.00001. (For a further discussion see p. 202 of Hierarchical Linear Models.)

9.4 Procedure for graphing equations

Note that in the case of graphing equations, the level-1 data file **must remain in the directory in which it was located when the SSM/MDM file was made, and it must keep the same filename.** This is because the graphing procedure requires access to the raw level-1 data.

HLM[2] provides graphing options to display the relationships between the outcome and the predictor(s). Below we provide a two-level example of a growth curve analysis of pro-deviant attitude for fourteen-year-old youth over a period of five years with data from the National Youth Survey (Elliot, Huizinga, & Menard, 1989; Raudenbush, 1999). This example is based on the data files NYS21.SAV and NYS22.SAV which can be found in the examples\chapter9 subfolder. As the graphing procedure requires access to the level-1 data file during analysis, the SSM file has to be made first.

In our example, the level-1 file, *NYS21.SAV*, has 1,066 observations collected from interviewing annually fourteen-year-old youths beginning in 1976:

ATTIT A nine-item scale assessing attitudes favorable to deviant behavior

    For each item, participants were asked how wrong (very wrong, wrong, a little bit wrong, not wrong at all) they believe it is for someone their age, for example, to damage and destroy property, use marijuana, use alcohol, sell hard drugs, or steal. The measure was positively skewed; so a logarithmic transformation was performed to reduce the skewness.

AGE16 Age of participant at a specific time minus 16

AGE16S AGE16 * AGE16

The level-2 data file, NYS22.SAV, consists of 241 youths and three variables per participant.

---

[2]Starting with version 5.04

FEMALE   An indicator for gender (1 = female, 0 = male)

MINORITY An indicator for ethnicity (1 = minority, 0 = other)

INCOME   Income

At level 1, we formulate a polynomial model of order 2 using AGE16 and AGE16S (see Figure 9.7) with FEMALE and MINORITY as covariates at level 2. The procedure for setting up the model is given in Section 2.5.2. We will ask HLM2 to graph the predicted values of pro-deviant attitude scores at different ages for different gender-by-ethnicity groups.

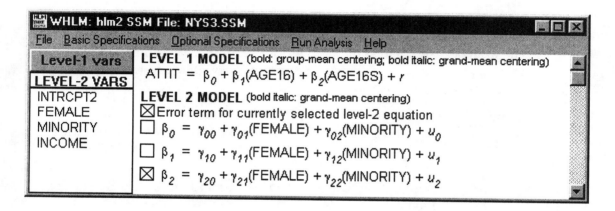

Figure 9.7
A polynomial model of order 2 with FEMALE and MINORITY as level-2 covariates

9.4.1 To prepare the graph

1. Select **Basic Specifications** to open the **Basic Model Specifications – HLM2** dialog box.

2. Click **Graph equations** to open the **Equation Graphing** dialog box (see Fig. 9.8).

3. Click **Yes** to **Graph equations?** (default) and enter a filename for the graph. The default name is **grapheq.geq**. Click **OK**.

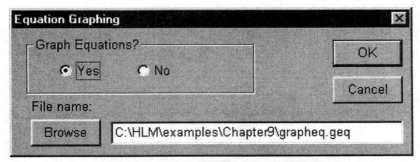

Figure 9.8   Equation Graphing dialog box

4. Enter a title and name the output filename, save the command file, and run the analysis as usual.

5. After the analysis has finished running, open the **File** menu and choose **Graph Equations**. Another **Equation Graphing – Specification** dialog box will open (see Fig. 9.9). Table 9.1 lists the definitions and options in the **Equation Graphing – Specification** dialog box. Note the linking numbers (1 through 9) in figure and table.

6. Select AGE16 in the **X focus Level-1** drop-down listbox to graph pro-deviant attitude score as a function of age.

7. Select **Entire Range** in the **For continuous x** drop-down listbox to include the entire range of age on the x-axis in the graph.

8. Click the selection button for **Smooth** for **Range of x focus** to display a smooth curve.

9. Click **1** and select **power of x/z**. An **Equation Graphing – power** dialog box will open (see Fig. 9.10).

10. The box to the left of the equal sign is for the transformed variable. Select AGE16S in the drop-down listbox. The box to the right is for the original variable. AGE16 will appear in the drop-down listbox. In this example, AGE16 is the only level-1 variable to select. Enter **2** in the box for the **power** to be raised (see Fig. 9.11). Click **OK**.

11. (Optional) Click **Select Range/Titles/Color** to specify the ranges for x- and y-axis (the default for each is the value computed), to enter legend and graph titles, and to select screen color (see Fig. 9.12). Enter **Fig. 1 Pro-deviant Attitude Score x Age x Gender x Ethnicity** into the **Graph title** box. Click **OK**.

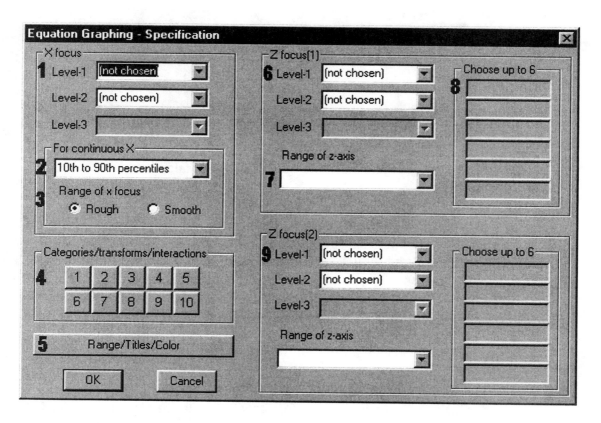

Figure 9.9   Equation Graphing – Specification dialog box

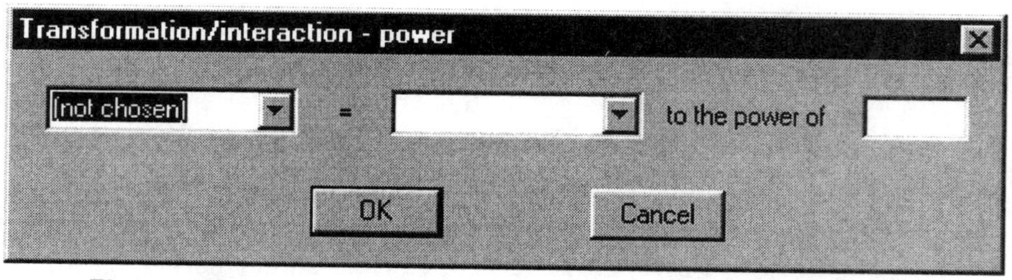

Figure 9.10   Transformation/interaction – power dialog box

Table 9.1   Options in the Equation Graphing – Specification dialog box

	Specification	Description	Options
1	X focus	Specify the variable to be displayed on the horizontal axis	1. level-1 predictor 2. level-2 predictor 3. level-3 predictor
2	For continuous X	Specify the maximum and minimum values of X to be displayed	1. 10th to 90th perc. (default) 2. 5th to 95th percentiles 3. 25th to 75th percentiles 4. $+/- 2$ s.e.'s 5. entire range
3	Range of x focus	Specify the type of curve displayed	1. rough (default) 2. smooth
4	Categories/ transforms/ interactions	Define categorical variable and specify the relation-ship(s) between the trans-formed and the original vars as well as interaction(s)	1. define categorical variable 2. interaction 3. power of x/z 4. square root 5. natural log
5	Range/	Specify the maximum and minimum values of X and Y to be displayed	Default for each is the value computed
	Titles/	Enter a graph title and/or axis titles	–
	Color	Select screen color	1. Color (default) 2. Black and white
6	Z focus (1)	Specify the first classification variable for X	1. level-1 predictor 2. level-2 predictor 3. level-3 predictor
7	Range of z-axis	Specify the specific values of Z focus (1) to be included	*If continuous:* 1. 25th and 75th percentiles 2. 25th/50th/75th perc. (default) 3. Averaged lower/upper quartiles 4. Choose up to six values *If discrete:* 1. Use the actual two values (default) 2. Choose one or two values
8	Choose up to 6	Enter 6 specific values for Z focus (1)	Six values for Z focus (1)
9	Z focus (2)	Specify the second classification variable for X	1. level-1 predictor 2. level-2 predictor 3. level-3 predictor

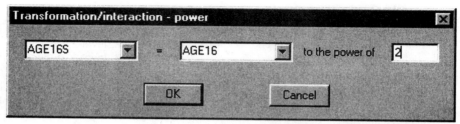

Figure 9.11   Equation for the transformed variable AGE16S

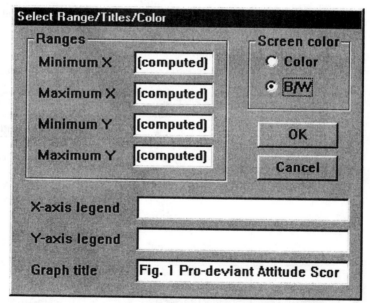

Figure 9.12   Select Range/Titles/Color dialog box

12. Select FEMALE in the **Z focus(1)** drop-down listbox to graph pro-deviant attitude score as a function of age for males and females. The option of **Use the actual two values** will appear in the text box for the **Range of z-axis** (see Fig. 9.13).

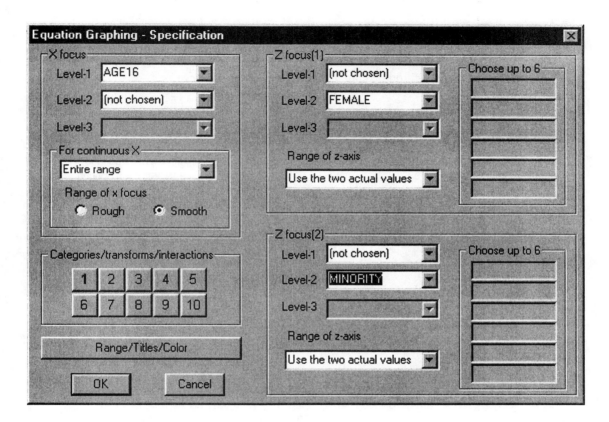

Figure 9.13   Specifications for the growth curve analysis example

13. Select MINORITY in the **Z focus(2)** drop-down listbox to graph pro-deviant attitude score as a function of age for minority and non-minority male and female youths. The option **Use the actual two values** appears in the text box for the **Range of z-axis** (see Fig. 9.13).

14. Click **OK**. A plot showing the relationship between pro-deviant attitude score and age for different gender-by-ethnicity groups will appear (see Fig. 9.14). The curves indicate that there is a nonmono-

tonic and nonlinear relationship between pro-deviant attitude score and age for minority and non-minority male youths over the five year period. Such relationship, however, does not exist for minority and non-minority female youths.

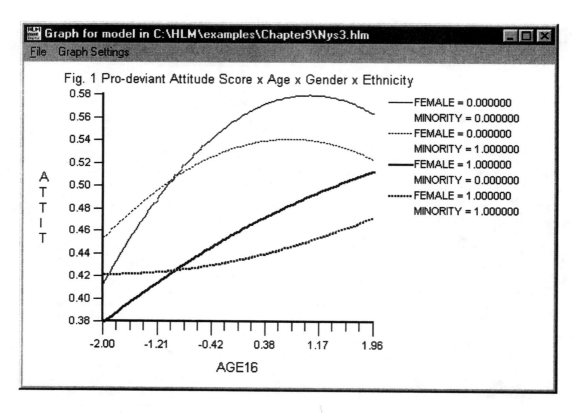

Figure 9.14
Plot showing the relationship between pro-deviant attitute score and age for different gender-by-ethnicity groups

15. Open the **File** menu and choose **Save color graph**. A **Save as** dialog box will open. Enter a filename for the file and click **OK**. The file is an Enhanced Windows Metafile (emf). One can insert this file into a Word document using **Insert Picture From file**. To print the graph, choose **Print black/white graph**.

16. (Optional) To make modifications, select **Graph Settings**. The **Equation Graphing** dialog box will appear.
17. Open the **File** menu and choose **Close**.

9.4.2 Using the define categorical variable option

Users can use the **define categorical variable** option of **Categories/transforms/ interactions** to prepare graphs illustrating the relationships between the predicted outcome with one or two variables for different categories of a third variable. For example, for the conditional model for the public school (eg2.hlm in the Examples\chapter4 folder) shown by Fig. 4.8 of Section 4.4, users can display a graph of growth curves of mathematics achievement over the six years for White (the reference group), Black, and Hispanic students. Fig. 9.15 below indicates that YEAR is chosen as the **X focus Level-1** and BLACK as the **Level-2 Z focus(1)** variable. Note that it makes no difference whether one selects **Black** or **Hispanic** as the **Level-2 Z focus(1)** variable.

9.4.3 To prepare the graph

1. Click **1** under the **Categories/transforms/interactions** section and select **define categorical variable**. A **Define categorical variable** dialog box will open (see Fig. 9.16).
2. Choose **Black** from the **Choose first category member from foci** drop-down listbox. **Hispanic** will appear in the **Possible choices** box.
3. Enter **White** in the **Name reference category** box.
4. Double click **Hispanic** to move it to the **Category members** box to tell the graphing subroutine that it is another category of the ethnicity variable (see Fig. 9.17).
5. Click **OK**.
6. Click **Select Range/Titles/Color** and enter **Fig. 2 Math. Ach. x Year x Ethnic Group** into the **Graph title** box, then click **OK**.
7. Click **OK** to close the **Equation Graphing – Specifications** dialog box. A plot showing the relationship between mathematics achievement and year for different ethnic groups will appear (see Fig. 9.18).

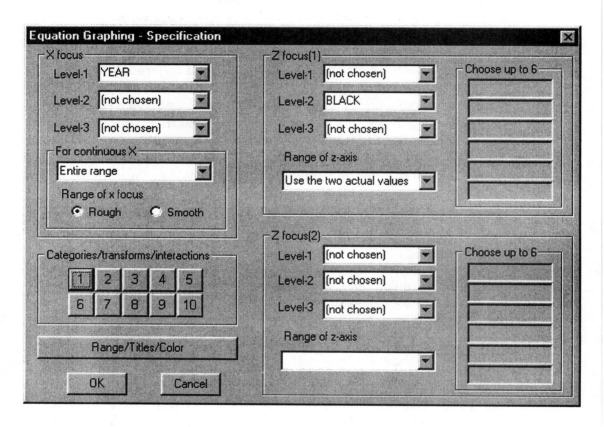

Figure 9.15
Specifications for the conditional model for the public school example

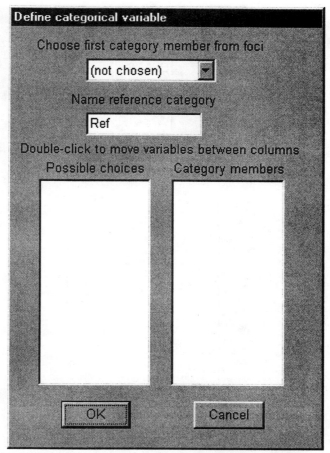

Figure 9.16   Define categorical variable dialog box

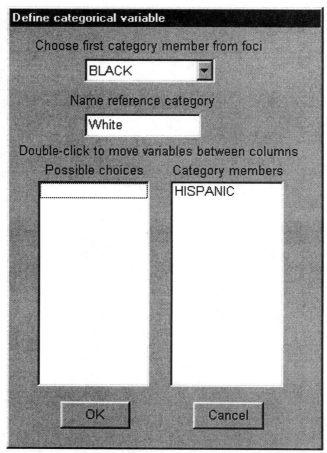

Figure 9.17   Specifications for the public school example

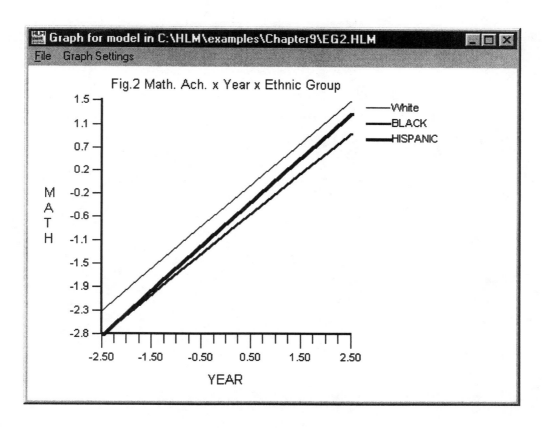

Figure 9.18
Plot showing the relationship between mathematics achievement and year for different ethnic groups

A   Using HLM2 in interactive and batch mode

This appendix describes and illustrates how to use HLM2 in interactive and batch mode to construct SSM files, to execute analyses based on the SSM file, and to specify a residual file to evaluate model fit. It also lists and describes command keywords and options. References are made to appropriate sections in the manual where the procedures are described in greater details.

A.1   Using HLM2 in interactive mode

A.1.1   Example: constructing an SSM file for the HS&B data using SPSS file input

In the computer session that follows, all responses entered by the user are typed in **boldface**. All text presented in *italics* represents additional commentary we have added to help the user understand what is happening in the program at that moment.

C:\HLM> **HLM2**   *(type the program name at the system prompt to start)*

```
Will you be starting with raw data?  Y
Is the input file a v-known file?  N
Enter type of raw data:
    for ASCII input              enter 1
    for SYSTAT .SYS file         enter 2
    for SAS V5 transport file    enter 3
    for SPSS file (UNIX or windows) enter 4
```

```
      for anything DBMSCOPY reads     enter 5
Type? 4
```

The "anything DBMSCOPY reads" prompt is only present on the PC version of HLM.

```
Input name of level-1 file: HSB1.SAV
```

```
Input name of level-2 file: HSB2.SAV
```

(See Section 2.5.1.1 for a description of the variables in HSB1.SAV and HSB2.SAV)

```
The available level-1 variables are:
For        ID enter 1    For MINORITY enter 2    For    FEMALE enter 3
For       SES enter 4    For MATHACH  enter 5
What variable is the group ID? 1
Please specify level-1 variable # 1 (enter 0 to end): 2
Please specify level-1 variable # 2 (enter 0 to end): 3
Please specify level-1 variable # 3 (enter 0 to end): 4
Please specify level-1 variable # 4 (enter 0 to end): 5

The available level-2 variables are:
For        ID enter 1    For      SIZE enter 2    For    SECTOR enter 3
For     PRACAD enter 4   For  DISCLIM enter 5     For    HIMNTY enter 6
For    MEANSES enter 7
What variable is the group ID? 1
Please specify level-2 variable # 1 (enter 0 to end): 2
Please specify level-2 variable # 2 (enter 0 to end): 3
Please specify level-2 variable # 3 (enter 0 to end): 4
Please specify level-2 variable # 4 (enter 0 to end): 5
Please specify level-2 variable # 5 (enter 0 to end): 6
Please specify level-2 variable # 6 (enter 0 to end): 7
Are there missing data in the level-1 file? N
```

Note, had we indicated that missing data were present in the level-1 file, the following additional prompts would have come to the screen:

```
Is the missing value the same for all variables?   Y
Do you want pair-wise or list-wise deletion? (enter p or l) L
```

See Section 2.6 on how HLM2 handles missing data.

```
Is there a level-1 weighting variable?  N
Is there a level-2 weighting variable?  N
```

Had we indicated that design weights been used, the user would be prompted with two questions about level-1 and level-2 weighting. The following is an example for level-1 population estimates (see Section 2.7 for details):

```
Is there a level-1 weighting variable?   Y
Will your generalizations principally involve level-1 effects or level-2 effects?
(enter 1 or 2)   1
Are the level-1 weights already normalized?   N
What is the name of the level-1 weighting variable?   LEV1WT
Is there a level-2 weighting variable?   N
```

Next is an example that uses weights at both levels:

```
Is there a level-1 weighting variable?   Y
Will your generalizations principally involve level-1 effects or level-2 effects?
(enter 1 or 2)   2
Are the level-1 weights already normalized?   N
What is the name of the level-1 weighting variable?   LEV1WT
Is there a level-2 weighting variable?   Y
Are the level-2 weights already normalized?   N
What is the name of the level-2 weighting variable?   LEV2WT
```

Section 2.7.3 describes when this weighting scheme is appropriate.

```
Enter name of SSM file:  HSB.SSM
```

HLM2 will now proceed to create a sufficient statistics file.

HLM2 will always write out a file named CREATESS.RSP that contains a log of the input responses given to create the SSM file. Should the SSM file appear incorrect for some reason, inspection of the log may provide a clue. Also, this file may be edited, renamed, and used as input to create a new SSM file. At the system prompt simply type, for example, HLM2L -R CREATESS.NEW where CREATESS.NEW is the edited, renamed input file. The interactive prompts will be quickly sent to the screen and "answered" (by responses read from the file CREATESS.NEW), and the program will proceed automatically to recreate the SSM file.

A.1.2 Example: constructing an SSM file for the HS&B data using ASCII file input

C:\HLM> **HLM2**

Will you be starting with raw data? **Y**

(type the program name at the system prompt to start)

Is the input file a v-known file? **N**

Enter type of raw data:

for ASCII input	enter 1
for SYSTAT .SYS file	enter 2
for SAS V5 transport file	enter 3
for SPSS file (UNIX or windows)	enter 4
for anything DBMSCOPY reads	enter 5

Type? **1**

Input number of level-1 variables (not including the character ID): **4**
Input format of level-1 file (the ID must be read as character data)
  format: **(A4,8X,4F12.3)**

See Section A.2 for rules for format statements.

Input name of level-1 file: **HSB1.DAT**

Input number of level-2 variables (not including the character ID): **6**
Input format of level-2 file (the ID must be read as character data)
  format: **(A2,8X,6F12.3)**
Input name of level-2 file: **HSB2.DAT**

Enter 8 character name for level-1 variable number 1: **MINORITY**
Enter 8 character name for level-1 variable number 2: **FEMALE**
Enter 8 character name for level-1 variable number 3: **SES**
Enter 8 character name for level-1 variable number 4: **MATHACH**

Enter 8 character name for level-2 variable number 1: **SIZE**
Enter 8 character name for level-2 variable number 2: **SECTOR**
Enter 8 character name for level-2 variable number 3: **PRACAD**
Enter 8 character name for level-2 variable number 4: **DISCLIM**
Enter 8 character name for level-2 variable number 5: **HIMINTY**
Enter 8 character name for level-2 variable number 6: **MEANSES**

Are there missing data in the level-1 file? **N**

Note, had we indicated that missing data were present in the level-1 file, the following additional prompts would have come to the screen:

```
Is the missing value the same for all variables?   Y
```

HLM2 allows for the possibility of a different missing value code for each variable. An answer of 'N' causes HLM2 to ask the user to enter a missing value for each level-1 variable.

```
Enter the number that represents missing data.   -99.0
Do you want pair-wise or list-wise deletion? (enter p or l)   L
Is there a level-1 weighting variable?   N
Is there a level-2 weighting variable?   N
```

See the section on weighting in the previous example in Section A.1.1 using SPSS input files and Section 2.7

```
Enter name of SSM file:   HSB.SSM
```

HLM2 will now proceed to create a sufficient statistics file.

A.2   Rules for Format Statements

While the input format statement for HLM resembles FORTRAN, only a subset of format options are acceptable. The user may specify:

1. The A format descriptor to read in the ID variable. This is followed by a number of columns that the ID occupies.
2. The F format descriptor (and the E, used to read in numbers with exponents). This may be preceded with a number specifying a repeat value, and needs to be followed by a decimal number specifying both the number of columns that variable occupies and the places to the right of the decimal.

   For example, 4F12.3 tells HLM that there are four variables in a row occupying 12 columns and that each value has three numbers to the right of the decimal point.
3. The X format descriptor. This is used to skip over a number of columns. For example, 8X skips over eight columns when reading the data.

4. The / (forward slash) format descriptor. This tells HLM to go to the next line of the input file to read data. It is used when each case takes more than one line in the raw data file.

5. Commas have to be inserted to separate each of the descriptors.

6. In contrast to FORTRAN, HLM does not allow nesting of parentheses (*e.g.*, (4A,4(1X,F12.3)) will not be read properly by HLM modules).

A.2.1 Example: executing an analysis using HSB.SSM

Here is an example of an HLM2 session in the interactive mode. At the system command line prompt, we first type the program name — HLM2 — followed by the name of the sufficient statistics file — HSB.SSM. The program now takes the user directly into the model specification process.

```
C:\HLM> HLM2 HSB.SSM

Do you want to do a non-linear analysis?  N (See Appendix C for non-linear analysis)

                 SPECIFYING A LEVEL-1 OUTCOME VARIABLE

Please specify a level-1 outcome variable

 The choices are:
 For MINORITY enter  1     For    FEMALE enter  2     For       SES enter  3
 For   MATHACH enter  4

What is the outcome variable:  4

Do you wish to:

    Examine means,variances,chi-squared, etc? Enter 1
    Specify an HLM model?                      Enter 2
    Define a new outcome variable?             Enter 3
    Exit?                                      Enter 4

What do you want to do?  2
```

Option 1 is detailed in Section A.6: "Preliminary exploratory analysis with HLM2."

Level-1 predictor variable specification

Which level-1 predictors do you wish to use?
 The choices are:
 For MINORITY enter 1   For   FEMALE enter 2   For   SES enter 3

 level-1 predictor? (Enter 0 to end)   **3**
 level-1 predictor? (Enter 0 to end)   **0**

 Do you want to center any level-1 predictors? **Y**
 (Enter 0 for no centering, enter 1 for group-mean, 2 for grand-mean)
 How do you want to center   SES? **1**

Note: we have selected group-mean centering for the level-1 predictor, SES.

 Do you want to set the level-1 intercept to zero in this analysis? **N**

An answer of "Y" here specifies a level-1 model without an intercept or constant term (see Section 2.9.6).

Level-2 predictor variable specification

Which level-2 variables do you wish to use?

 The choices are:
 For   SIZE enter 1   For   SECTOR enter 2   For   PRACAD enter 3
 For DISCLIM enter 4   For   HIMNTY enter 5   For   MEANSES enter 6

 Which level-2 predictors to model INTRCPT1?
  Level-2 predictor? (Enter 0 to end)   **2**
  Level-2 predictor? (Enter 0 to end)   **6**
  Level-2 predictor? (Enter 0 to end)   **0**

 Which level-2 predictors to model   SES slope?
  Level-2 predictor? (Enter 0 to end)   **2**
  Level-2 predictor? (Enter 0 to end)   **6**
  Level-2 predictor? (Enter 0 to end)   **0**

 Do you want to constrain the variances in any of the level-2 random
  effects to zero? **N**

An answer of "Y" here causes HLM2 to list out the level-1 coefficients and asks the user whether the corresponding random effect should be set to zero. An answer of "Y" to one of these probes is equivalent to specifying that level-1 coefficient as a fixed (or non-randomly varying) effect.

```
Do you want to center any level-2 predictors? N
```

Note: the user has the option of selecting grand-mean centering for each of the level-2 predictors.

```
                    ADDITIONAL PROGRAM FEATURES

Select the level-2 variables that you might consider for
inclusion as predictors in subsequent models.

The choices are:
For      SIZE enter  1    For    SECTOR enter  2    For    PRACAD enter  3
For   DISCLIM enter  4    For    HIMNTY enter  5    For   MEANSES enter  6

Which level-2 variables to model INTRCPT1?
 Level-2 variable? (Enter 0 to end)  1
 Level-2 variable? (Enter 0 to end)  3
 Level-2 variable? (Enter 0 to end)  4
 Level-2 variable? (Enter 0 to end)  5
 Level-2 variable? (Enter 0 to end)  0

Which level-2 variables to model      SES slope?
 Level-2 variable? (Enter 0 to end)  -1
```

For all of the level-2 predictors selected here, HLM2 will compute approximate "t-to-enter statistics" that can be used to guide specification of subsequent HLM2 models. Note, the code "–1" tells HLM2 to use for the SES slope model the same set of level-2 predictors as selected for the previous level-2 equation (i.e., the model for INTRCPT1).

```
Do you want to run this analysis with a heterogeneous sigma²? N
```

An answer of "Y" here causes HLM2 to ask which variables to be included in modeling sigma² (see Section 2.9.3 for details) and the number of macro- and micro-iterations. See also Section A.4.

```
Do you want to constrain any (more) of the gammas? N
```

An answer of "Y" here causes HLM2 to ask the user which gamma is to be constrained (see Section 2.9.8 and Section A.4).

```
Do you wish to use any of the optional hypothesis testing procedures? N
```

HLM2 allows multivariate hypothesis tests among the fixed effects and of variance-covariance components specification. The first example below illustrates how a multivariate hypothesis test for fixed effects is implemented (See Section 2.9.2 for details).

```
Do you wish to use any of the optional hypothesis testing procedures?   Y
Do you wish to specify a multivariate hypothesis for the fixed effects?  Y
Enter contrast value for INTRCPT1/INTRCPT2 (0 to ignore) 0
Enter contrast value for          /  SECTOR (0 to ignore) 1
Enter contrast value for          / MEANSES (0 to ignore) 0
Enter contrast value for     SES/INTRCPT2 (0 to ignore) 0
Enter contrast value for          /  SECTOR (0 to ignore) 0
Enter contrast value for          / MEANSES (0 to ignore) 0

Do you wish to specify another contrast as part of this hypothesis? Y
Enter contrast value for INTRCPT1/INTRCPT2 (0 to ignore)  0
Enter contrast value for          /  SECTOR (0 to ignore) 0
Enter contrast value for          / MEANSES (0 to ignore) 0
Enter contrast value for     SES/INTRCPT2 (0 to ignore) 0
Enter contrast value for          /  SECTOR (0 to ignore) 1
Enter contrast value for          / MEANSES (0 to ignore) 0

Do you wish to specify another contrast as part of this hypothesis?  N
Do you wish to specify another hypothesis?  N
```

The second example illustrates how a multivariate test of variance-covariance components is specified.

```
Do you wish to test the specification for the variance-covariance components
against an alternative model? (Note: the same fixed effects must be specified
in both models) Y
Enter the deviance statistic value   46512.978
Enter the number of variance-covariance parameters   4

                         OUTPUT SPECIFICATION

Do you want a residual file? N
```

Had we answered yes, we would be prompted:

```
Enter type of stat package you will use:
    for SYSTAT      enter 1
    for SAS         enter 2
    for SPSS        enter 3
Type? 3

Enter additional variables to go in residual file

The choices are:
For      SIZE enter  1    For    SECTOR enter  2    For    PRACAD enter  3
For   DISCLIM enter  4    For    HIMNTY enter  5    For   MEANSES enter  6

Level-2 variable? (Enter 0 to end)  1
Level-2 variable? (Enter 0 to end)  3
Level-2 variable? (Enter 0 to end)  5
Level-2 variable? (Enter 0 to end)  0
```

An SPSS syntax file, RESFIL2.SPS, will be written out as HLM2 runs. See Sections 2.5.4.1 and 2.5.4.2 on structure of the residual file and possible residual analyses.

```
How many iterations do you want to do?  100
Do you want to see OLS estimates for all of the level-2 units?  N
 Enter a problem title: Intercept and Slopes-as-Outcomes Model
 Enter name of output file: HSB1.OUT

Computing . . ., please wait

Starting values computed.  Iterations begun.
```

While the program is running, HLM2 sends the value of the likelihood function computed for each iteration to the screen. We have printed below just the first and last three. Because the change between the 60th and 61st iterations was very small, the program automatically terminated before the requested 100 iterations were computed. The sensitivity of this "automatic stopping value" can be controlled by the user. See Section A.3 for details.

Produced along with the output file is a file called NEWCMD.HLM which is a command file constructed by HLM based on the interactive session just completed.

```
Should you wish to terminate the iterations prior to convergence, enter cntl-c
The value of the likelihood function at iteration 1 = -2.325291E+004
The value of the likelihood function at iteration 2 = -2.325274E+004
The value of the likelihood function at iteration 3 = -2.325266E+004
  . . .
  . . .
  . . .
The value of the likelihood function at iteration 59 = -2.325186E+004
The value of the likelihood function at iteration 60 = -2.325186E+004
The value of the likelihood function at iteration 61 = -2.325186E+004
```

See Section 2.5.3 for an annotated example of the output for this model.

A.3 Using HLM in batch and/or interactive mode

HLM users can control which questions come to the screen by means of a command file. At one extreme, the command file is virtually empty and questions regarding every possible optional procedure or output will come to the screen. At the other extreme, the command file specifies the answer to every question that might arise, in which case the analysis is performed completely in batch mode. In between the two extremes are a large number of possibilities in which various questions are answered in the command file while other questions come to the screen. Hence, the execution can be partly batch and partly interactive.

The file presented below is produced along with the list output by HLM for the *Intercept and Slopes-as-Outcomes Model* using the HS&B data specified in Section A.2.1. The italicized comments provide a brief description of each command function. A complete overview of all the possible keywords and related options in the command file appears in Section A.4.

```
#This command file was run with hsb.ssm        Indicates which SSM was used.
NUMIT:100                                 Sets the maximum number of iterations.
STOPVAL:0.0000010000         Sets the criteria for automatically stopping the iterations.
NONLIN:N                                     Switch to do a non-linear analysis.
LEVEL1:MATHACH=INTRCPT1+SES,1+RANDOM                  Specifies the level-1 model.
LEVEL2:INTRCPT1=INTRCPT2+SECTOR+MEANSES+RANDOM/SIZE,PRACAD,DISCLIM,HIMNTY
LEVEL2:SES=INTRCPT2+SECTOR+MEANSES+RANDOM/SIZE,PRACAD,DISCLIM,HIMNTY
                    Specifies the level-2 model and other level-2 predictors for possible
                    inclusion in subsequent models for both INTRCPT1 and the SES slope.
```

RESFIL:N	Controls whether a residual file is created.
HETEROL1VAR:N	Specifies an analysis with a heterogeneous sigma^2.
ACCEL:5	Controls frequency of use of accelerator.
LVR:N	Specifies a latent variable regression model.
LEV1OLS:10	Controls the number of level-1 OLS regressions printed out.
HYPOTH:N	Disables some optional hypothesis testing procedures.
FIXTAU:3	Alternative options for generating starting values.
CONSTRAIN:N	Estimates a model with constrained level-2 coefficients.
OUTPUT:HSB1.OUT	File where HLM2 output will be saved.
TITLE:Intercept and Slopes-as-Outcome Model	Title on page 1 of output.

A user can rename the file with or without modification with a plain text (ASCII) editor for subsequent batch-mode application. For instance, he or she may request the program to print out all the level-1 OLS regressions by changing the LEV1OLS:10 to LEV1OLS:160 and rename the file to HSB2.HLM. The user can execute the analysis by typing

```
HLM2 HSB.SSM HSB2.HLM
```

at the system prompt. As the run is fully specified in the command file HSB2.HLM, no questions will come to the screen during its execution. This is full batch mode. The user may choose a fully interactive execution mode or an execution mode that is partly interactive and partly batch. With partly interactive, partly batch mode, some specification occurs in the command file; the program prompts the user with questions for the remaining program features. Some users may find this a useful way to suppress some of the questions relating to less often used features of the programs. Fully interactive mode is invoked when one of the programs is invoked without a second argument, *i.e.*,

```
HLM2 HSB.SSM
```

In this case, all of the possible questions will be asked with the exception relating to type of estimation used (mlf:y must be specified in the command file).

A.4 Using HLM2 in batch mode

A command file consists of a series of lines. Each line begins with a keyword followed by a colon, after the colon is the option chosen by the user, *i.e.*,

KEYWORD:OPTION

For example, HLM2 provides several optional hypothesis-testing procedures, described in detail in the Sections 2.9.2 through 2.9.4. Suppose the user does not wish to use these optional procedures in a given analysis. Then the following line would be included in the command file:

HYPOTH:N

The keyword HYPOTH concerns the optional hypothesis testing procedures; the option chosen ('N') indicates that the user does not wish to employ these procedures. Alternatively, the user might include the line:

HYPOTH:Y

This causes HLM2 to send the optional hypothesis testing menu to the screen during model specification in the interactive mode. Lines beginning with a pound sign (#; also called hash mark) are ignored and may be used to put comments in the command file.

HLM2, by default, has set up the following options unless the user specifies an alternative command file.

```
STOPVAL:0.0000010000              Sets convergence criterion to be 0.000001.
ACCEL:5                           Use accelerator once after five iterations.
FIXTAU:3
        Use the "standard" computer-generated values for the variances and covariances.
MLF:N                             Use the restricted maximum likelihood approach.
```

A.4.1 Table of keywords and options

Table A.1 presents the list of keywords and options recognized by HLM2.

A.5 Printing of Variance and Covariance Matrices for Fixed Effects and Level-2 Variances

The variance-covariance matrices of estimates of fixed effects and variance-covariance parameters based on HLM2 or HLM3 can be saved by checking "print variance-covariance matrices" in the **Basic Specifications** dialog

Table A.1   Keywords and options for the HLM2 command file

Keyword	Function	Option	Definition
LEVEL1	Level-1 model specification	INTRCPT1 +*VARNAME* +*VARNAME*,1 +*VARNAME*,2	Level-1 intercept Level-1 predictor (no centering) Level-1 predictor centered around group (or level-2 unit) mean Level-1 predictor centered around grand mean
		(Note: variable names may be specified in either upper or lower case.)	
LEVEL2	Level-2 model specification	INTRCPT2 +*VARNAME* +*VARNAME*,2 /*VARLIST*	Level-2 intercept Level-2 predictor (no centering) Level-2 predictor centered around grand mean List after the slash level-2 variables for exploratory analysis and "t-to-enter" statistics on subsequent runs. A slash without a subsequent variable list suppresses the interactive prompt.
NUMIT	Maximum number of iterations	*POSITIVE INTEGER*	
ACCEL	Controls iteration acceleration	*INTEGER* ≥ 3	Selects how often the accelerator is used. Default is 5.
LEV1OLS	Number of units for which OL equations should be printed	*POSITIVE INTEGER*	Default is 10.
CONSTRAIN	Constraining of gammas	N Y	No constraining Yes: two or more gammas will be constrained.

The program will prompt the user interactively to set the constraints. Alternatively, constraints can be set in the command file. For example, suppose the following coefficients were estimated: γ_{10}, γ_{11}, γ_{20}, γ_{21} and we wish to specify $\gamma_{20} = \gamma_{21}$, we add the following command line: CONSTRAIN: 0,0,1,1. *For the following coefficients:* γ_{00}, γ_{01}, γ_{02}, γ_{10}, γ_{11}, γ_{12}, *the command line:* CONSTRAIN: 0,1,2,0,1,2 *will have the following result:* $\gamma_{01} = \gamma_{11}$ *and* $\gamma_{02} = \gamma_{12}$.
Note all coefficients sharing the value "0" are free to be estimated independently.

Keyword	Function	Option	Definition
HYPOTH	Select optional hypothesis testing menu	Y N	Yes: sends optional hypothesis testing menu to the screen during interactive mode use. No. (Note, during batch execution, HYPOTH:N should be selected in order to suppress screen prompt. Select desired options through keywords below.)

Continues

Keyword	Function	Option	Definition
GAMMA#	Specifies a particular multivariate contrast to be tested		In any single run, HLM2 will test up to 5 multivariate hypotheses. Each hypothesis may consist of up to 5 contrasts.

Each contrast is specified by its own line in the command file. The contrast associated with the first hypothesis is specified with the keyword GAMMA1. *For example, the contrast shown in Fig. 2.31 can be specified by adding the following lines:*
GAMMA1:0.0,1.0,0.0,0.0,0.0,0.0
GAMMA1:0.0,0.0,0.0,0.0,1.0,0.0
For the second hypothesis, the keyword is GAMMA2 *and for the third it is* GAMMA3. *(See Section 2.9.2 for further discussion and illustration.)*

Keyword	Function	Option	Definition
HOMVAR	Test homogeneity of level-1 variance	N Y	No Yes
DEVIANCE	Deviance statistic from prior analysis	*POSITIVE REAL NUMBER*	$-2*$ log-likelihood at maximum-likelihood estimate
DF	Degrees of freedom associated with deviance statistic from prior analysis (use only if "DEVIANCE" has been specified)	*POSITIVE INTEGER*	
FIXTAU	Method of correcting unacceptable starting values	1 2 3 4 5	Set all off-diagonal elements to 0 Manually reset starting values Automatic fix-up (default) Terminate run Stop program even if starting values are acceptable; display starting values and then allow user to manually reset them.
HETEROL1VAR		N *VARLIST*	No Variable list
FIXSIGMA2	Controls σ^2	N *REAL NUMBER* > 0	Default: does not restrict σ^2. Fixes σ^2 to the specified value.
STOPVAL	Convergence criterion for maximum likelihood estimation	*POSITIVE REAL NUMBER*	Example: .000001. Can be specified to be more (or less) restrictive.

Continues

Keywords and options for the HLM2 command file (Continued)

Keyword	Function	Option	Definition
MLF	Controls maximum likeli-hood estimation method	N Y	No Yes, full maximum likelihood. Produces standard errors of $\mathbf{T}$ and σ^2.
RESFIL	Create a residual file	Y N */VARLIST*	Yes No List after the slash additional level-2 variables to be included in the residual file.
RESFILNAME	Name of residual file	*FILENAME*	Changes the default. Defaults are: RESFIL.CMD for SYSTAT, RESFIL.SYS for SPSS, and RESFIL.SAS for SAS.
RESFILTYPE	Type for residual file	SYSTAT SAS SPSS	Selects program type to be used in subsequent analysis of residual file.
PRINTVARIANCE-COVARIANCE	Output files containing the variance-covariance matrices of Tau and Gammas	N Y A	No Yes Append the files in consecutive runs. See Section A.5 for details.
TITLE			Program label up to 64 characters
OUTPUT	Filename of file that contains output	*FILENAME*	Will be written to disk; output will overwrite a file of same name.

Continues

Keyword	Function	Option	Definition
		The following keywords are specific to nonlinear, latent variable, and multiply-imputed data analysis	
NONLIN	Selects a nonlinear analysis	BERNOULLI POISSON BINOMIAL, *COUNTVAR* POISSON, *COUNTVAR* MULTINOMIAL, *COUNTVAR* ORDINAL, *COUNTVAR*	These options are explained in detail in Chapter 6.
MACROIT	Maximum number of macro iterations	*POSITIVE INTEGER*	Used in non-linear models
MICROIT	Maximum number of micro iterations	*POSITIVE INTEGER*	Used in non-linear models
STOPMACRO	Convergence criterion for change in parameters across macro iterations	*POSITIVE INTEGER*	
STOPMICRO	Convergence criterion for micro iterations	*POSITIVE REAL NUMBER*	Note: same function as STOPVAL in a linear analysis.
LAPLACE	Requests Laplace-6 iterations	N Y, *NO. OF ITERATIONS*	No Yes, maximum number of iterations; uses a sixth order approximation to the likelihood based on a Laplace transform for Bernoulli models. See Sections 5.6.3 and 6.8.2 for details.
LVR	Performs a latent variable regression	N I P O	No Ignore Predictor Outcome (See Section 9.1 for details)
PLAUSVALS	Selects a list of plausible values for multiple imputation application	*VARLIST*	See Section 9.2.1 for details.

box. The keyword PRINTVARIANCE-COVARIANCE facilitates the same purpose in batch mode.

The following gives a description of the files containing critical statistics and their variances that are provided by the program upon request.

Let:

$r =$ number of random effects at level-1

$f =$ number of fixed effects

$p =$ number of outcomes in a latent variable run

$pm =$ number of coefficients in a latent variable run

1. **For HLM2:**

   (a) TAUVC.DAT contains tau in r columns and r rows and then the inverse of the information matrix (the standard errors of tau are the square roots of the diagonals). The dimensions of this matrix are $r * (r + 1)/2 \times r * (r + 1)/2$.

   (b) GAMVC.DAT contains the gammas and the gamma variance-covariance matrix. After the gammas, there are f more rows of f entries containing the variance-covariance matrix.

   (c) GAMVCR.DAT contains the gamma and the gamma variance-covariance matrix used to compute the robust standard errors. After the gammas, there are f rows of f entries containing the variance-covariance matrix.

2. **For HGLM:**

   (a) TAUVC.DAT contains tau for the final unit-specific results in r columns and r rows and then the inverse of the information matrix (the standard errors of tau are the square roots of the diagonals). The dimensions of this matrix are $r * (r + 1)/2 \times r * (r + 1)/2$.

   (b) GAMVCUS.DAT contains the final unit-specific gammas and the gamma variance-covariance matrix. The gammas are in the first line and this line has f entries. Then there are f more rows of f entries containing the variance and covariance matrix.

(c) GAMVCPA.DAT contains the final unit-specific gammas and the gamma variance-covariance matrix. The gammas are in the first line and this line has f entries. Then there are f more rows of f entries containing the variance and covariance matrix.

(d) GAMVCPAR.DAT contains the final unit-specific gammas and the gamma variance-covariance matrix used to compute the population-averaged robust standard errors. The gammas are in the first line and this line has f entries. Then there are f more rows of f entries containing the variance and covariance matrix.

3. **For Bernoulli models, if Laplace iterations are requested:**

(e) GAMVCL.DAT contains the gammas and the variance-covariance matrix used to compute the Laplace standard errors. There are f rows of f entries containing the variance and covariance matrix.

4. **For latent variable regression:**

(a) LVRALPHA.DAT contains pm lines each containing a regression coefficient and its standard error. The order is the same as in the output table. The final p lines of p columns contain the $\mathrm{Var}(u^*)$ matrix printed in the list output.

5. **For plausible values analysis:**

(a) GAMVC.DAT (and GAMVCR.DAT and TAUVC.DAT) are from the last run and TAUVCPV.DAT, GAMVCPV.DAT, and GAMVCPVR.DAT are the PV average files.

All of the above files are created with an n(F15.7,1X) format. That is, each entry is fifteen characters wide with seven decimal places, followed by a space (blank character).

If the value of r or f or $r * (r + 1)/2$ exceeds 60, the line is split into two or more pieces.

A.6 Preliminary exploratory analysis with HLM2

The first option in the basic HLM2 menu "Examine means, variances, chi-squared, etc.?" provides a variety of statistics useful as we begin to formulate HLM problems. The use of this option is available only in interactive mode and a description of the output appears below.

```
HLM2 HSB.SSM

                 SPECIFYING A LEVEL-1 OUTCOME VARIABLE
Please specify a level-1 outcome variable

The choices are:
For MINORITY enter  1    For    FEMALE enter  2    For       SES enter  3
For  MATHACH enter  4 What is the outcome variable:   4

Do you wish to:

Examine means,variances,chi-squared, etc? Enter 1
Specify an HLM model?                      Enter 2
Define a new outcome variable?             Enter 3
Exit?                                      Enter 4

What do you want to do?   1
```

Below is the output that HLM2 sends to the screen.

```
The outcome variable is  MATHACH
```

potential level-1 predictors	mean univariate regression coefficient	ANOVA estimate of variance in regression coefficient	reliability	chi-squared	j
MEANS	12.74785	8.76642	0.90192	1618.70998	160
MINORITY	-2.72109	5.60227	0.30517	228.41290	136
FEMALE	-0.94302	0.27533	0.05944	143.41090	123
SES	2.10355	0.46634	0.17531	212.38315	160

```
0 level-2 units were deleted because of no variance in  MATHACH
```

The display above presents information from a series of univariate regressions conducted separately on each unit. The outcome variable selected for these regressions is displayed at the top (MATHACH). The row entitled MEANS *provides the statistics from a one-way* ANOVA *on the outcome variable in the 160 schools. The remaining lines summarize the result from the respective univariate regressions estimated separately in each school. The mean univariate coefficient averaged across the J schools is reported in the first column. Column 2 provides an* ANOVA-*type estimate of the parameter variability in these univariate coefficients. The average reliability and chi-squared test statistics for homogeneity among the univariate regressions are reported in the third and fourth columns.*

These data provide our first information about which level-1 coefficients might be specified as random. Though very preliminary results, they suggest that both MINORITY *and* SES *coefficients might be specified as random. Note, these are just univariate regression coefficients and are not adjusted for any other level-1 effects as they would be in a full level-1 model.*

```
Hit return to continue < HRt >

Do you wish to:

Examine correlations among univariate
coefficients and level-2 variables?        Enter 1
Specify an HLM model?                       Enter 2
Define a new outcome variable?              Enter 3
Exit?                                       Enter 4

What do you want to do?   1
```

At this point, the user identifies which of the univariate regression coefficients computed above are to be considered further. In this instance, we will choose all three. (The unit mean is automatically included.)

```
Please enter the level-1 univariate slopes you wish to estimate

The choices are:
For MINORITY enter  1   For   FEMALE enter  2   For      SES enter  3

level-1 predictor? (Enter 0 to end)   1
level-1 predictor? (Enter 0 to end)   2
level-1 predictor? (Enter 0 to end)   3
```

Next, we select the level-2 predictors that might be used to model the means and univariate regression slopes.

```
Please enter the level-2 predictors you wish to estimate

The choices are:

For      SIZE enter  1    For    SECTOR enter  2    For    PRACAD enter  3
For    DISCLIM enter  4    For    HIMINTY enter  5    For    MEANSES enter  6

level-2 predictor? (Enter 0 to end)   1
level-2 predictor? (Enter 0 to end)   2
level-2 predictor? (Enter 0 to end)   3
level-2 predictor? (Enter 0 to end)   4
level-2 predictor? (Enter 0 to end)   5
level-2 predictor? (Enter 0 to end)   6

The correlation matrix among level-1 univariate coefficients
(Diagonal elements are standard deviations)

Predictors MEANS    MINORITY    FEMALE       SES

MEANS      3.1177
MINORITY   0.1238    4.2846
FEMALE    -0.0639    0.0978    2.1522
SES        0.0135   -0.5121   -0.2078    1.6310

Hit return to continue < HRt >
```

*These are simple correlations and standard deviations among the univari-
ate regression coefficients estimated in the 160 schools.*

```
The correlation matrix among level-2 predictors
(Diagonal elements are standard deviations)

Predictors     SIZE      SECTOR     PRACAD    DISCLIM    HIMINTY    MEANSES

SIZE        629.5064
SECTOR       -0.4519    0.4976
PRACAD       -0.3150    0.6724    0.2559
DISCLIM       0.3554   -0.7125   -0.6119    0.9770
HIMINTY       0.1150    0.0494   -0.0792    0.0373    0.4479
MEANSES      -0.1296    0.3553    0.6491   -0.3493   -0.4056    0.4140

Hit return to continue < HRt >
```

These are simple correlations among the level-2 predictors.

APPENDIX A: USING HLM2 IN INTERACTIVE AND BATCH MODE

```
Correlations between level-2 predictors and level-1 univariate coefficients

Level-2          Level-1 univariate coefficients
Predictors     MEANS    MINORITY    FEMALE       SES

SIZE          -0.0982   -0.1862    -0.2591     0.2008
SECTOR         0.4492    0.3680     0.1199    -0.3977
PRACAD         0.6821    0.2152     0.0612    -0.2017
DISCLIM       -0.4678   -0.4343    -0.1038     0.3355
HIMINTY       -0.3752    0.0790    -0.0004    -0.1964
MEANSES        0.7847    0.0626     0.0576     0.0496

Hit return to continue < HRt >
```

The display above contains our first cross-level information. It presents information on the level-2 predictors that might be associated with the unit means and univariate regression coefficients. It suggests a list of candidate variables that might be included in the level-2 model for each level-1 coefficient. Again, this too is preliminary because the level-2 coefficients used here are univariate. Nonetheless they are informative.

```
Do you wish to:

Specify an HLM model?                  Enter 1
Define a new outcome variable?         Enter 2
Exit?                                  Enter 3

What do you want to do?   3
```

B Using HLM3 in interactive and batch mode

This appendix describes and illustrates how to use HLM3 in interactive and batch mode to construct SSM files, and to execute analyses based on the SSM file. It also lists and defines command keywords and options unique to HLM3. References are made to appropriate sections in the manual where the procedures are described in greater details.

As in the case of HLM2, formulation, estimation, and testing of models using HLM3 can be achieved in several ways: Windows mode (PC users only), interactive mode, or batch mode. Interactive execution guides the user through the steps of the analysis by posing questions and providing a menu of options. However, batch mode can be considerably faster once the user becomes skilled in working with the program. In between the two extremes — fully interactive and fully batch — is a range of execution modes that are partly interactive and partly batch. The degree to which the execution is automated (via batch mode) is controlled by the command file, as in the case of HLM2.

B.1 Using HLM3 in interactive mode

B.1.1 Example: constructing an SSM file for the public school data using SPSS file input

```
c:HLM> HLM3
```
(type the program name at the system prompt to start)

```
Will you be starting with raw data?   Y
```

263

```
Enter type of raw data:
    for ASCII input                    enter 1
    for SYSTAT .SYS file               enter 2
    for SAS V5 transport file          enter 3
    for SPSS file (UNIX or windows)    enter 4
    for anything DBMSCOPY reads        enter 5
Type?  4
```

The "anything DBMSCOPY reads" prompt is only present in the PC version of HLM.

```
Input name of level-1 file:  EG1.SAV
Input name of level-2 file:  EG2.SAV
Input name of level-3 file:  EG3.SAV
```

See Section 4.1.1.1 for a description of the variables in the data files.

```
The available level-1 variables are:

For      GID enter 1   For     PLID enter 2   For     YEAR enter 3
For    GRADE enter 4   For     MATH enter 5   For RETAINED enter 6

What variable is the level-3 ID?  1
What variable is the level-2 ID?  2
```

Note: there are two linking IDs in the level-1 data file.

```
Please specify level-1 variable # 1 (enter 0 to end):  3
Please specify level-1 variable # 2 (enter 0 to end):  4
Please specify level-1 variable # 3 (enter 0 to end):  5
Please specify level-1 variable # 4 (enter 0 to end):  6

The available level-2 variables are:

For      GID enter 1   For     PLID enter 2   For   FEMALE enter 3
For    BLACK enter 4   For HISPANIC enter 5

What variable is the level-3 ID?  1
What variable is the level-2 ID?  2
```

Note: there are two linking IDs in the level-2 data file.

```
Please specify level-2 variable # 1 (enter 0 to end):  3
Please specify level-2 variable # 2 (enter 0 to end):  4
Please specify level-2 variable # 3 (enter 0 to end):  5

The available level-3 variables are:

For      GID  enter  1    For     SIZE  enter  2    For    LOWINC  enter  3
For MOBILITY  enter  4

What variable is the level-3 ID?  1
```

Note: there is only one linking ID in the level-3 data file.

```
Please specify level-3 variable # 1 (enter 0 to end):  2
Please specify level-3 variable # 2 (enter 0 to end):  3
Please specify level-3 variable # 3 (enter 0 to end):  4

Are there missing data in the level-1 file?  N
```

Note: had we indicated that missing data were present in the level-1 file, the following additional prompts would have come to the screen.

```
Is the missing value the same for all variables?   Y
Do you want pair-wise or list-wise deletion? (enter p or l)  L
```

See Section 2.6 on how HLM2 handles missing data.

```
Is there a level-1 weighting variable?  N
```

Had we indicated that design weights had been used, the user would be prompted with a question regarding the name of the level-1 weighting variable (see Section 2.7 for details):

```
Note that HLM3 expects that the weight variable(s) is already normalized.
What is the name of the level-1 weighting variable?  GRADE

Enter name of ssm file:  EG.SSM
```

After the SSM file is computed, descriptive statistics for each file are sent to the screen. It is important to examine these carefully to guarantee that no errors were made in specifying the format of the data. HLM3 will save these statistics in a file named HLM3SSM.STS. These results are helpful as a reference and when constructing a descriptive table about the data for a written report.

B.1.2 Example: constructing an SSM file for the public school data using ASCII file input

`c:HLM> HLM3 -R EGASCII.RSP`

```
Will you be starting with raw data?  Enter type of raw data:
    for ASCII input              enter 1
    for SYSTAT .SYS file         enter 2
    for SAS V5 transport file    enter 3
    for SPSS file (UNIX or windows) enter 4
    for anything DBMSCOPY reads  enter 5

Type? 1

Input number of level-1 variables (not including the character ID): 4
The first A field must be a character level-3 id, the second, the level-2 id
Input format of level-1 file: (A4,1X,A9,1X,2F5.1,F7.3,F2.0)
```

See Section A.2 for rules for format statements.

```
Input name of level-1 file: EG1.DAT

Input number of level-2 variables (not including the character ID): 3
The first A field must be a character level-3 id, the second, the level-2 id
 Input format of level-2 file: (A4,1X,A9,3F2.0)
Input name of level-2 file: EG2.DAT

Input number of level-3 variables (not including the character ID): 3
The first A field must be a character level-3 id
 Input format of level-3 file: (A4,1X,3F7.1)
Input name of level-3 file: EG3.DAT

Enter 8 character name for level-1 variable number 1: YEAR
Enter 8 character name for level-1 variable number 2: GRADE
Enter 8 character name for level-1 variable number 3: MATH
Enter 8 character name for level-1 variable number 4: RETAINED

Enter 8 character name for level-2 variable number 1: GENDER
Enter 8 character name for level-2 variable number 2: BLACK
Enter 8 character name for level-2 variable number 3: HISPANIC

Enter 8 character name for level-3 variable number 1: SIZE
Enter 8 character name for level-3 variable number 2: LOWINC
Enter 8 character name for level-3 variable number 3: MOBILE
```

```
Are there missing data in the level-1 file?  N
Is there a level-1 weighting variable?  N

Enter name of ssm file:  EG.SSM
```

*HLM3 automatically creates a file named CREATESS.RSP that lists the
stream of responses typed by the user while creating the SSM file. The
CREATESS.RSP file has several uses. It can help the user discover errors in
the format or variable name specification. Once these are identified, CRE-
ATESS.RSP can be copied, for example, to NEWSS.RSP, and then edited.
Alternatively, if the user wishes to delete or add variables, the copy of CRE-
ATESS.RSP can be edited. To reconstruct the SSM file using this new set of
commands, simply type:*

```
HLM3 -R NEWSS.RSP
```

B.1.3   Example: Executing an analysis using EG.SSM

```
c:HLM>  HLM3 EG.SSM
```

*As in HLM2, the first argument, HLM3, tells the computer to execute the
three-level HLM program; the second argument specifies the SSM file to be
analyzed. An optional third argument specifies a command file that can
be used to automate aspects of model specification via batch-mode.*

```
Do you want to do a non-linear analysis?  N

                SPECIFYING A LEVEL-1 OUTCOME VARIABLE

Please specify a level-1 outcome variable

The choices are:
  For      YEAR enter  1    For    GRADE enter  2    For     MATH enter  3
  For RETAINED enter  4

What is the outcome variable:  3

                     SPECIFYING AN HLM MODEL

Level-1 predictor variable specification
```

```
Which level-1 predictors do you wish to use?

The choices are:
 For      YEAR enter  1    For     GRADE enter  2
 For RETAINED enter  4

level-1 predictor? (Enter 0 to end)   1
level-1 predictor? (Enter 0 to end)   0

Do you want to center any level-1 predictors?  N
```

If you answer "Y" here, the program will offer the option of centering each predictor around the unit mean, a_{jk}, or the grand mean, a....

```
Do you want to set the level-1 intercept to zero in this analysis?  N
```

This allows you to formulate a model with no intercept term at level 1.

```
Level-2 predictor variable specification

Which level-2 variables do you wish to use?

The choices are:
 For     FEMALE enter  1    For      BLACK enter  2    For HISPANIC enter  3

Which level-2 predictor to model INTRCPT1, P0?
 Level-2 predictor? (Enter 0 to end)   0
Which level-2 predictor to model      YEAR, P1 slope?
 Level-2 predictor? (Enter 0 to end)   0
Do you want to set the level-2 intercept to zero for INTRCPT1, P0?  N
```

This allows you to formulate a model with no intercept term at level 2.

```
Do you want to set the level-2 intercept to zero for      YEAR, P1?  N

Do you want to constrain the variances in any of the level-2 random
 effect to zero?  N
```

If you answer "Y" here, HLM3 will allow you to fix one or more level-2 variances (and associated covariances) to zero. Through this process the corresponding level-2 outcome is specified as fixed (no predictors) or non-randomly varying (some predictors included.) Notice that the model *above contains no level-2 predictors. Had level-2 predictors been included, the user would have been prompted about possible centering options. The choices are: centering around the group mean, $X_{\cdot k}$, centering around the grand mean, $X_{\cdot\cdot}$, or no centering.*

```
Level-3 predictor variable specification

Which level-3 predictors do you wish to use?

The choices are:
  For     SIZE enter  1    For   LOWINC enter  2    For MOBILITY enter  3

Which level-3 predictors to model INTRCPT1/INTRCPT2, B00?
Level-3 predictor? (Enter 0 to end)  0
Which level-3 predictors to model     YEAR/INTRCPT2, B10 slope?
Level-3 predictor? (Enter 0 to end)  0
```

Notice also that this model contains no level-3 predictors. Had level-3 predictors been included, the user would have been prompted about possible centering options. The choices are: centering around the grand mean, $W_{\cdot}$, or no centering.

```
Do you want to constrain the variances in any of the level-3 random
 effect to zero?  N
```

By answering "Y" here, you can specify level-3 outcomes as fixed or non-randomly varying.

```
                    ADDITIONAL PROGRAM FEATURES

Select the level-2 variables that you might consider for
inclusion as predictors in subsequent models.

The choices are:
  For    FEMALE enter  1    For    BLACK enter  2    For HISPANIC enter  3

Which level-2 variables to model INTRCPT1, P0?
Level-2 predictor? (Enter 0 to end)   1
Level-2 predictor? (Enter 0 to end)   2
Level-2 predictor? (Enter 0 to end)   3

Which level-2 variables to model     YEAR, P1 slope?
Level-2 predictor? (Enter 0 to end)  -1
```

As in HLM2, HLM3 will interpret the response of "−1" to repeat the selections made for the previous prompt, i.e., 1, 2, 3.

```
Select the level-3 predictor variables that you might consider for
inclusion as predictors in subsequent models.

The choices are:
 For     SIZE enter  1    For   LOWINC enter  2    For MOBILITY enter  3

Which level-3 variables to model INTRCPT1/INTRCPT2, B00?
 Level-3 predictor? (Enter 0 to end)  1
 Level-3 predictor? (Enter 0 to end)  2
 Level-3 predictor? (Enter 0 to end)  3

Which level-3 variables to model     YEAR/INTRCPT2, B10 slope?
 Level-3 predictor? (Enter 0 to end)  1
 Level-3 predictor? (Enter 0 to end)  2
 Level-3 predictor? (Enter 0 to end)  3

Do you want to constrain any (more) of the gammas? N
Do you wish to use any of the optional hypothesis testing procedures? N
```

The options available here are a multivariate hypothesis test for the fixed effects and a likelihood ratio test for comparison of nested models.

```
Do you want to do a latent variable regression on tau(beta)? N

                         OUTPUT SPECIFICATION

Do you want a level-2 residual file? Y

Enter additional variables to go in residual file

The choices are:
 For   FEMALE enter  1    For    BLACK enter  2    For HISPANIC enter  3

 Level-2 variable? (Enter 0 to end)  0
Do you want a level-3 residual file? Y

Enter additional variables to go in residual file

The choices are:
 For     SIZE enter  1    For   LOWINC enter  2    For MOBILITY enter  3

 Level-3 variable? (Enter 0 to end)  0
```

```
Enter type of stat package you will use:
   for SYSTAT      enter 1
   for SAS         enter 2
   for SPSS        enter 3
Type? 3

How many iterations do you want to do? 100
Enter a problem title: Unconditional Linear Growth Model
Enter name of output file: EG1.OUT

Computing . . ., please wait
Starting values computed.  Iterations begun.
Should you wish to terminate the iterations prior to convergence, enter cntl-c
The value of the likelihood function at iteration 1 = -8.169527E+003
The value of the likelihood function at iteration 2 = -8.165377E+003
The value of the likelihood function at iteration 3 = -8.165024E+003
The value of the likelihood function at iteration 4 = -8.164872E+003
The value of the likelihood function at iteration 5 = -8.164748E+003
The value of the likelihood function at iteration 6 = -8.163118E+003
The value of the likelihood function at iteration 7 = -8.163116E+003
The value of the likelihood function at iteration 8 = -8.163116E+003
The value of the likelihood function at iteration 9 = -8.163116E+003
```

See Section 4.2.1 for an annotated output of EG1.OUT.

B.2   Using HLM3 in batch mode

The command file structure for HLM3 closely parallels that of HLM2. Each line begins with a keyword followed by a colon. After the colon is the option chosen by the user, *i.e.*,

KEYWORD:OPTION

As with HLM2, a pound sign (#; also called hash mark) as the first character of a line can be used to introduce a comment into the command file.

The following keywords have the same definitions and options in HLM3 as in HLM2 (see Table A.1):

ACCEL	CONSTRAIN	DEVIANCE	DF	FIXTAU
FIXSIGMA2	GAMMA#	HYPOTH	LAPLACE	MACROIT

```
MICROIT         NONLIN        NUMIT         OUTPUT        PLAUSVALS
PRINTVARIANCE-COVARIANCE RESFIL          RESFILNAME    RESFILTYPE
SIGMA2          STOPMACRO     STOPMICRO     STOPVAL       TITLE
```

The following keywords are available only for HLM2:

```
LEV1OLS        HOMVAR        HETEROL1VAR   MLF           LVR
```

B.2.1 Table of keywords and options

Table B.1 presents the list of keywords and options unique to HLM3.

B.3 Printing of Variance and Covariance Matrices

Besides the files described in Section A.5, HLM3 can provide the following files upon request.

Note that issuing this request by adding the command line

PRINTVARIANCE-COVARIANCE:Y

to the command file will produce statistics for both tau(pi) and tau(beta).

Let:

$r = $ number of random effects at level-1

$r2 = $ number of random effects at level-2

1. **For HLM3:**

   TAUVC.DAT contains tau (tau(pi)) in r columns and r rows, the next $r2$ lines are the tau(beta), and then the inverse of the information matrix (the standard errors of tau(s) are the square roots of the diagonals).

   The dimensions of this matrix are $(r * (r + 1)/2 + r2 * (r2 + 1)/2) \times (r * (r + 1)/2 + r2 * (r2 + 1)/2)$.

Table B.1   Keywords and/or options unique to the HLM3 command file

Keyword	Function	Option	Definition
LEVEL1	Level-1 model specification	INTRCPT1	Level-1 intercept
		$+VARNAME$	Level-1 predictor (no centering)
		$+VARNAME$,1	Level-1 predictor centered around unit mean $a_{.jk}$
		$+VARNAME$,2	Level-1 predictor centered around grand mean $a_{...}$
(Note: variable names may be specified in either upper or lower case)			
LEVEL2	Level-2 model specification	INTRCPT2	Level-2 intercept
		$+VARNAME$	Level-2 predictor (no centering)
		$+VARNAME$,1	Level-2 predictor centered around group mean, $X_{.k}$
		$+VARNAME$,2	Level-2 predictor centered around grand mean, $X_{..}$
		/VARLIST	List after the slash level-2 variables for exploratory analysis and "t-to-enter statistics" on subsequent runs. A slash without a subsequent variable list suppresses the interactive prompt.
LEVEL3	Level-3 model specification	INTRCPT3	Level-3 intercept (must be included in the level-3 model)
		$+VARNAME$	Level-3 predictor (no centering)
		$+VARNAME$,2	Level-3 predictor centered around grand mean W.
		/VARLIST	List after the slash level-3 variables for exploratory analysis and "t-to-enter statistics" on subsequent runs. A slash without a subsequent variable list suppresses the interactive prompt.

Continues

Keyword	Function	Option	Definition
RESFIL2	Create a residual file	Y N /VARLIST	Yes No List after the slash additional level-2 variables to be included in the residual file.
RESFIL2NAME	Name of residual file	FILENAME	Changes the default. Defaults are: RESFIL.CMD for SYSTAT, RESFIL.SYS for SPSS, and RESFIL.SAS for SAS.
RESFIL3	Create a residual file	Y N /VARLIST	Yes No List after the slash additional level-2 variables to be included in the residual file.
RESFIL3NAME	Name of residual file	FILENAME	Changes the default. Defaults are: RESFIL.CMD for SYSTAT, RESFIL.SYS for SPSS, and RESFIL.SAS for SAS.
RESFILTYPE	Type for residual file	SYSTAT SAS SPSS	Selects program type to be used in subsequent analysis of residual file.
FIXTAU2	Method of correcting unacceptable starting values for $\mathbf{T}_\pi$	1 2 3 4 5	Set all off-diagonal elements to 0. Manually reset starting values. Automatic fix-up. Terminate run. Stop program after computing starting values even if acceptable; display starting values and then allow user to manually reset them.
FIXTAU3	Method of correcting unacceptable starting values for $\mathbf{T}_\beta$	1 2 3 4 5	Set all off-diagonal elements to 0. Manually reset starting values. Automatic fix-up. Terminate run. Stop program after computing starting values even if acceptable; display starting values and then allow user to manually reset them.
LVR-BETA	Performs a latent variable regression	N P,O	No P for predictor(s); O for outcome(s) See Section 9.1 for details.

2. **For three-level HGLM:**

TAUVC.DAT has the same format as the one for HLM2. The tau(s) are the final unit-specific results.

The files for the gammas have the identical structure as those for two-level models (see Section A.5).

All files are created with an n(F15.7,1X) format. That is, each entry is fifteen characters wide with seven decimal places, followed by a space (blank character).

If the value of r or $r2$ or $r * (r + 1)/2 + r2 * (r2 + 1)/2$ exceeds 60, the line is split into two or more pieces.

C Using HGLM in interactive and batch mode

This appendix describes and illustrates how to use HGLM in interactive and batch mode to execute analyses based on the SSM files. References are made to appropriate sections in the manual where the procedures are described in greater details.

C.1 Example: Executing an analysis using THAIUGRP.SSM

Here is an example of an HLM2 session in the interactive mode. At the system command line prompt, we first type the program name — HLM2 — followed by the name of the sufficient statistics file — THAIUGRP.SSM. The program now takes the user directly into the model specification process.

```
c:HLM>  HLM2 THAIUGRP.SSM

Do you want to do a non-linear analysis?  Y

Enter type of non-linear analysis:
```

See Chapter 5 for details regarding type of non-linear analysis.

```
        1) Bernoulli (0 or 1)
        2) Binomial (count)
        3) Poisson   (constant exposure)
        4) Poisson   (variable exposure)
        5) Multinomial
        6) Ordinal

type of analysis: 1
```

As mentioned, with one binary outcome per level-1 unit, the model choice is "1" (Bernoulli).

If "2" (Binomial) is chosen, the user will be asked:

```
For the non-linear analysis, which variable indicates the number of trials?
```

If "4" (Poisson (variable exposure)) is chosen, the user will be asked:

```
For the non-linear analysis, which variable indicates the exposure?
```

If "4" (Multinomial) or "5" (Ordinal) is chosen, the user will be asked:

```
How many categories does the "OUTCOME" have?

Enter maximum number of macro iterations: 25
Enter maximum number of micro iterations: 20
```

Specifying 25 macro iterations sets an upper limit; if, after the 25th iteration the algorithm has not converged, the program will nonetheless terminate and print the results at that iteration. Similarly, setting 20 as the number of micro iterations insures that, after 20 micro iterations, the current macro iteration will terminate even if the micro iteration convergence criterion has not been met.

```
Do you wish to allow over-dispersion at level 1? N
```

An answer of "Y" here allows a user to estimate a level-1 dispersion parameter σ^2. If the assumption of no dispersion holds, $sigma^2 = 1.0$. If the data are over-dispersed, $\sigma^2 > 1.0$; if the data are under-dispersed, $\sigma^2 < 1.0$.

```
Do you want to do the Laplace-6 iterations? N
```

An answer of "Y" here allows a user to obtain a highly accurate Laplace approximation to the maximum likelihood. See Sections 5.6.3 and 6.8.2. The user will be prompted to enter maximum number of Laplace macro iterations.

SPECIFYING A LEVEL-1 OUTCOME VARIABLE

Please specify a level-1 outcome variable

The choices are:

For   MALE enter 1   For   PPED enter 2   For   REP1 enter 3

What is the outcome variable: **3**

Do you wish to:

    Examine means,variances,chi-squared, etc? Enter 1
    Specify an HLM model?   Enter 2
    Define a new outcome variable?   Enter 3
    Exit?   Enter 4
What do you want to do? **2**

SPECIFYING AN HLM MODEL

Level-1 predictor variable specification

Which level-1 predictors do you wish to use?

The choices are:

For   MALE enter 1   For   PPED enter 2

  level-1 predictor? (Enter 0 to end) **1**
  level-1 predictor? (Enter 0 to end) **2**

Thus, we have set up a level-1 model with repetition (REP1) as the outcome and with gender (MALE) and pre-primary experience (PPED) as predictors.

Do you want to center any level-1 predictors? **N**

Do you want to set the level-1 intercept to zero in this analysis? **N**

Level-2 predictor variable specification

Which level-2 variables do you wish to use?

The choices are:

For   MSESC enter   1

Which level-2 predictors to model INTRCPT1?
  Level-2 predictor? (Enter 0 to end) **1**

```
Which level-2 predictors to model     MALE slope?
  Level-2 predictor? (Enter 0 to end)  0

Which level-2 predictors to model     PPED slope?
  Level-2 predictor? (Enter 0 to end)  0
```

Thus we have modeled the level-1 intercept as depending on the mean SES (MSESC) of the school. The coefficients associated with gender and pre-primary experience are fixed. Mean SES has been centered around its grand mean.

```
Do you want to constrain the variances in any of the level-2 random
effects to zero? Y

  Do you want to fix INTRCPT1?   N
  Do you want to fix     MALE?   Y
  Do you want to fix     PPED?   Y

  Do you want to center any level-2 predictors?  Y

  (Enter 0 for no centering, 2 for grand-mean)
  How do you want to center    MSESC? 2
```

                    ADDITIONAL PROGRAM FEATURES

```
Select the level-2 variables that you might consider for
inclusion as predictors in subsequent models.

  The choices are:
  For    MSESC enter   1

Which level-2 variables to model INTRCPT1?
  Level-2 variable? (Enter 0 to end)   0

Do you want to constrain any (more) of the gammas?  N
Do you wish to use any of the optional hypothesis testing procedures?  N
Do you want to do a latent variable regression?  Y
Setting method of estimation to full.

Enter o for outcome, p for predictor, or i to ignore
How do you want to model INTRCPT1?  P
```

                       OUTPUT SPECIFICATION

Do you want a residual file? **Y**

Enter type of stat package you will use:
    for SYSTAT   enter 1
    for SAS   enter 2
    for SPSS   enter 3

Type? **3**

Enter additional variables to go in residual file
 The choices are:
 For   MSESC enter 1

 Level-2 variable? (Enter 0 to end) **1**

Do you want to see OLS estimates for all of the level-2 units? **N**

 Enter a problem title: **Bernoulli output, Thailand data**
 Enter name of output file: **THAIBERN.OUT**

MACRO ITERATION 1

Starting values computed. Iterations begun.
Should you wish to terminate the iterations prior to convergence, enter cntl-c
The value of the likelihood function at iteration 1 = -2.400265E+003
The value of the likelihood function at iteration 2 = -2.399651E+003
The value of the likelihood function at iteration 3 = -2.399620E+003
The value of the likelihood function at iteration 4 = -2.399614E+003
The value of the likelihood function at iteration 5 = -2.399612E+003
The value of the likelihood function at iteration 6 = -2.399612E+003
The value of the likelihood function at iteration 7 = -2.399612E+003

Macro iteration number 1 has converged after seven micro iterations. This macro iteration actually computes the linear-model estimates (using the identity link function as if the level-1 errors were assumed normal). These results are then transformed and input to start macro iteration 2, which is, in fact, the first non-linear iteration.

MACRO ITERATION 2

Starting values computed. Iterations begun.
Should you wish to terminate the iterations prior to convergence, enter cntl-c
The value of the likelihood function at iteration 1 = -1.067218E+004
The value of the likelihood function at iteration 2 = -1.013726E+004
The value of the likelihood function at iteration 3 = -1.011008E+004

```
The value of the likelihood function at iteration 4 = -1.010428E+004
The value of the likelihood function at iteration 5 = -1.010265E+004
The value of the likelihood function at iteration 6 = -1.010193E+004
The value of the likelihood function at iteration 7 = -1.010188E+004
The value of the likelihood function at iteration 8 = -1.010188E+004
The value of the likelihood function at iteration 9 = -1.010187E+004
The value of the likelihood function at iteration 10 = -1.010187E+004
The value of the likelihood function at iteration 11 = -1.010187E+004
The value of the likelihood function at iteration 12 = -1.010187E+004
```

Macro interaction 2, the first non-linear macro iteration, converged after twelve micro iterations.

MACRO ITERATION 3

```
Starting values computed.  Iterations begun.
Should you wish to terminate the iterations prior to convergence, enter cntl-c
The value of the likelihood function at iteration 1 = -9.954836E+003
The value of the likelihood function at iteration 2 = -9.954596E+003
The value of the likelihood function at iteration 3 = -9.954567E+003
The value of the likelihood function at iteration 4 = -9.954558E+003
The value of the likelihood function at iteration 5 = -9.954555E+003
The value of the likelihood function at iteration 6 = -9.954554E+003
The value of the likelihood function at iteration 7 = -9.954553E+003
```

MACRO ITERATION 4

```
Starting values computed.  Iterations begun.
Should you wish to terminate the iterations prior to convergence, enter cntl-c
The value of the likelihood function at iteration 1 = -1.000019E+004
The value of the likelihood function at iteration 2 = -1.000018E+004
The value of the likelihood function at iteration 3 = -1.000018E+004
The value of the likelihood function at iteration 4 = -1.000017E+004
The value of the likelihood function at iteration 5 = -1.000017E+004
The value of the likelihood function at iteration 6 = -1.000017E+004
The value of the likelihood function at iteration 7 = -1.000017E+004
```

MACRO ITERATION 5

```
Starting values computed.  Iterations begun.
Should you wish to terminate the iterations prior to convergence, enter cntl-c
The value of the likelihood function at iteration 1 = -1.000347E+004
The value of the likelihood function at iteration 2 = -1.000347E+004
The value of the likelihood function at iteration 3 = -1.000347E+004
```

APPENDIX C: USING HGLM IN INTERACTIVE AND BATCH MODE

```
Starting values computed.  Iterations begun.
Should you wish to terminate the iterations prior to convergence, enter cntl-c
The value of the likelihood function at iteration 1 = -1.000375E+004
The value of the likelihood function at iteration 2 = -1.000375E+004
```

```
Starting values computed.  Iterations begun.
Should you wish to terminate the iterations prior to convergence, enter cntl-c
The value of the likelihood function at iteration 1 = -1.000375E+004
The value of the likelihood function at iteration 2 = -1.000375E+004
```

Note that macro iteration 7 converged with just 2 micro iterations. Also, the change in parameter estimates between macro iterations 6 and 7 was found negligible (less than the criterion for convergence) so that macro iteration 8 was the final "unit-specific" macro iteration. One final "population average" iteration is computed, and screen output for that is given below.

```
Starting values computed.  Iterations begun.
Should you wish to terminate the iterations prior to convergence, enter cntl-c
The value of the likelihood function at iteration 1 = -1.000374E+004
The value of the likelihood function at iteration 2 = -1.000374E+004
```

Thus concludes the interactive terminal session. See Section 6.2 for an annotated output for this run.

The interactive session annotated above produced the following command file (NEWCMD.HLM).

```
#This command file was run with thaiugrp.ssm
LEVEL1:REP1=INTRCPT1+SEX+PPED+RANDOM
LEVEL2:INTRCPT1=INTRCPT2+MSESC,2+RANDOM/
LEVEL2:SEX=INTRCPT2/
LEVEL2:PPED=INTRCPT2/
RESFIL:N
STOPMICRO:0.000010
STOPMACRO:0.000100
MACROIT:25
MICROIT:20
```

```
NONLIN:BERNOULLI
LEV1OLS:0
HYPOTH:n
FIXTAU:3
CONSTRAIN:N
OUTPUT:thaibern.out
TITLE:Bernoulli output, Thailand data
ACCEL:5
```

If one now types at the system prompt:

HLM2 THAIUGRP.SSM NEWCMD.HLM

the output above would be reproduced. It is a good idea to rename the NEWCMD.HLM file if it is to be edited and re-used. Each execution of the program will produce a NEWCMD.HLM file that will overwrite the old one.

Note that the NEWCMD.HLM file above is similar to the same file produced by a linear-model analysis, with the addition of the following lines:

`STOPMICRO:0.000010`	*(default convergence criterion for micro iterations)*
`STOPMACRO:0.000100`	*(default convergence criterion for macro iterations)*
`MACROIT:25`	*(maximum number of macro iterations)*
`MICROIT:20`	*(maximum number if micro iterations per macro iteration)*
`NONLIN:BERNOULLI`	*(type of non-linear model)*

See Tables A.1 and B.1 for a description of the keywords and options.

D   Using HMLM in interactive and batch mode

This appendix describes prompts and commands for creating MDM files and executing analyses based on the MDM files. References are made to appropriate sections in the manual where the procedures are described in greater details. To start HMLM or HMLM2, type HMLM or HMLM2 at the system prompt.

D.1   Constructing an MDM file

The procedure for MDM creation is similar to the one for SSM (see Sections A.1.1 and A.1.2). The only difference is that the user will be prompted with questions regarding the number of occasions contained in the data and which variables are the indicator variables. To create an MDM file using the NYS data sets described in Section 8.1.1, for example, HMLM will display the following prompts to request the needed information.

```
How many occasions are contained in the data? 5

Please select the 5 indicator variables:
Is    ATTIT    an indicator variable?   N
Is      AGE    an indicator variable?   N
Is    AGE11    an indicator variable?   N
Is    AGE13    an indicator variable?   N
Is   AGE11S    an indicator variable?   N
Is   AGE13S    an indicator variable?   N
Is     IND1    an indicator variable?   Y
Is     IND2    an indicator variable?   Y
Is     IND3    an indicator variable?   Y
```

```
Is    IND4    an indicator variable?  Y
Is    IND5    an indicator variable?  Y
```

D.2   Executing analyses based on MDM files

The procedure for executing analyses based on MDM files is similar to the one based on SSM files. A major difference is that only coefficients associated with variables that are invariant across all level-1 units, *i.e.*, their values do not vary across the units, can be specified as random. Otherwise, the coefficients will be automatically set as non-random by the program. The following displays prompts unique to HMLM and HMLM2 for the NYS example described in Section 8.2.

c:HLM> **HMLM NYS.MDM**

```
Enter type HMLM analysis:
```

See Chapter 7 for details regarding type of HMLM analysis.

```
1) Unrestricted
2) Random effects model with homogeneous level-1 variance
3) Random effects model with heterogeneous level-1 variance
4) Random effects model with log-linear model for level-1 variance
5) Random effects model with first-order autoregressive level-1 variance

type of analysis: 3
```

For choices 2 to 5, the user will be prompted:

```
Do you want to skip the unrestricted iterations?  N
```

If "4" (log-linear model for level-1 variance) is chosen, HMLM will ask the user to enter variables to model sigma^2, for example:

```
Should VAR1 be in C?
```

An interactive session will output a command file NEWCMD.MLM. An example for one of the analyses discussed in Section 8.2 is given below.

```
#WHLM CMD FILE FOR C:\HLM\NYS.MDM
NUMIT:50
STOPVAL:0.0000010000
LEVEL1:ATTIT=INTRCPT1+AGE13+AGE13S+RANDOM
LEVEL2:INTRCPT1=INTRCPT2+RANDOM
LEVEL2:AGE13=INTRCPT2+RANDOM
LEVEL2:AGE13S=INTRCPT2+RANDOM
FIXTAU:3
ACCEL:5
R_E_MODEL:UNRESTRICTED
LVR:N
TITLE:HMLM OUTPUT, NYS DATA
OUTPUT:C:\HLM\NYS1.OUT
```

If one types at the system prompt

HMLM NYS.MDM NEWCMD.MLM

the result will be the output for a model with an unrestricted covariance structure as given in Section 8.3. It is a good idea to rename the NEWCMD.MLM file if it is to be edited and re-used. Each execution of the program will produce a NEWCMD.MLM file that will overwrite the old one.

Note that the NEWCMD.MLM file above is similar to the same file produced by a linear-model analysis, with the addition of the following line.

```
R_E_MODEL:UNRESTRICTED
```

It indicates that the unrestricted covariance structure is chosen. The command lines for the other four choices are:

```
R_E_MODEL:HOMOL1VAR            (a model with homogeneous level-1 variance)
R_E_MODEL:HETL1VAR            (a model with heterogeneous variance at level 1)
R_E_MODEL:LOGLIN/VAR  (a model that includes a log-linear structure for the level-1 variance,
                      VAR contains the list of variables used to model the level-1 variance)
R_E_MODEL:AUTOREG        (a model with first-order auto-regressive level-1 random errors)
```

Note that HMLM and HMLM2 do not allow optional hypothesis testing, nonlinear outcomes, use of plausible values and multiply-imputed values, constraints of gammas, and they do not write out any residual files.

A description of the keywords and options for HMLM and HMLM2 commands can be found in Tables A.1 (for two-level models) and Table B.1 (for three-level models).

APPENDIX D: USING HMLM IN INTERACTIVE AND BATCH MODE

E | Using Special Features in interactive and batch mode

This appendix describes and illustrates how to use the special features in interactive and batch mode to execute analyses. References are made to appropriate sections in the manual where the procedures are described in greater details.

E.1 Example: Latent variable analysis using the National Youth Study datasets

The following interactive session illustrates a latent variable analysis example using the National Youth Study (NYS) datasets. A description of the data files and the model specification can be found in Sections 8.1.1 and 9.1.1.

```
c:HLM>  HMLM NYS.MDM

Enter type HMLM analysis:

  1) Unrestricted
  2) Random effects model with homogeneous level-1 variance
  3) Random effects model with heterogeneous level-1 variance
  4) Random effects model with log-linear model for level-1 variance
  5) Random effects model with first-order autoregressive level-1 variance

type of analysis: 2
```

We select the homogeneous level-1 variance option for this model. Thus, using HLM2 will yield identical results in this case.

Do you want to skip the unrestricted iterations? **Y**

Please specify a level-1 outcome variable

The choices are:

For	ATTIT enter	1	For	AGE enter	2	For	AGE11 enter	3
For	AGE13 enter	4	For	AGE11S enter	5	For	AGE13S enter	6
For	IND1 enter	7	For	IND2 enter	8	For	IND3 enter	9
For	IND4 enter	10	For	IND5 enter	11			

What is the outcome variable: **1**

The outcome is tolerance towards deviant behavior.

SPECIFYING AN HMLM MODEL

Level-1 predictor variable specification

Which level-1 predictors do you wish to use?

The choices are:

			For	AGE enter	2	For	AGE11 enter	3
For	AGE13 enter	4	For	AGE11S enter	5	For	AGE13S enter	6
For	IND1 enter	7	For	IND2 enter	8	For	IND3 enter	9
For	IND4 enter	10	For	IND5 enter	11			

level-1 predictor? (Enter 0 to end) **3**
level-1 predictor? (Enter 0 to end) **0**

AGE11 is the age of participant at a specific time minus 11.

Do you want to center any level-1 predictors? **N**

Do you want to set the level-1 intercept to zero in this analysis? **N**

Level-2 predictor variable specification

Which level-2 variables do you wish to use?

The choices are:

For	FEMALE enter	1	For MINORITY enter	2	For	INCOME enter	3

Which level-2 predictors to model INTRCPT1?
Level-2 predictor? (Enter 0 to end) **1**

```
         Level-2 predictor? (Enter 0 to end)    0

     Which level-2 predictors to model    AGE11 slope?
       Level-2 predictor? (Enter 0 to end)    1
       Level-2 predictor? (Enter 0 to end)    0

   Do you want to constrain the variances in any of the level-2 random
    effects to zero?  N

                      ADDITIONAL PROGRAM FEATURES

   Do you want to do a latent variable regression?  Y

   Enter o for outcome, p for predictor, or i to ignore

   How do you want to handle INTRCPT1?  P
   How do you want to handle    AGE11?  O
```

INTRCPT1, the level of tolerance at age 11, is used as a predictor to model the outcome, AGE11, the linear growth rate. Note that INTRCPT1 and AGE11 are latent variables, that is, they are free of measurement error.

```
                       OUTPUT SPECIFICATION

   How many iterations do you want to do?  50
     Enter a problem title:  Latent variable regression, NYS Data
     Enter name of output file:  NYS2.OUT

   Computing . . ., please wait
```

Partial output for this analysis is given in Section 9.1.1.

E.2   A latent variable analysis to run regression with missing data

The following interactive session illustrates a latent variable analysis to run regression with missing data with an artificial data set. A description of the data files and the model specification can be found in Section 9.1.2.

```
c:HLM>  HMLM MISSING.MDM

   Enter type HMLM analysis:
```

```
1) Unrestricted
2) Random effects model with homogeneous level-1 variance
3) Random effects model with heterogeneous level-1 variance
4) Random effects model with log-linear model for level-1 variance
5) Random effects model with first-order autoregressive level-1 variance
```

type of analysis: **1**

SPECIFYING A LEVEL-1 OUTCOME VARIABLE

Please specify a level-1 outcome variable

```
The choices are:
For MEASURES enter  1    For    IND1 enter  2    For    IND2 enter  3
For    IND3 enter  4
```

What is the outcome variable: **1**

SPECIFYING AN HMLM MODEL

Level-1 predictor variable specification

Which level-1 predictors do you wish to use?

```
The choices are:
For    IND1 enter  2    For    IND2 enter  3    For    IND3 enter  4

level-1 predictor? (Enter 0 to end)   1
That is the outcome variable!
level-1 predictor? (Enter 0 to end)   2
level-1 predictor? (Enter 0 to end)   3
level-1 predictor? (Enter 0 to end)   4
```

Do you want to center any level-1 predictors? **N**

Do you want to set the level-1 intercept to zero in this analysis? **Y**

Note that a no-intercept model is formulated (see Section 2.9.6.

Level-2 predictor variable specification

Which level-2 variables do you wish to use?

```
The choices are:
For    DUMMY enter  1
```

```
Which level-2 predictors to model      IND1 slope?
  Level-2 predictor? (Enter 0 to end)  0
Which level-2 predictors to model      IND2 slope?
  Level-2 predictor? (Enter 0 to end)  0
Which level-2 predictors to model      IND3 slope?
  Level-2 predictor? (Enter 0 to end)  0
```

IND2 and IND3 are selected to predict IND1.

```
Do you want to constrain the variances in any of the level-2 random
  effects to zero?  N

                    ADDITIONAL PROGRAM FEATURES

Do you want to do a latent variable regression?  Y

Enter o for outcome, p for predictor, or i to ignore
How do you want to handle      IND1?  O
How do you want to handle      IND2?  P
How do you want to handle      IND3?  P

                     OUTPUT SPECIFICATION

How many iterations do you want to do?  50
  Enter a problem title:  Latent variable analysis, Missing data example
  Enter name of output file:  MISSING1.OUT
```

Partial output for this analysis is given in Section 9.1.2.

E.3 Commands to apply HLM to multiply-imputed data

To analyze data with multiply-imputed values for the outcome variable or
only one covariate, the user needs to add the following line manually into
the command file.

PLAUSVALS:*VARLIST*

where *VARLIST* lists variables containing the multiply-imputed values.

To analyze data with multiply-imputed values for the outcome and/or covariates, the user needs to prepare multiple SSM files. After setting up

the multiple SSM files, the user has to submit the command files to HLM2 or HLM3 as many times as the number of multiple SSM files with an extra flag, –MI#, where # is the sequence number, starting from 0. On the last run, you also need the –E flag, (E for estimate).

Suppose there are 4 sets of multiply-imputed data for a two-level model, called MDATA1.SSM, MDATA2.SSM, MDATA3.SSM, and MDATA4.SSM, and the command file is ANALYSE.HLM. The following commands need to be typed in at the system prompt.

HLM2 –MI0 MDATA1.SSM ANALYSE.HLM

HLM2 –MI1 MDATA2.SSM ANALYSE.HLM

HLM2 –MI2 MDATA3.SSM ANALYSE.HLM

HLM2 –MI3 –E MDATA4.SSM ANALYSE.HLM

F Overview of Files and Options

This appendix gives an comparitive overview of the input and output files as well as the options available in the four different modules in HLM.

The differences between HLM2, HLM3, HMLM, and HMLM2 with regard to the creation of the SSM file or the MDM file are summarized in Table F.1.

Table F.1   Options for creating SSM/MDM files

Option	HLM2	HLM3	HMLM	HMLM2
Level-1 weight	Y	Y	N	N
Normalization of level-1 weight	Y	N	N	N
Generalization of weights	Y	N	N	N
Level-2 weight	Y	N	N	N
Normalization of level-2 weight	Y	N	N	N
Missing data	Y*	Y*	N	N
Listwise/pairwise deletion	Y	Y	N	N

* Specify missing data codes prior to importing into HLM when using stat package data. When using ASCII data, use options provided in WHLM for missing data code specification.

The next two tables (F.2 and F.3) summarize the basic and optional specifications available for the data analysis under the four modules.

The four figures present an overview of the input files that are needed and the output files that are created by the four modules. Fig. F.1 for HLM2, Fig. F.2 for HLM3, Fig. F.3 for HMLM, and Fig. F.4 for HMLM2.

Table F.2   Basic Modeling Specifications

Option	HLM2	HLM3	HMLM	HMLM2
No of iterations	Y	Y	Y	Y
Mode of iteration acceleration	N	Y	N	N
Frequency of accelerator	Y	Y	Y	Y
# of OLS estimates shown	Y	N	N	N
% change to stop iterating	Y	Y	Y	Y
Action when convergence not reached	Y	Y	Y	Y
Print var-cov matrices	Y	Y	N	N
Type of likelihood (REML/FML)	Y	N	N	N
How to handle bad Tau(pi)	Y	Y	Y	Y
How to handle bad Tau(beta)	N	Y	N	Y
Treatment of level-1 variance	N	N	Y	Y
Title	Y	Y	Y	Y
Output file specification	Y	Y	Y	Y
Residual file (level-2)	Y	Y	N	N
Residual file (level-3)	N	Y	N	N

Note that the RSP file and the HLM or MLM file have arrows in both directions, because they are generated by the program as output and they can function as input for a subsequent run.

Table F.3   Optional Modeling Specifications

Option	HLM2	HLM3	HMLM	HMLM2
Optional Hypothesis Testing				
Multivariate hypothesis tests	Y	Y	N	N
Test against another model (deviance, no of parameters)	Y	Y	N	N
Test homogeneity of level-1 variance	Y	Y	N	N
Fix sigma^2 to specified value	Y	Y	N	N
Exploratory Analysis				
Level-2	Y	N	N	N
Level-3	Y	Y	N	N
Setup Nonlinear Model				
Bernoulli	Y	Y	N	N
Poisson (constant exposure)	Y	Y	N	N
Binomial	Y	Y	N	N
Poisson (variable exposure)	Y	Y	N	N
Multinomial	Y	N	N	N
Ordinal	Y	N	N	N
Macro iterations	Y	Y	N	N
Stopping criterion (macro)	Y	Y	N	N
Micro iterations	Y	Y	N	N
Stopping criterion (micro)	Y	Y	N	N
Over-dispersion	Y	Y	N	N
Laplace iterations	Y*	N	N	N
No of Laplace iterations	Y*	N	N	N
Plausible Values	Y	Y	N	N
V–known Model[†]	Y	N	N	N
Multiple Imputation	Y	Y	N	N
Latent Variable Regression	Y	Y	Y	N
Constraint of gammas	Y	Y	N	N
Heterogeneous sigma^2 (predictors of level-1 variance)	Y	N	N	N
Macro iterations	Y	N	N	N
Stopping criterion (macro)	Y	N	N	N
Micro iterations	Y	N	N	N
Stopping criterion (micro)	Y	N	N	N
Predictors of level-1 variance	N	N	Y[‡]	Y[‡]

*   Only with Bernoulli
†   Not available in Windows mode   ‡   Only for log-linear level-1 variance

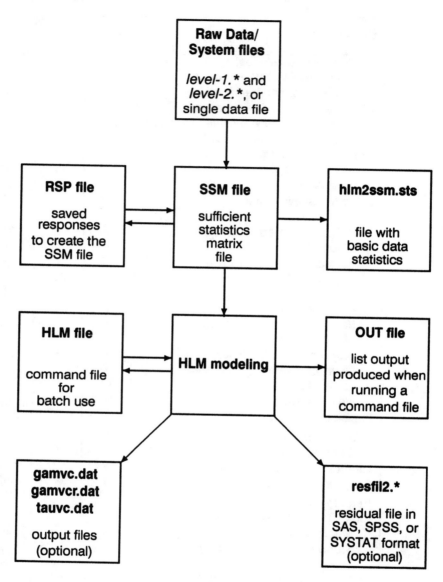

Figure F.1   HLM2 Files

APPENDIX F: OVERVIEW OF FILES AND OPTIONS

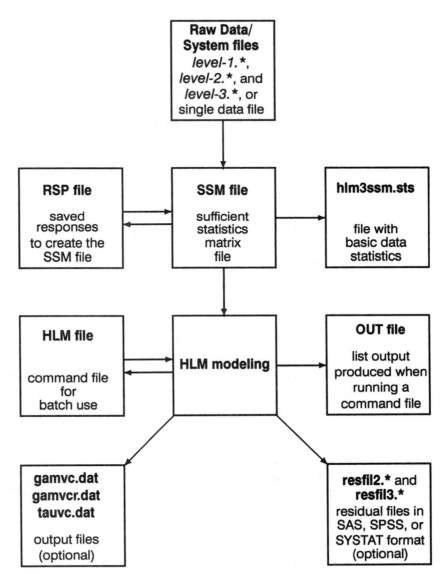

Figure F.2   HLM3 Files

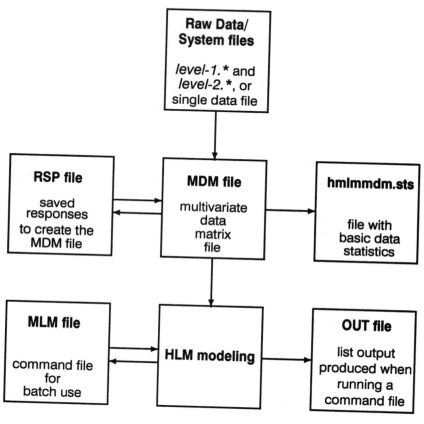

Figure F.3   HMLM Files

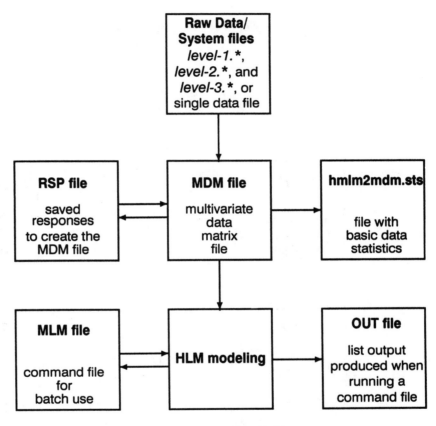

Figure F.4   HMLM2 Files

References

Barnett, R.C., Marshall, N.L., Raudenbush, S.W., & Brennan, R.T. (1993)
Gender and the relationship between job experience and psychological distress: a study of dual-earner couples.
Journal of Personality and Social Psychology, **64**, 794–806.

Bock, R.D. (1985)
Multivariate Statistical Methods in Behavioral Research.
Scientific Software International, Inc.

Breslow, N. & Clayton, D.G. (1993)
Approximate inference in generalized linear mixed models.
Journal of the American Statistical Association, **88**, 9–25.

Bryk, A., & Raudenbush, S. W. (1992)
Hierarchical Linear Models for Social and Behavioral Research: Applications and Data Analysis Methods.
Newbury Park, CA: Sage.

Cheong, Y. F., Fotiu, R., & Raudenbush, S. W. (in press)
Analytic alternatives in the analysis of NAEP.
Journal of Educational and Behavioral Statistics.

Dempster, A., Laird, N., & Rubin, D. (1977)
Maximum likelihood from incomplete data via the EM algorithm.
Journal of the Royal Statistical Society, Series B, **39**), 1–8.

Elliot, D., Huizinga, D., & Menard, S. (1989)
Multiple Problem Youth: Delinquency, Substance Use, and Mental Health Problems.
New York: Springer-Verlag.

Goldstein, H. (1991)

Nonlinear multilevel models with an application to discrete response data.

Biometrika, **78**, 45–51.

Hedeker, D., & Gibbons, R. (1994)

A random-effects ordinal regression model for multilevel analysis.

Biometrics, **50**, 933–44.

Jennrich, R., & Schluchter, M. (1986)

Unbalanced repeated-measures models with structured covariance matrices.

Biometrics, **42**, 805–820.

Little, R., & Rubin, D. (1987)

Statistical analysis with missing data.

New York: Wiley.

Little, R., & Schenker, N. (1995)

Missing data.

In Arminger, G., Clogg, C.C., & Sobel, M.E. (Eds.): *Handbook of Statistical Modeling for the Social and Behavioral Sciences.*

New York: Plenum Press.

Longford, N. (1993)

Random Coefficient Models.

Oxford: Clarendon Press.

McCullagh, P., & Nelder, J. (1989)

Generalized Linear Models, 2nd Edition.

London: Chapman and Hill.

Raudenbush, S. W. (1999)

Hierarchical models.

In S. Kotz (Ed.): Encyclopedia of Statistical Sciences, Update Volume 3 (pp. 318–323).

New York: Wiley.

Raudenbush, S. W. (in press)

Toward a coherent framework for comparing trajectories of individual change.

To appear in Collins, L., & Sayer, A. (Eds.): *Best Methods for Studying Change.*

Washington, DC: The American Psychological Association.

Raudenbush, S.W., & Bhumirat, C. (1992)

The distribution of resources for primary education and its consequences for educational achievement in Thailand.

International Journal of Education Research, **17(2)**, 143–164.

Raudenbush, S.W., & Bryk, A.S. (1987)

Examining correlates of diversity.

Journal of Educational Statistics, **12**, 241–269.

Raudenbush, S. W., & Bryk, A. S. (forthcoming)

Hierarchical Linear Models: Applications and Data Analysis Methods, Second Edition.

Newbury Park, CA: Sage.

Raudenbush, S. W., & Sampson, R. (1999).

Assessing direct and indirect associations in multilevel designs with latent variables,

Sociological Methods and Research, **28(2)**, 123–153.

Raudenbush, S.W., Yang, M.L., & Yosef, M. (in press).

Maximum likelihood for hierarchical models via high-order, multivariate Laplace approximation.

To appear in the *Journal of Computational and Graphical Statistics.*

Rodriguez, G., & Goldman, N. (1995)

An assessment of estimation procedures for multilevel models with binary responses.

Journal of the Royal Statistical Society, Series A, **158**, 73–89.

Rogers, A., *et al.* (1992)

National Assessment of Educational Progress: 1990 Secondary-use Data Files User Guide
Princeton, New Jersey: Educational Testing Service.

Rowan, B., Raudenbush, S.W., & Cheong, Y.F. (1993)

Teaching as a non-routine task: Implications for the organizational design of schools.
Educational Administration Quarterly, **29(4)**, 479–500.

Rowan, R., Raudenbush, S.W., & Kang, S. (1991)

Organizational design in high schools: A multilevel analysis.
American Journal of Education, **99(2)**, 238–266.

Rubin, D. (1987)

Multiple Imputation for Nonresponse in Surveys.
New York: Wiley.

Schafer, J. (1997)

Analysis of Incomplete Multivariate Data.
London: Chapman & Hall.

Schall, R. (1991)

Estimation in generalized linear models with random effects.
Biometrika, **40**, 719–727.

Stiratelli, R., Laird, N., & Ware, J. (1984)

Random effects models for serial observations with binary response.
Biometrics, **40**, 961–971.

Wong, G., & Mason, W. (1985)

The hierarchical logistic regression model for multilevel analysis.
Journal of the American Statistical Association, **80**(391), 513–524.

Yang, M. (1995)

A simulation study for the assessment of the non-linear hierarchical model estimation via approximate maximum likelihood.
Unpublished apprenticeship paper, College of Education, Michigan State University.

Yang, M.L. (1998)

Increasing the efficiency in estimating multilevel Bernoulli models, [Dissertation]

East Lansing, MI: Michigan State University.

Zeger, S., Liang, K., & Albert, P. (1988)

Models for longitudinal data: A likelihood approach.

Biometrics, **44**, 1049–1060.

Zeger, S., & Liang, L. (1986)

Longitudinal data analysis using generalized linear models.

Biometrika, **73**, 13–22.

Author Index

AUTHOR INDEX

Subject Index

Dummy variable, 118

E in format, 243
EB
    estimate, 5, 13, 41, 100, 101,
        103
    prefix, 6
    residual, 41, 46, 100
EB00, 102
EBINTRCP, 100
Effect size, 220
EG1.DAT, 88
EG1.HLM, 93
EG1.SAV, 84, 195
EG1HMLM2.SAV, 195
EG2.HLM, 100, 103
EG2.SAV, 86
EGASCII.RSP, 88
EGHMLM1.MLM, 196
EM algorithm, 5, 164
EMF file, 232
Empirical Bayes estimate, 5, 6, 79
Equal exposure, 146
Equation Graphing
    dialog box, 226
    options, 229
    specification dialog box, 227
Event rate, 116
Example, High School & Beyond,
    14
Example, Thailand education
    study, 134
Example, Vocabulary growth
    study, 70
EXPECT.DAT, 221
EXPECT.HLM, 221
EXPECT.OUT, 222

EXPECT.RSP, 220
Exploratory analysis, 58
Exposure, 116
Extra-binomial dispersion,
    131, 134
Extra-Poisson dispersion,
    131, 134

F in format, 243
File input rules, 14
filename.1 file, 214
Fisher iterations, 109
Fisher scoring, 5
Fitted value, 6, 41
Fixed coefficient, 77, 80
Fixed effect, 7, 36, 59, 71, 79, 80,
    100, 102
Fixed effect, delete, 71
Fixed effects model, 45
Fixed, specification, 31
FIXSIGMA2 keyword, 252, 272
FIXTAU keyword, 252, 272
FIXTAU2 keyword, 273
FIXTAU3 keyword, 273
Format statement, 243
FORTRAN, 243
Forward slash, in format, 244
Frequency of accelerator, 110
Full batch mode, 250
Full maximum likelihood, 80
Full ML, 7, 131
Full PQL, 131
Fully interactive mode, 250
FV00, 102
FVINTRCP, 100

GAMMA# keyword, 252, 272

MISSING1.SAV, 210
MISSING2.SAV, 210
ML, 7
MLF keyword, 272
Model
    checking, 13, 100
    fit, 190
    specification, 12, 28, 92, 133
MQL, 127
Multi-category data, 114
Multinomial model, 112, 118
    example, 150
Multiple imputation, 212
Multiple-measures model, 167
Multivariate data matrix (MDM), 175
Multivariate tests, 61

NAEP, 213
National Youth Survey, 175, 205
Nested data, 163
Nested model, 81
Nested structure, 1
Nesting, 75
Nesting of IDs, 15
NEWCMD.HLM, 248, 283
NEWCMD.MLM, 286
NJ, 44
NJK, 100
NK, 102
No accelerator, 109
No-intercept model, 69, 109
NONLIN keyword, 252, 272
Nonlinear analysis, 112, 133
Nonlinear Specification dialog box, 133
Normality assumption, 111

Normalizing weights, 52
Number of iterations, 158, 224
Numeric variable, 15
NUMIT keyword, 252, 272
NYS data, 285, 289
NYS.MDM, 286
NYS1.MLM, 178
NYS1.SAV, 176, 205
NYS2.MLM, 205
NYS2.SAV, 177, 205
NYS21.SAV, 225
NYS22.SAV, 225

OL estimate, 13
OL prefix, 6
OL residual, 41, 46
OL00, 102
OLINTRCP, 100
OLS estimate, 9
OLSRSVAR, 44
Omnibus test, 80
One-way ANOVA, 259
Option, 250, 251, 271
Optional hypothesis test, 61
Ordinal model, 112
    example, 156
Original coefficient, 209
Outcome, 2
Outcome variable, 77
Outlier, 13
OUTPUT keyword, 252, 272
Over-dispersion, 131, 144, 147, 160
Over-sampling, 51

Pairwise deletion, 49
Parameter estimation, 4, 79

SSM file, creation, 87
Starting value, 95
STOPMACRO keyword, 252, 272
STOPMICRO keyword, 252, 272
STOPVAL keyword, 252, 272
Sufficient statistics matrix
        (SSM), 11, 83
SYSTAT input, 88
System file, 12

"t-to-enter" statistics, 58
TAU, 5
Tau(beta), 78, 79, 199
Tau(pi), 77, 78
Tau, dispersion matrix, 3, 77
TAUVC.DAT, 109, 256, 257, 272
TAUVCPV.DAT, 257
TCHR.SSM, 150
TCHR1.HLM, 152
TCHR2.HLM, 156
Teacher expectancy effects data,
        219
Technical support, 138
THAIBNML.HLM, 145
Thailand data, 136
THAIU1.HLM, 136
THAIUGRP.SSM, 136, 277
Three-level model, 75, 76
Threshold, 121, 159
TITLE keyword, 252, 272

Unbiased estimate, 54
Under-dispersion, 131, 160
Unit-specific iteration, 138
Unit-specific model, 128, 130, 143
Univariate regression, 259

Unrestricted covariance
        structure, 164
Unrestricted model, 180
US Public Schools study, 75

V-known analysis, 219
V-known program, 45
Variable exposure, 148
Variance-covariance matrix, 161
Vocabulary growth study, 70

Weighting, 51, 54
Windows mode, 14, 92
Within-person variation, 166

X focus, 227
X in format, 243

Z focus, 231